中/青/文/库

本书得到中国青年政治学院出版基金资助

美语新词语与当代美国文化研究

周丽娜◎著

中国社会科学出版社

图书在版编目(CIP)数据

美语新词语与当代美国文化研究/周丽娜著 . —北京：中国社会科学
出版社，2015.2

ISBN 978 – 7 – 5161 – 5582 – 0

Ⅰ.①美… Ⅱ.①周… Ⅲ.①英语—新词语—研究—美国②文化—
研究—美国—现代 Ⅳ.①H313②G171.2

中国版本图书馆 CIP 数据核字 （2015） 第 037419 号

出 版 人	赵剑英	
责任编辑	李炳青	
责任校对	闫 萃	
责任印制	李寡寡	

出　　　版	中国社会科学出版社	
社　　　址	北京鼓楼西大街甲 158 号 （邮编 100720）	
网　　　址	http：//www. csspw. cn	
	中文域名：中国社科网　　　010 – 64070619	
发 行 部	010 – 84083685	
门 市 部	010 – 84029450	
经　　　销	新华书店及其他书店	

印　　　刷	北京市大兴区新魏印刷厂	
装　　　订	廊坊市广阳区广增装订厂	
版　　　次	2015 年 2 月第 1 版	
印　　　次	2015 年 2 月第 1 次印刷	

开　　　本	710 × 1000　　1/16	
印　　　张	20	
插　　　页	2	
字　　　数	338 千字	
定　　　价	66.00 元	

凡购买中国社会科学出版社图书，如有质量问题请与本社联系调换
电话：010 – 84083683

《中青文库》编辑说明

中国青年政治学院是在中央团校基础上于 1985 年 12 月成立的，是共青团中央直属的唯一一所普通高等学校，由教育部和共青团中央共建。中国青年政治学院成立以来，坚持"质量立校、特色兴校"的办学思想，艰苦奋斗、开拓创新，教育质量和办学水平不断提高。学校是教育部批准的国家大学生文化素质教育基地，中华全国青年联合会和国际劳工组织命名的大学生 KAB 创业教育基地。学校与中央编译局共建青年政治人才培养研究基地，与北京市共建社会工作人才发展研究院和青少年生命教育基地。

目前，学校已建立起包括本科教育、研究生教育、留学生教育、继续教育和团干部培训等在内的多形式、多层次的教育格局。设有中国马克思主义学院、青少年工作系、社会工作学院、法律系、经济系、新闻与传播系、公共管理系、中国语言文学系、外国语言文学系等 9 个教学院系，文化基础部、外语教学研究中心、计算机教学与应用中心、体育教学中心等 4 个教学中心（部），轮训部、继续教育学院、国际教育交流学院等 3 个教学培训机构。

学校现有专业以人文社会科学为主，涵盖哲学、经济学、法学、文学、管理学 5 个学科门类。学校设有思想政治教育、法学、社会工作、劳动与社会保障、社会学、经济学、财务管理、国际经济与贸易、新闻学、广播电视学、政治学与行政学、汉语言文学和英语等 13 个学士学位专业，其中社会工作、思想政治教育、法学、政治学与行政学为教育部特色专业。目前，学校拥有哲学、马克思主义理论、法学、社会学、新闻传播学和应用经济学等 6 个一级学科硕士授权点和 1 个专业硕士学位点，同时设有青少年研究院、中国马克思主义研究中心、中国志愿服务信息资料研究中心、大学生发展研究中心、大学生素质拓展研究中心等科研机构。

在学校的跨越式发展中，科研工作一直作为体现学校质量和特色的重要内容而被予以高度重视。2002年，学校制定了教师学术著作出版基金资助条例，旨在鼓励教师的个性化研究与著述，更期之以兼具人文精神与思想智慧的精品的涌现。出版基金创设之初，有学术丛书和学术译丛两个系列，意在开掘本校资源与移译域外菁华。随着年轻教师的剧增和学校科研支持力度的加大，2007年又增设了博士论文文库系列，用以鼓励新人，成就学术。三个系列共同构成了对教师学术研究成果的多层次支持体系。

十几年来，学校共资助教师出版学术著作百余部，内容涉及哲学、政治学、法学、社会学、经济学、文学艺术、历史学、管理学、新闻与传播等学科。学校资助出版的初具规模，激励了教师的科研热情，活跃了校内的学术气氛，也获得了很好的社会影响。在特色化办学愈益成为当下各高校发展之路的共识中，2010年，校学术委员会将遴选出的一批学术著作，辑为《中青文库》，予以资助出版。《中青文库》第一批（15本）、第二批（6本）、第三批（6本）出版后，有效展示了学校的科研水平和实力，在学术界和社会上产生了很好的反响。本辑作为第四批共推出12本著作，并希冀通过这项工作的陆续展开而更加突出学校特色，形成自身的学术风格与学术品牌。

在《中青文库》的编辑、审校过程中，中国社会科学出版社的编辑人员认真负责，用力颇勤，在此一并予以感谢！

目　　录

前　言

　　语言既是文化的载体，又是文化的一部分。二者关系紧密相连。英语是根植于西方文化土壤中的奇葩。从很大程度来说，仅仅掌握英语语法、词汇，具有听、说、读、写的能力并不能成功地进行跨文化交际，充其量只能应付考试。原因是，英语语言中的一些语言习惯、话语内涵与汉语迥然不同。因此，要准确理解不同文化中的现象需要了解跨文化知识。但是跨文化知识的获取并不是一蹴而就的。这就要求我们具有获取跨文化知识的意识并且持之以恒地进行学习。

　　语言的另外一个特点是，它是不断变化的。仅仅靠书本上所学到的语言文化知识并不能成功地进行跨文化交际。许多人所说的英语经常会让本地人感觉很怪，不自然，有时甚至会造成交际的失败，原因就是书本上的英语知识落后于语言的发展，甚至与社会流行语言大相径庭。如：美国人对糖和甜食喜爱有加，因而创造出新词 arm candy，指那些陪伴名流和富人甚至是普通人出入社交场合、但没有实质性感情的男女，可以翻译成"花瓶"或"蜜糖伴侣"。如果不了解其引申义和内涵，望文生义，定会在跨文化交际中影响正常交往。

　　综上所述，学习者必须不断了解并学习新的语言和文化现象，跟上这种变化。语言是文化的载体和交流的工具，反映社会文明进步的成果，并且对文化的传承有举足轻重的作用。反过来，任何人类社会都离不开文化，文化是语言形成和发展的基础，文化的发展推动了语言的发展。因此语言与文化密不可分，二者是相辅相成的。最为活跃、最富于变化的新词是语言的组成部分，它与文化的关系也是同样密不可分的。透视当代美国文化必须透视美语新词，研究美语新词必须研究当代美国文化，二者相辅相成。

　　本书通过总结归纳前人新词与文化研究成果，对于美语新词语现象和当代美国文化从概念上进行了界定，详细系统地论述了新词语和文化的特征、二者之间的关系、研究意义，描述和归纳出新词语构成方式，对于美国文化发展和美语新词语构词趋势进行了预测，从而形成研究框架和体系，以图丰富词汇学与文化的研究。

　　本书由十二章组成：第一章为语言文化新词语的概念界定和特征；第二章为三者间关系及研究意义；第三章为美语新词语产生的文化因素；第四章为当代美国文化特征；第五章为美语新词语构成的方法；第六章为美语新词语的构成趋势；第七章为美语委婉语；第八章为当代美国习语；第九章为美语新词语研究；第十章为美语新词语的翻译方法及原则；第十一章为美语新词语发展趋势；第十二章为当代美国文化发展趋势。

　　本书适用于语言研究者、大中学教师、英语专业研究生及本科生使用。通过本书的学习，读者能够对美国文化与美语新词语有深入的了解。也希望通过这本书为语言文化研究领域尽微薄之力。

第一篇
语言、文化、新词语概念、关系
及研究意义

第一章 语言、文化、新词语

一 语言

（一）语言的概念

语言的定义多种多样，大致分为四种。第一种强调历史文化属性，代表人物为洪堡特；第二种强调自然属性，代表人物为索绪尔；第三种强调社会属性；第四种强调人类自身的自然属性，代表人物为乔姆斯基。

洪堡特认为，语言是一个民族生存的必要的"呼吸"，是一个民族灵魂。语言是精神的创造活动，或者"是精神自然的流射"，"语言从精神出发，再反作用于精神"（洪堡特，1999）。语言介于人与世界之间，人必须通过自己生成的语言去认识世界并把握世界。语言记录下人们对于世界的看法和经验，加上其自身的规律和组织，于是逐渐形成独特的世界观，所以说，语言就是世界观。

到了 20 世纪初，语言学发展成为一门独立学科，得到巨大发展。代表人物有索绪尔和乔姆斯基。索绪尔强调语言的社会性。他认为语言是一种自足的结构系统，同时又是一种分类原则。它是社会制度、事实和制度。语言本体论基于 langue，parole 和 language 三者的区分。Langue 是一种符号系统，parole 存在于言语社团心理之中，是个人的自由话语行为，language 是全球语言现象，它包括 langue 和 parole。

乔姆斯基认为，语言是一组有限与无限句子的结合，其中每个句子的长度都是有限的，并且由一组有限的成分构成。它是一种心智实体，他以其《句法结构》创立了转换生成语法（1957）。索绪尔认为，语言是一个社团话语总体，即语言外在观。而乔姆斯基提出 internalized language（内在化语言），language acquisition device（语言习得机制）和

language faculty（语言官能）的理论，强调语言的内在化。

《语言与语言学百科辞典》是这样定义语言的：人类社会用来交际或自我表现的、约定俗成的声音、手势或文字系统。

《牛津英语大辞典》对于语言的定义：它是一个国家、一个民族或种族使用的全部词及词的组合方式。

综合所有语言学家及权威字典的定义，可以这样认为，语言是人类认知世界进行表述的方式和过程。

（二）语言的属性

语言的重要属性就是"人类社会最重要的信息交际工具"，可以概括为以下几点：

1. 规范性，即约定性。语言是社会约定俗成的，是所有成员以不同形式参与、约定和服从这种约定的结果。语言工具在运用过程中，还不断完善自己的系统功能，这是促进语言发展的动力。

2. 交际性。语言的存在价值之一就在于交际。语言从某种意义上来看，是人类文化得以传承和储存的有效载体。因此，它在自身的发展当中，逐步体现出很强的传承性和交际性。

3. 传承性。传承性是指语言以自己的风格特色吸引或者促使人们在生活生产中自觉不自觉地通过语言这个工具直接或者间接影响着相关的人群，或者波及更广泛的区域，达到传承的效果。另外，语言在人类社会发展当中，不仅在人与人之间、古代人与现代人之间、中国人与外国人之间储存了文明的精华信息，承担文明发展的桥梁。

4. 符号性与系统性。语言是社会约定俗成的、表达观念的符号。符号的本质是社会的。它在某种程度上要逃避社会上某些小集体、小圈子的意识。这是语言最主要的特征。语言是一种社会契约，一个社会接受一种表达手段而排斥另一种表达手段其实都是社会上的集体意识的习惯。或者可以说，没有好坏之分，关键是使用哪一种表达方式。

语言符号是一种包含着两面性的实体。一方面语言是表示事物名称的，所以任何语言都是概念的映像，即具有所指性；另外，语言要依托声音这种媒介来表达所指，所以说语言也是声音的映像，声音是语言的另一个侧面，也就是说语言具有能指性。

5. 发展性。任何事物都是不断地运动变化发展的，新事物不断地产生，旧事物不断地消亡。语言也是这样，语言系统的变化受到使用的推动以及社会、文化等很多因素的影响，不断发展，并表现出简练、实用、包容力、表现力强的发展趋势。

6. 载体性。一个民族的语言面貌是由该民族的文化所规定的，它是该民族文化的一种表现形式。民族文化的价值观念、风俗习惯等都在语言上打下了烙印。便得人们可以从语言中去探寻其民族文化的烙印，揭示其中的积淀。从这个意义上来看，语言就是文化的载体。可以说，任何一种语言要素都蕴含着一定的文化内容，体现一定的文化风格。

二 文化

（一）文化概念

英国人类学家、文化史和人类学进化论开创者 E. B. Tylor 是最先提出文化定义的学者。他在 1871 年出版的《原始文化》一书中对文化进行了界定：文化或文明是一种复合体，其中包括知识、信仰、艺术、道德、法律、风俗以及作为社会成员的人所获得的任何能力和习惯。美国著名语言学家 Sapir 认为，文化是"一个社会所做的和所想的是什么"。而现代文化学之父、美国文化人类学家 C. Kluckhohn 认为，在人类学中，所谓文化就是一个民族的生活方式的总体，以及个人从某集团得来的具有社会性的遗产。美国另一位人类学家 W. Goodenough 在《人类学和语言学》的论文中把文化视为人们所获得的具有社会性的知识。他认为，一个社会的文化包括一个人用社会成员所接受的方式生活而必须了解或相信的任何东西。

文化涵盖的内容丰富多样，仅美国 *Webster's New Collegiate Dictionary* 就给出了 6 个定义。而澳大利亚出版的 *The Macquarie Dictionary* 则给出了 10 个定义。据统计，仅文化的定义就有 200 个之多。

总体而言，人类学把文化分为三个层面，即高级文化、大众文化、深层文化。高级文化包括文学、艺术、宗教、哲学等；大众文化有衣食住行、风俗、礼仪等生活方式；深层文化则指价值观念、解决问题方式、社会交际等。三种层次的文化紧密相连，互相影响。高级文化和大众文化扎根于深层文化，而深层文化则以某种艺术形式反映在高级文化中。可以说人类学角度的文化是 inclusive，包括人类生活的各个方面及其创造的各个成果。

而文化学则把文化分为表层、中层和深层三个层面。表层指物质文化，涵盖物质的精神产品。中层也被称为制度文化，包括行为、习俗、礼仪等人际关系。深层是指观念文化，包括价值观念、思维习惯方式、审美方式等。

关于文化的分类，H. H. Stern（1992：208）根据文化的结构和范畴把文化分为广义和狭义两种概念。广义的文化即大写的文化（Culture with a big C），狭义的文化即小写的文化（Culture with a small c）。广义地说，文化指的是人类在社会历史发展过程中所创造的物质和精神财富的总和。它包括物质文化、制度文化和心理文化三个方面。

物质文化是指人类创造的种种物质文明，包括交通工具、服饰、日常用品等，是一种可见的显性文化。制度文化和心理文化分别指生活制度、家庭制度、社会制度以及思维方式、宗教信仰、审美情趣，它们属于不可见的隐性文化。包括文学、哲学、政治等方面内容。狭义的文化是指人们普遍的社会习惯，如衣食住行、风俗习惯、生活方式、行为规范等。

小写的 c 则是普遍的习惯或某一社会成员对文化的适应能力。

总而言之，文化是人类创造的一切物质产品和精神产品的总和，同时又是语言、文学、艺术及一切意识形态在内的精神产品。

（二）文化的本质特征

1. 继承性。文化是后天习得的，它必须包括习得的知识。文化是社会成员获得和共同拥有的一种生活方式。新的一代在不断扬弃原有文化的同时，继承原有文化的一部分或精髓。文化向下一代流传，下一代也认同、共享上一代的文化，因而具有继承性。

2. 社会性。一切文化，不管是物质的，还是精神的，都是人类创造的产品。文化属于社会，不属于个人。可以说，人既是社会的人，也是文化的人。

3. 引导性。文化的引导功能是指文化可以为人们的行动提供方向和可供选择的方式。通过共享文化，行动者可以知道自己的何种行为是适宜的、可以引起积极回应的，并选择有效的行动。文化的形成和确立，是通过符号被习得并得以传播的。这就意味着某种价值观和行为规范的被认可和被遵从。在语言上更是如此。语言的规范、语法规律、遣词规则、使用习惯是约定俗成的。每个社会成员都要遵守，违反了这些约定，就会受到惩罚，交际就会失败。

4. 文化是动态变化的。纵观历史长河，发明创造贯穿其中，科学技术不断进步。人们的思想、世界观、价值观等深层文化随之发生巨大变化。而风俗习惯、生活方式、语言等表层文化的变化更明显。

5. 民族性。文化是人类共有的。但是各个社会的文化有所不同。这是因为人类经历或处于文化发展不同的过程。文化因而通过民族独有的形式表现出来，具有鲜明的民族特色。

三　新词语

（一）新词语的概念与美语新词语

新词语的英文对应单词为 neologism。根据英文权威词典 *Webster's New World Dictionary* 的解释，它有两条含义：第一条是 a new word or a new meaning for an established word；第二条是 the use of, or the practice of creating, new words or new meanings for established words。根据第一条意义，新词语又有两层含义：第一层是指由于社会的变迁而衍生出来的新词语；第二层是指那些旧词随着社会的变化必然出现的语言变迁而衍生出来的新义和新用法。第二条意义指的是新词语的发明和使用、旧词新意的约定俗成及其用法。而由此观之，新的词语是受到一定的时间和范围限制的，而且它还必须是在与现在不远的时间段内产生或者被吸收到人们所使用的词汇中来的词语。据此我们认为，一个词语能否被认为是一个新词语，就在于它是否满足以下三个条件：第一，这个词语是近段时期所产生的；第二，产生之后该词语应被相关的权威的英语词典所吸收；第三，属于旧词的词语随着时代变迁被人们赋予了新的含义且已经约定俗成，否则旧词语就难以新用。

广义上来说，现有的词汇中没有的都可以称为新词语。本书主要研究的是美语新词语。美语新词语指的是 20 世纪 50 年代以来出现在美语中的新词语，涉及美国社会生活、科学技术、政治、经济、艺术教育、亚文化群体等。

新词语产生后有三种生存可能，一是不稳定新词。它们被小部分人使用或问世后不久就无人使用，消失、"夭折"了；二是中庸性新词。它们继续不稳定地、小范围地存在；三是稳定性新词。它们被普遍使用、广泛流传而逐渐稳定，进入词汇系统而成为其中一分子，这时这样的词语也就不"新"了。

（二）新词语的产生形式

新词语产生的形式多种多样。新词语可以是崭新的词语，它们通过复合法、派生法、类比法、缩合词构成崭新词汇。复合词是由两个或两个以上的根词（base）构成一个词。如 soft power（软实力）。派生法也称为词缀法。在一个词根前或后加上一个词缀，变成一个新词。例如 hoplophobia（持枪械恐惧症）。缩略法（shortening）是对原词进行剪裁，缩略其中一部分。这些词语的缩略方法主要有首字母缩略法、首字母拼音法、同音借用法、数字缩略法、截短缩略法、拼缀词。如 Chimerica（China + America，中美），LOHAS（lifestyles of health and sustainability，乐活族），LAT（living apart together）等。

新词语也可以是旧词新意。如 cookie 原指"小甜饼"，网语则指"为响应客户请求而由服务器返回给客户的一块数据"。美国人对糖和甜食喜爱有加，因而创造出 eye candy。eye candy 表示"某些人和东西只能用来养眼，但拿不来或不属于自己"。后来人们用 eye candy 指那些"非常性感、吸引人的女性"。

创造新词语的另外一个方法就是词类的转换（conversion），即不依靠词形变化，直接把一个词从一种词类转换成另一种词类。例如名词的 friend 转换成动词变成网络用语"加为好友"。

外来语也是构建新词的主要手段之一。外来语是指语言中的某些词语从一个民族的语言传到另一个民族的语言中。英语中有着大量外来语的存在。分别来自汉语、法语、德语、意大利语、西班牙语、北欧语系、日语等。如汉语的 fengshui（风水），qinghaosu（青蒿素）；法语的 déjà vu（已经见过），parkour（跑酷）；希腊语的 megahouse（大房子），cyberspace；西班牙语的 tortilla（墨西哥煎玉米饼），savvy（有知识的）；日语的 manga（动漫），tamagotchi（电子宠物），karoshi（过劳死）；德语的 Gummi bear（小熊糖）；俄语的 Lunik（探月使命），sputnik（人造卫星），icon（标记）；阿拉伯语的 gala（狂欢），Alqaida（基地组织）等。

（三）新词语言产生的文化背景

新词语的产生总是与社会、人口、物质、道德、观念、文化、习俗等的变迁密切相关的，所以最能产生新词语的地方总是来自社会的某些最活跃的领域、人群、媒体，甚至某些地区。它不仅仅是作为新的语言载体、新的交际工具出现在我们的生活中，而且真切地反映了社会生活，记录了整个社会的每一步进程。

新词语产生的领域涉及政治、经济、科技、社会、文化等方面。语言是文化的载体，文化是语言的内蕴。各民族文化的个性特征，经过历史的积淀而结晶在词汇、语法、语音层面上。而一个民族语言的词汇系统能够最直接、最敏感地反映出该民族的文化价值取向。反之，一个民族的文化心理对词汇的影响也最深。词汇与文化是互动关系，词汇能反映文化，而文化的发展更制约和推动词汇的发展。稳定下来的词汇又能考证、记载、传播、比较文化。词汇发展趋势是，数量越来越大，速度越来越快，性质越来越趋向统一、多样和不稳定。其文化原因主要有三个：全球化和文化交流加剧、科学知识的普及和新文化繁荣。

1. 全球化和文化交流加剧。全球化以经济为主导，辐射政治、军事、文化各领域，走向统一、联合、协调，因此全球化不管是出于互惠互利的需要，还是殖民主义的掠夺，都会使交往的双方相互影响。表现在文化和语言方面，从经济实力角度看，通常是上层文化影响低级文化比较多些。

2. 科学知识的普及。人们文化水平的提高，现代传媒的广泛影响，科学专业术语的普通词语化，使得词汇不断丰富和更新。如"blog、Email"等词，既是科技术语，又是一般老百姓口中常用的普通词语。texting（发信息），organic（有机的）等词语已经走进千家万户。可以预见，现在经济、科技、电脑、金融领域内的术语，有的将很快成为大众词语。

3. 新文化繁荣。新兴领域的兴起和新文化繁荣促进新词语的发展及流传。例如，随着信息产业的兴起和计算机领域的开发，网络语言如wifi（无线保真），flashmob（快闪族），hacker（黑客），social networking（社交网络）等作为一种文化现象影响深远。绿色生活方式深入人心。

人们倡导并推崇健康的生活方式。如 go green, green wedding 日益受到民众的欢迎，越来越多的人选择 Lohas（乐活族）生活方式和 eco-friendly（环境友好）的居住环境，他们无论是开车还是购买食物都会计算 food mile（食物英里）和 footprint（碳足迹）。

（四）新词语的特性

1. 新词语只有人类才有，也是人类所创造的，是独一无二的。2. 新词语的社会性也是语言的本质属性。3. 新词语也是后天才习得的。4. 新词语不断发展变化。随着社会生活的发展，词语也在进行着变化和发展。5. 语言的变化也反映着文化的变迁。这在词汇方面表现得尤为紧密，词汇可以敏感地反映社会生活。词汇有渐变性，反映社会生活的词语有一部分随着旧事物和旧概念的消失而消失；词汇还有稳固性的一面。事物和概念本身经历了变化，可是与此有关的大部分词语却沿用下来。

（五）流行语与新词语的区别

1. "流行语"常与"新词"混淆。但是它们有着很大差别和不同：流行语只在一定的时间内非常流行，可称为流行语。它们可以是新产生的词语，也可以是原有的词语，如 cold 一词原是"冷"的意思，后来经传播才成为流行语，表示"酷"。

2. 流行语的固定程度比较短，绝大部分都经历由盛转衰直至销声匿迹的过程，只有很少部分能长期被大众使用，进而成为惯用语和常用语。

3. 流行语虽然使用的时间比较短，但流行期间的使用范围广，形式多样，传播快，因而引起的社会效应也比较大。许多新词却不同。

第二章 语言、文化新词语的
关系与研究意义

一 语言文化新词语的关系

语言与文化密不可分。语言是文化的载体和交流工具,反映社会文明进步的成果,并且对文化的传承有举足轻重的作用。反过来,任何人类社会都离不开文化,文化是语言形成和发展的基础,文化的发展推动了语言的发展。因此二者是相辅相成的。

(一) 语言是文化的一部分

语言是文化的有机组成部分。正如马林诺夫斯基指出的那样:"语言是文化整体中的一部分,但是它并不是一个工具的体系,而是一套发音的风俗及精神文化的一部分"(马林诺夫斯基,1987)。文化是通过社会习得的知识,而语言是人类在后天的社会语言环境中习得的知识系统。语言是人类创造性加工的产品,是一种制度,一种规范,一种价值体系,因此具有社会性、传承性和变异性,是文化的一部分。一个民族的语言是由该民族的文化所约定俗成的,它是这个民族文化的一种表现形式。

(二) 语言是文化的载体

民族文化的价值、观点、习俗等都在语言上打下印迹,使得人们从民族语言中去寻求民族文化的遗迹,揭示其中的积淀。同时人的思想的形成借助语言,而人的思想又以语言的形式来表达。从这些角度来看,语言就是文化的载体,蕴含着一定的文化内容,体现一定的文化风格。

（三）语言反映社会现实

具有文化传承功能的语言是反映社会现实的一面镜子。语言正是在同等程度上反映着社会体制，带有社会制度的影子。由于语言能够反映一段时期的社会现象，也能够反映动态的社会，因此语言具有时间性，属于语言学上研究的历时语言学的范畴。通过语言，人类可以了解各个时期社会的各种文化，包括当时的历史社会、信仰、制度以及风俗习惯。然而，虽然语言反映文化，但是它脱离不开文化，它不能脱离其所在的社会文化环境，深受社会文化影响。

（四）文化是语言形成和发展的基础

也就是说，没有文化的语言是不存在的，正如萨丕尔在《语言》中所说："语言不能脱离文化而存在，不能脱离社会继承下来的各种做法和观念。"语言中的许多方面，如句法结构、词汇意义等，都含有许多文化因素。

（五）文化制约语言

语言的运用受到文化的制约。了解文化是避免言语误解的一个不可缺少的环节，因为在不同的文化背景下，同样的话语在一种文化中是礼貌、得体的，而在另一种文化中有可能被视为冒犯、无礼。即使在相同的文化背景下，语言文字的运用也要受文化的制约。

（六）新词语反映社会文化

词语是构成语言的基本成分，是语言系统中最活跃、最富于变化的成分，一种语言中的词汇同社会文化紧密相连，往往反映了这种语言的文化和环境。这说明了文化对语言的影响主要是通过词汇来表现的。而新词语则是词汇的一部分，它是反映当代社会文化的一面镜子，新词语的学习和研究有助于理解目标语社会和文化。

二　新词语与当代美国文化研究意义

长期以来，学者在新词语和当代美国文化方面做出不懈的努力。汪榕培在《英语词汇学教程》、《英语词汇学研究》及《英语新词认知语言学研究——漫谈英语中的"9·11"词汇》等研究成果中比较详细地论及英语新词，金圣华出版了《英语新词词汇》，毛荣贵在《英语词汇热点透视》中对新词问题也有专门研究。当代美国文化的研究有王恩铭的《当代美国社会与文化》、王作民的《美国万花筒》、刘永涛的《当代美国文化》、朱世达的《当代美国文化》、郑立信的《美国英语与美国文化》和吴斐的《美国社会与文化》等。国内也有些新词语、文化研究论文，但都不是系统全面的研究。文化和新词语相结合进行的研究更是寥寥无几。美国文化与新词语的著述几乎是空白，对它们的纵向与横向研究更是有待于深入和完善。随着时代的发展和研究水平的提高，新词语与文化的系统研究尤为重要，并具有深刻的现实意义和理论意义：

1. 有助于了解社会文化。对于新词语和当代文化的学习与研究有助于了解文化、社会、经济政治等现代文明，时代的变迁也能通过新词得到反映，人们在一定时期内的思维方式、文化、生活也通过新词语得到反映。对于它们的研究有助于学习者对其进行全面深入的了解。

2. 对新词语和文化的发展做出预测。作为研究者，不仅要观察追踪收集整理新词和文化现象，还应预测词汇文化发展趋势。英语新词的发展前景将会是：英语新词语的数量与日俱增、英语新词语的来源多种多样、英语新词语的形式趋向简洁。文化发展更是如此。根据新词语文化特征，我们对于未来文化趋势做出预测。

3. 可以为语言文化研究工作者和语言学习者提供丰富厚实的资料。在梳理新词语、新词义的形成、演变的过程及动因，探究文化特点等方面，为揭示当代词汇和文化的动态发展规律服务。

4. 为当代的文化词汇研究服务。通过文化和词汇的研究能使研究者和语言习得者适应国际上新词语整理和研究形势的需要，有利于开展国际交流。

5. 对新词语的规范及新词语词典编纂提供指导性意见。关于新词语在词典尤其是新词语词典中收录应该遵循以下基本原则：填充语言空白原则，丰富原则，简洁明了原则，品位原则，引导原则，符合语言结构规律原则。新词研究为词典编纂提供原始资料和理论框架，使得词典编纂有据可依。

　　6. 有助于跨文化交际。对文化新词的归纳分析，为学习者提供翔实的材料，使他们持有"宽容"的态度对待语言和文化现象，使得跨文化交际得以成功进行。

第二篇
美语新词语产生的文化背景
和美国文化特征

第三章 新词语产生的文化因素

一 新词语与美国社会生活

（一）婚恋

20 世纪中期，随着美国工业化和城市化进程的加快，社会得到高速发展，人们的生活水平大大提高，个人主义和自由至上的价值观念增强。法律条文的变更、妇女接受高等教育和就业机会的增多、妇女地位的变化，使得美国传统的婚姻家庭模式，即核心家庭模式，遭受到前所未有的挑战，出现了多元化家庭模式。

DINK（double income no kids，丁克家庭）是已婚夫妇选择不生育孩子的一种家庭类型，他们选择献身于对事业的追求或享受二人世界。由此结构而来的 DINs（double income no sex）则表示"双收入无性家庭"。而 SITCOM 家庭（single income two children oppressive mortgage，单份工资、两个孩子及沉重房贷负担的家庭）则过着负担比较重的生活。一些人为了节省费用，举办 wedding moon（婚礼加蜜月旅行）和 destination marriage（目的地结婚），还有一些人寻求公司赞助举行 sponsored wedding。近些年来，green wedding（绿色婚礼）受到美国年轻人欢迎。环保婚礼中的新人非常关心生态环境，持有环保社交的概念，因而他们选择的婚礼是绿色婚礼。美国新人在 wedding shower（婚前送礼会）上可以收到很多礼品，但许多人把自己不需要的礼品重新包装后再转送出去，这种行为被称为 regift（转赠礼品）。有的客人甚至把收据放在礼品里，新人就可以把礼品兑换成现金。这是因为美国具有无条件退款政策。结婚之后如果夫妇双方不在一地，一方追随另一方而居住在异地的被称为 trailing spouse（随迁配偶），夫妻双方不指望白头偕老而举行的婚礼为 starter marriage，而晚年结婚则是 elderweds。

　　由于女性地位得到提升，有的妇女薪水甚至比男性配偶还要高，人们称她们为 alpha earner（养家太太）。有些 househusband（家庭妇男）辞职在家带孩子做家务。一些大公司高级管理女性一旦有了孩子就辞职在家，目的是培养一流的孩子，她们是 Alpha Mom（强势妈妈）。而有些妈妈则是 stay at work mom（生完孩子就去上班）。tiger mom 表示"严厉却爱孩子的虎妈"，hockey mom 是"带孩子参加冰球比赛及训练的冰球妈妈"，soccer mom 是"那些带孩子参加棒球比赛和训练的白人中产阶级妈妈"，waitress mom 则是"工资低从事服务行业工作的劳动阶层的妈妈"。与此同时，各种与 dad 有关的新词应运而生。例如：office park daddy（已婚居住于郊区的白领父亲），NASCAR dad（白领工人父亲）。伊拉克战争迫使许多美国兵奔向战场，把孩子和妻子留在身后。为了安慰妻子和孩子，他们和家人制作与自己的真人大小一样的画像，陪伴妻子和孩子，这种画像被称为 flat daddy。21 世纪初，美国出现了 helicopter parent（采用直升机式教育的家长）和 lawn mower parent（割草机父母）两个新词。这些父母多为 20 世纪 80 年代生人，过分溺爱关注孩子。helicopter parent 不管孩子是否真的需要，过分关注孩子生活中的经历和问题，他们像直升机一样整天盘旋在孩子的身边，时刻等待孩子的召唤。与直升机父母不同，lawn mower parent 随时赶在孩子前面，帮助他们扫清道路上的障碍。在父母不同的教育方式下，出现了 trophy child（奖杯孩子），hurried child（过分早教的孩子），severely gifted child（极度有天分的孩子），free range child（被散养有许多自由活动的孩子），wikipedia child（研究与思考能力差的孩子）。

　　美国最高法院在索纳斯诉爱德华州一案中，支持爱德华州的规定，即一个提出要与住在本州的配偶离婚的人，必须是在本州居住长达一年以上的居民。它的目的是希望让打算分手的夫妻冷静下来，寻求和解的可能。但实际上多数已破裂的婚姻很难挽救。结果是许多人到南部的佛罗里达州或西部的内华达去办离婚，在这里几个星期即可获得离婚的终审。这样的离婚被称为 migratory divorce（移居离婚）或 renovate（到雷诺市解除婚姻）。这种非最终判决的规定显然达不到预期的目的，各州陆续取消这一规定，以使法律更符合实际。1970 年，美国统一国家法律委员会一致通过了 Uniform Marriage and Divorce Act，简称 UMDA（统一结婚—离婚法），确认只要夫妻一方提出离婚就可以将"婚姻无可挽回的破裂"作为离婚的唯一的理由准判离婚。自此，No Fault Divorce Law（无过错离婚法）相继在各州开始实施。无过错离婚法是促使美国家庭破裂的主要原因之一。splitters（分开者）这个新词成为离婚的委婉语。unwedding ceremony（婚姻解除仪式）替代 divorce，表明人们对于离婚开放的胸怀。

由于美国离婚率大幅上升，高达 50%，一些家庭重新组合，出现了 blended family（重组家庭）。在 blended family 中，男女双方各自带着前婚所生的孩子再婚，一起度 family moon（全家蜜月），这种家庭也被称为 step family（继亲家庭）。婚后所生的孩子成为 mutual child（共生孩子）。mother-out-law（前岳母），step wife（丈夫的前妻，前夫的妻子），wasband（妻子的前夫）让人应接不暇。夫妻离婚后，有的丈夫 pay the support due（定时支付抚养费），有的是 deadbeat father（不尽赡养孩子义务的父亲）。有的夫妻为了 custody rights（共同监护权）或为了获得 visitation right（看望子女权利）而打上法庭。parellel parenting（共同抚养），virtual visitation（虚拟探访）等成为解决问题的一种方法而出现。父母离婚导致一些孩子精神颓废，借酒浇愁，吸毒而不能自拔，孩子只能交给祖父母领养，这种情况称为 skipped generation。有些婚姻名存实亡，双方忍气吞声凑合了一辈子。当一方过世，另一方马上写出 post motem divorce（分葬离婚书），声明生不同时、死不同穴。

离婚率大幅上升，导致美国的单亲家庭也越来越多，催生大量问题。美国各州尝试各种方法来解决这个问题。一些州提倡人们缔结 prenuptial agreement 或 premarital agreement（契约婚姻）。它是夫妻双方完全自愿订立的一种新的婚姻形式，但男女双方必须在结婚前进行选择。当男女双方一致选择契约婚姻形式时，双方要订立协议：保证终身相伴，不轻易离婚，除非一方有明显的严重过错。即通过契约的形式来约束人们对离婚的选择的随意性。因而，所谓契约婚姻，指的是夫妻双方完全自愿订立的一种新的婚姻形式。

1967 年，美国最高法院规定各州过去制定的禁止黑白通婚的法律裁决为无效。在洛芬诉弗吉尼一案中，最高法院否决了种族间禁止通婚的各州法令。判决认为，结婚自由历来就被认为是个人神圣不可侵犯的权利，对一个自由人来说，它是自然而然的追求人生幸福的基本权利。自此以后，mixed family（异族通婚）有所增加。现在美国大约有 100 万儿童生活在收养家庭中，而这些家庭基本上都是由不同种族混合组成的家庭，所以也是 mixed marriage（异族通婚）或 salt and pepper（黑白种族通婚）家庭。

20 世纪 70 年代末 80 年代初，随着同性恋权益运动的发展，美国公众对同性恋者趋于宽容，在各地方、各州和联邦政府的反歧视政策、法律中，都加进了反对歧视性倾向的条款。继 Massachusetts 之后，Connecticut，Iowa，New Hampshire，New York，Vermont 等相继承认 same sex marriage（同性恋婚姻）。据 1990 年社会性别组织估测，美国大约有 170 万—340 万女性的丈夫曾经或正在与男性同性有性关系。据估测，大约 2%—4% 的美国已婚女性公开或秘密地经历过 bisexual（双性）婚姻或 same sex marriage（同性婚姻）。brokeback marriage（断背婚姻）是指"婚姻中的一方是同性恋或者曾经有过 a gay affair（同性恋经历）"。男女同性恋家庭分别被称为 gay family 和 lesbian family，如此一来，同性恋家庭所要的孩子就会有 two dads 或 two moms。到了 20 世纪 90 年代，同性恋解放运动使得同性恋身份逐渐得到社会认同，一度出现了 gabyboom（同性恋婴儿潮）。有上千万儿童生活在女同性恋者或者男同性恋者组建的家庭中，大多数同性恋家庭中的孩子是他们的父亲或母亲在成为同性恋者之前所生，那些孩子的父母在离婚或者分手以后成为同性恋者。也有的孩子是同性恋者婚姻后通过科学手段生育的。有的孩子则是同性恋者收养的孩子。

美国一些大城市每年都会有 gay parade（同性恋大游行）。libber（同性恋活动分子）要求同性恋拥有民权，呼吁同性恋者 come out of closet（出柜）。他们建立了 gay bar（同性恋酒吧），gay community（同性恋社区），gaybourhood（同性恋街区），gay bookstore（同性恋书店），gay bathroom（同性恋浴室），gay club（同性恋俱乐部）。同性恋被称为 queer，homo，same sex person。男同性恋者被称为 gayboy，queen，closet queen。女同性恋者叫做 lesbian，leslie，fair lady，dyke。lipstick lesbian 为"漂亮优雅的女同性恋"，luppie 表示"女同性恋雅皮士"。当然同性恋中不乏名人，他们中有很多人是很有名的艺术家、影视明星、体育明星和政治家，被称为 celesbian（名人同性恋者），他们曝光率高，承受巨大压力，如果是同性恋有时不得不 lanced（名人被迫承认是同性恋）。还有一些人是异性恋但常常有同性恋关系，他们被称为 heteroflexibility。

late-breaking gays 是"到了晚年才意识到自己是同性恋者"，hasbian 是
"曾为同性恋但是现在处于异性恋中的人"。同性恋艺术家表演的嘻哈
被称做 homohop。有些人为了吸引他人的注意使自己看上去像同性恋但
实际不是，这些人被称为 faux-mosexual（假同性恋者）。同性恋的声势
之浩大使得美国总统奥巴马不得不采取各种措施支持同性伴侣拥有各种
权利。2012 年 5 月他在接受美国广播公司采访时表示，他改变了自己
先前的反对态度转而支持同性恋婚姻。经过长期权益的抗争，有些同性
恋者不再对自己的身份感到恐惧，而是勇敢地承认自己的身份。他们不
仅仅谈论同性恋话题，还关心其他问题，他们的谈话涵盖各种内容，希
望被大众所接受。这类人被称为 post gay。然而，虽然同性恋者地位得
到提升，但是还会有一类人认为异性恋优于同性恋，这些人被大众称为
straight supremacist。他们对同性恋很敏感，有着敏感的 gaydar（同性恋
雷达）。这就是为什么每年六月份同性恋大游行时都会有反同性恋者与
赞同者在大街上辩论同性恋存在的合理性的原因。

在美国，大多数人相信婚姻的基础是爱情。年轻人已不再接受 ar-
ranged marriage（包办婚姻），而转向以互相爱慕（浪漫式爱情）为基础
而缔结婚约。人们认为现代婚姻的主要功能是提供伴侣和亲密关系，因
而强调个人自由选择配偶。这种选择的后果不会直接影响其他任何人，
而只会关系到这对夫妇本身及其将生育的儿女。虽然现代美国社会被认
为择偶有充分自由，实际上很多人受 homogamy（同类婚）影响。即在
择偶时人们愿意选取一个其背景、素养都同自己较相近的对象，而不是
地位悬殊的 morganatic marriage（异类婚）。

然而，快节奏的生活使得美国人很难找到爱情。于是美国人 Yaacov
Deyo 在 1998 年于好莱坞贝夫利山上的 Pete's Café 组织了 speed date（速
配）活动。这一概念迅速传到美国许多社区包括纽约，甚至英国。没时
间恋爱的美国人奔上了情感的高速公路。除了 speed date（速配）外，
美国人还推出 one minute date，three minute date，five minute date，intelli-
dating（知识型约会），hyper dating（超级约会，一晚约会多人）等速度
约会形式。

在恋爱过程中，出现了各种类型的恋爱关系，cradle robber 是指
"年龄大的男性找了一个年龄小的女性为友或为妻"，意为"老牛吃嫩
草者"。gold digger（掘金女）以美色骗取老男人钱财或提高社会地位，

意在从他们身上挖出点儿金子来。而这些腰缠万贯的老色男则被称为 dirty old man（色迷迷、肮脏的老头）或是 sugar daddy（蜜糖老爹）。有了 sugar daddy，sugar mom（蜜糖老妈）的出现也就不足为怪了。sugar mom 用钱财博取年轻男友的欢心。boy toy 或 toy boy 是指恋爱婚姻关系中，年龄比女方小很多的男性，而且这些女人大多是为了性满足。cougar 是中年女性与年轻男性的恋爱关系，manther 则是指"中年男性与年轻女性持有的恋爱关系"。

到了 20 世纪 80 年代，美国一些成功职业女士虽然到了已婚年龄甚至大龄却不急于结婚，而且为此而骄傲。这类人被称为 leather spinster（坚硬的女独身者）。有些 quirky alone（乐单族）并不因为年龄问题急于嫁人，而是耐心地等待合适的"那个他"的到来。那些类似"钻石王老五"的单身汉则被称为 toxic bachelor（有杀伤力的单身汉）。另外还有 nevermarrieds（终身不婚者），himbo（只有外在没有内在美的帅哥）等形容单身人士的新词。

几十年来美国非婚同居现象呈上升趋势，不但年轻人趋之若鹜，中老年人也不乏其例。有的两性之间长期同居，形同夫妻。有的因为工作地点与居住地点太远而只一周同居一次，被称作 living together apart（分开同居）。有的人同居后又散伙，或者与多名异性同居，如 badhop（随意换性伴侣），multipartner relationshons（多名性伴侣），poluamory（一人多爱）。这种两性关系使得 common-law marriage（习惯法婚姻），live-in relationship（同居关系），domestic partner（非婚姻同居伴侣）大有等同法律所承认的事实婚姻的趋势，使得许多同居伴侣都拥有已婚夫妻的权利。

因特网的高速发展使得许多人在谷歌搜索寻找异性朋友，这种行为被称为 google（谷歌搜索寻找异性朋友），双方下线后进一步互动，进行 fleshmeet（面对面的会晤）。网恋被称为 internet love。新婚夫妇在因特网上发布婚礼视频被称作 webcast wedding，即将结婚的新人在网上发布婚礼消息被称为 wedsite。

（二）衣着美容

美国的 shopping mall 是由数百家专业商店聚集在一起组成，坐落于美国郊区。它有供顾客使用的大型停车场。anchor store 也称作 draw tenant，被称作锚店，是知名的零售商，锚店是必不可少的"领头羊"。大型的购物中心都会引进知名的零售商，以吸引 retail traffic（购物人流），稳定市场收入。但近几十年由于激烈的竞争，顾客总希望看到各种服务与购物、饮食等结合在一起的购物中心。Urban Entertainment Center（城市娱乐中心）后来居上，成为最热门的概念之一。它将娱乐、餐饮与零售业集中在一幢建筑内。人们在购物中心购物后，在 foodcourt（美食广场）或 eatery（简餐店）解决午餐。也可以在这里的饭店吃完大餐在电影院里看 bluckbuster（大片）。有的男士不愿意陪伴妻子或女朋友购物，那她可以雇用商店里的 shopping boyfriend（购物男友）为她们提供周到的全程陪伴服务，提供购物咨询。在许多购物中心，buy one get one free（买一送一）的广告随处可见，这是商家主要的促销手段之一。美国商家提供三包服务，即 3R policy（replace，repair，refund，包换、包修、包退）。有些购物者钻这种服务的空子，买了东西，用上几天就去退货。这种行为被称为 shopgrifting（购物欺诈）或 wardrobing（使用后退货现象）。

20 世纪 90 年代，明星们爱穿名牌与佩戴珠宝，井市大街上也流行闪亮饰物，出现 bling（亮晶）一族。他们既不是黑帮，也不是社会的底层。甚至越来越多的女 bling 也加入其中，使得各种衣服首饰比从前更加炫目耀眼，多彩纷呈，有的甚至显得肤浅、无聊、俗气。2002 年科罗拉多州的三位设计师设计并制作名为 Crocs 的鞋类产品，全名为 Croslite，简称 Crocs。如今它已经成为美国人夏天必备的休闲鞋。近年来在美国颇为流行的还有 flip flop，它是人字形拖鞋。虽然起源于日本，但近年来在美国颇为流行。它如此流行以至于人们用它来指"那些政策立场上摇摆不定的人和政客"。设计师 Marc Jacobs 设计出 layering（叠层穿衣），在英美大行其道，颇受大众欢迎。年轻女士经常在里面穿一件长 T 恤，在外面套上一件不同颜色的短 T 恤，两种和谐的颜色搭配在一起，煞是好看。2008 年，形容词 T-shirtable 进入英语语言，成为流行语。它是指"适合被印制在 T 恤上作为标语或标志的东西"。2008 年11 月，奥巴马在芝加哥的格兰特公园举行百万民众参加的"竞选之夜"大集会，由于芝加哥是奥巴马竞选总部，他是当地出来的参议员，因而，芝加哥是民主党铁杆支持者。当时，这里 60% 的人都穿着印有奥巴马头像的 T 恤，以此表明自己的立场。奥巴马的形象成为 T-shirtable

pictures。

美国人在节假日、生日喜欢送礼物。有时礼物不是自己喜欢的种类，人们就会把它转赠他人。美国著名网站 www. regiftable. com（礼物可转送性）最近的一项调查显示，52%的美国人曾经把他人给予的礼物转给朋友或亲戚。78%的人认为转赠礼物可以接受。to regift 用作动词，指"把礼物转送别人"，regifting 表示转赠礼，而 regifter 是转赠礼物的人。

穆斯林的服饰文化强调服饰必须遮盖羞体，以免因暴露引发道德沉沦等不良社会后果。穆斯林服饰文化强调衣饰必须庄重，因为它向外界展示人们的气质、风度和品格。穆斯林妇女游泳时必须穿 burqini（遮挡全身的游泳衣），穿 camikini（吊带背心比基尼裤衩）是不允许的。有些反传统的妇女可能会 Dejab（停止戴头巾）。近些年，美国还出现了 hijabista（穿着既符合穆斯林传统又很时髦的穆斯林妇女或专门为穆斯林妇女设计时髦服装的设计师）一词，这些穆斯林妇女可能住在新泽西也可能是雅加达。

lipstick indicator（口红指数）这个术语指"口红销售量在经济萧条前或萧条期间陡然大增现象"。在 20 世纪 90 年代末和 2001 年"9·11"恐怖袭击事件后，美国的经济出现下滑，但口红却出现热销。同样，男士领带销量也大幅度上升。据统计，2002 年 8—10 月间口红的销量比上一年同期增长 11%。同样，受金融危机影响一些妇女精打细算但依然打扮得时髦漂亮，她们被称作 recessionista（不景气时尚达人）。还有一些人为了节省费用，自己做衣服，成为 sewist（缝衣匠）。有的父母把年轻孩子不穿的衣服拿来自己穿，这种衣服被称作 hand-me-up（穿孩子的旧衣服），还有的年轻人把衣服传给弟弟妹妹，后者把其称为 hand-me-down（别人用过的旧衣服）。

Casual Friday（休闲星期五，同义词为 Dress-down Friday，Bis-Cas-Fri 或 Casual Day）最早起源于美国，现今已经流传到世界各地。在这一天，员工可以穿休闲服上班。20 世纪 90 年代，休闲星期五已经成为一种社会时尚，尤其是在旧金山湾区。"休闲星期五"原本是要为办公场所注入无拘无束、轻松的气氛，但结果似乎适得其反，办公室的气氛反而比以前更加沉重。表面上看，员工似乎可以摆脱制服的呆板形象及套装的严肃气氛，但他们却开始为了要穿什么便服而大伤脑筋。结果，这些周五穿的非正式服装反而成了 business casual（商务休闲）。大约在 2000 年，美国男性服装公司又创出 Dress-up Thursday 概念，试图重振西装昔日的辉煌。于是，许多公司开始重拾着装理念，一些曾经允许职员穿牛仔服装的公司也规定他们必须着 formal business casual（正式的工作休闲装），甚至是 business formal（工作正装上班）。但是，对于一部分职业女性来说，为了符合工作职场对女性的期待和要求，女性无形中必须穿着某种类型的服饰，这样才会被认为是得体的，才可以顺利地在职场上升迁。因而她们还要注重 dress correctness（服装的正确性），深色的套装或是白色的衬衣是最得体的服饰。除了上班时必穿的衣饰和平时所穿的休闲装外，人们还准备 third wardrobe（第三衣橱），它是介于正装与休闲装之间的服装。根据这个词汇，人们创出了 floordrobe（地板衣橱）一词，表示"满地摊放的衣服"。

与此同时，美国出现多种与衣饰有关的非主流文化。hyperwhite（超级白人，电脑精英）穿着不同于白人的衣饰，喜欢带着口袋保护套，防止钢笔墨水漏到衬衣上，皮带套里装着各种小玩意儿，他们还喜欢穿防热短裤。这些人包括 the Bill Gates nerd, Screech nerd, Millhouse nerd, Dwight Schrewt nerd 和 Michael Scott nerd 等技术精英。另外一种亚文化是 shoefiti（鞋子涂鸦）。毕业生为了纪念毕业并表示人生新开始而把鞋子系在电线上，这种行为被称作 shoefiti（鞋子涂鸦），成了像 graffiti（涂鸦）一样的街头艺术。yarn bombing（针织涂鸦）是一些妈妈或奶奶级别的人物，出于迷信或好意在公共场所，如门把手或椅子上留下她们所织的针织物，就好像涂鸦一般，留待公众欣赏。extreme ironing（极限熨烫）是西方近几年颇为流行且颇具危险的新式运动。在极限熨烫运动中，参赛者带着衣服、熨斗和熨衣板攀登险峻的山峰，潜入水中，在雪地中、在沙漠里，在悬崖之间的钢丝绳上熨烫衣服。这种运动结合了户外运动的挑战性和烫衣服的温馨及成就感。

美国是世界整形美容超级大国，各种整形手术都有可能被完美地实现。美国整形协会 2008 年发布的信息表明，最受美国人欢迎的 cougar lift（整形）分别是 liposuction（吸脂手术），breast augmentation（丰胸手术），blepharoplas 或 eyelid surgeryty（眼皮手术），abdominoplasty（tummy tuck，缩腹手术），breast reduction（缩胸手术），rhinoplasty（隆鼻手术）和 facelift（去皱整容手术）。为了 perma-youth（驻颜）和美丽，他们举行 Botox party（肉毒素派对）和 pumping party（注射硅胶聚会）。近年来美容界推出各种新型手术，包括 Bozilian（去除阴毛手术），voice lift（声音整形），mommy makeover（孕后复原手术），liposculpture（脂肪去除术），scar management（疤痕去除术）等。一些人沉迷于整形不能自拔，进行几十次整形手术，变成 surgiholic（整形狂）。美国人非常在意牙齿的美白，他们花在牙齿美白的费用是所有美容中最多的，热衷于牙齿美白的人被称为 bleachorexia（亮白牙齿迷）。

当代美国男性对于一些整形或美容也颇为热衷，美国媒体 2010 年 10 月 30 日援引一份消费者调查报告称，2009 年美国男性在面霜、眼霜、除纹霜等化妆护肤产品方面的花销达到 48 亿美元（约人民币 320 亿元），是 1997 年的两倍，当时这个数字仅为 24 亿美元。他们穿 Manny Hose（男士丝袜裤），Mandals（罗马式凉鞋），挎着 Murses（小型类似女用包），使用 guyliner（画眼线）和 manscara（男士睫毛膏）。在纽约等大城市有专门为男士服务的男士美容院，在这里，男人们可以享受各种类型的护理，比如对眼疲劳的治疗、修眉或者画眉。boyzilian（男士巴西式蜜蜡脱毛）和 manscaping（男生脱毛）也是这里的一个服务项目。男性一直认为如果女性穿深 V 衬衣或裙子，或是性感或大胆，或是不雅。但是近年来男士开始穿露胸衬衣，展示他们的性感，这种穿着被称为 he-vage（露胸衣）。美国男人们刚刚了解 metrosexual 的定义，开始关心品牌、美容和品位，努力向 homosexual 看齐，时尚预言家们又纷纷宣布：精心甚至过度修饰自己外表的 metrosexual（都市玉面男）风潮，典型如贝克汉姆，已经过时了。男人们必须要 ubersexual（都市阳刚男）——具有男人的阳刚之气，但仍然得保持女性化的那一面。而在不久以前，时尚预测专家又宣布，technosexual（科技型男）已取代都市阳刚男，成为现代流行词。

（三）饮食

快餐文化发源于美国，美国人创作出许多与快餐有关的词汇。例如：convenience foods（方便食品），TV dinner（电视餐），take out（外卖），fast food cluster（快餐店聚集地），grab and go（拿着食品就走），fast casual（快餐加随意的就餐方式），toy food（速食品）等词。

与快餐文化紧密相连的是美国的汽车文化。由于美国是汽车大国，被称为"轮子上的国家"。家家有车，户户出行选择驾车。只要到了16岁，人们都会学习驾车，拿到一个驾照。为了方便人们开车，快餐公司推出许多食品。如 cup-holder cuisine（杯装食品），dashboard dining（仪表盘食物），one-handed food（手指食物，方便工作或开车），deskfast（桌边早餐），drive-through cuisine（汽车食品），drive time dining（边开车边吃饭）等。

在美国，一些人只喜欢吃 white food（白色加工食品），Frankenfood（转基因食品），stealth fat（反式脂肪酸食品）和 Chichenability（鸡肉味食品）。有些人是 meat tooth（喜欢吃肉），有些人是 salad dodger（不吃沙拉的人）。一味地食用快餐和不健康的生活方式，如 passive overeating（被动多吃），auto-eating（机械地吃）带来各种疾病和肥胖现象：globesity（全球性肥胖），freshmen 15（大一15磅），Generation XL（超重儿），gurgitator（大胃王），milkaholic（牛奶狂），couch potato（沙发土豆）。

随着这些现象的增加，美国人意识到问题的严重性。政府开始提倡健康的生活方式，2011年，美国农业部和第一夫人米歇尔推介了 Food Plate（全新饮食指南），取代20年来人们所熟知的 Food Pyramid（食物金字塔）。新的饮食指南将引导人们更合理地饮食，包括食用更多的水果和蔬菜。越来越多的人开始注重健康饮食，他们推崇有机、绿色、环保食品。许多人选择吃 heirloom pork（有机猪肉），pharma food（含有保健药物的食品），deprivation cuisine（健康但无味的食品），推崇 ape diet（素食），grazing（多吃少餐）。他们发明了 tofurkey（豆腐火鸡），unturkey（素食火鸡），只做 ethical eater（素食者），freegan（免费素食者），locavore（只吃当地食品的人），locapour（只喝本地酒的人），vegivore（蔬菜迷）。素食者更是大行其道，flextarian 只是偶尔吃肉的素食者，lacto-vegetarian 是食用奶制品素食者，但是拒绝蛋类食品。ovo vegetarian 不食肉类也不食用奶制品，但是食用蛋类和蜂类产品。vegan 不食用任何奶类、蛋类或任何动物食品。近十几年来，一些人出于健康和喜好等各种原因，选择食用鱼类和禽类等动物食品。semi-vegetarian 除了吃素食外，还食用鱼类产品、禽类和蛋类食品，甚至牛奶。而 pescatarian 除了食用鱼类及贝类产品外，拒绝食用所有的肉类产品。二者被统称为"新素食主义者"。fruitarian 只食用水果、坚果、果仁等食物。su vegetarian 起源于印度，他们拒吃所有的动物产品和某些蔬菜，如洋葱、大蒜、大葱、韭菜等。macrobiotics 只食用全麦食品和豆类食品，还有一些 macrobiotics 并不是素食者，他们有些人会吃鱼类产品。而 raw vegan 只食用生鲜水果、蔬菜及坚果。

越来越多的美国人认识到快餐的危害。他们推崇慢餐的理念。除非万不得已，否则不会选择吃快餐。slow food 注重传统和有机种植方式，倡导美食和美酒、放慢进餐节奏、享受生活，主流食品减少了肉和土豆。越来越多的饭店增设了 salad bar（沙拉吧），供人们选择新鲜的蔬菜。

美国人还发明创造了各种饮料，以完善健康生活方式。如 relaxation drink（无酒精提神饮料），beersicle（啤酒冰棒），garage wine（产量小且质量高的酒），在各种饮料中加入苏打、盐、矿物质制成 energy drink（能量饮料）。

异族食品被引进美国人的餐桌。美国人很享受 Wok（锅）中的 stir frying（炒）。tofu（豆腐），tempeh（天贝），soy milk（豆奶）经常出现在高档食谱中。人们对于 Pita bread（口袋面包）中加入 hammus（鹰嘴豆）习以为常。其他食品如 tahini（芝麻酱），falafel（沙拉三明治），gyros（沙威玛）更是大受欢迎。Babka（巴步卡蛋糕），cannoli（菜油），coquille St. Jacques（扇贝），refried beans（炸豆泥），gorp（花生、葡萄干、谷物及巧克力混合的能量小吃）等词逐渐被大众所熟知，成为美语词语，进入字典。

自从美国第一夫人米歇尔在白宫开辟菜园，种植绿色有机蔬菜以此倡导健康生活后，美国掀起了在家中阳台或花园种植食物的热潮。人们吃 100-foot diet（100 英尺食物）和 garden to fork（自家花园产食物）。有些人在自家后院进行小块地密集种植，称为 SPIN，有些人租地种菜。城市里开始有了 window farm（窗口种农作物）和 farm scraper（顶层种庄稼的高楼）。

更有意思的是，许多食物被赋予更多的寓意：candy bar phone 是无盖手机，在某个部门增长极快而其他部门稳定增长的经济被称为 cappuccino economy（cappuccino 经济），champagne problem 是"两个理想之事间的决定"，小钱上不注意、大手大脚终成浪费的行为被称为 latte factor（拿铁因素）。令人震惊之事被形象地称为 coffee spitter（晴天霹雳），marmalade dropper（震惊之事）或 muffin choker（晴天霹雳）。票房收益不高但极有教育意义的电影被称作 spinach cinema（菠菜电影）。

（四）运动健康

随着科技的进步，现代人变得越来越懒惰。人们每天坐在电视、电脑前的时间日渐增多，出现了许多 couch potato（沙发土豆）和 mouse potato（鼠标土豆）。运动量减少，零食、便利食品等加工食品的消费也随之增加。人们做饭时间减少，越来越多的人去餐馆就餐。Obesity epidemic（肥胖的流行）已经不是个人的体形问题，已经成为国家问题。鉴于此，美国国会通过了一些致力于解决肥胖问题的议案，许多州也设定了 school food standard（学校餐饮标准）。美国卫生组织在社区范围内推动健康计划，如在社区中修建更多人行道，鼓励人们步行，在公园中修建 jogging trail（跑步小道），在学校推广健康午餐等。在政府的教育及推动下，全民健身运动意识得到提升。

越来越多的人开始进行 jogging（慢跑）之类的 aerobics（有氧运动），更多的城市开设自行车道，为骑车人乘 ten speeds（十变速自行车）锻炼提供方便。各种各样的运动项目应运而生，例如：sightjogging（观景慢跑），strollerobics（推婴儿车有氧运动），chariobics（椅子运动），core training（肚皮后背运动），retro running（倒走），off road skating（越野滑冰），parkour（跑酷），slacklining（走尼龙绳），fastpacking（背包跑步），dancesport（室内舞竞赛），glaming（豪华露营），Zorbing（左宾球锻炼）。

美国人最喜欢的运动是橄榄球、棒球和篮球。但是冲浪和橄榄球是新词产生最多的运动领域。如：double inverse（双反），blitzing（虎扑式），suicide squad（敢死队，橄榄球赛中负责开球和踢悬空球队），delay（拖延比赛）。冲浪运动中你可以 hot dogging（炫耀技艺），你可以是一个 gremmie（生手），也可以做 beach bunny（一个不冲浪女孩），但是不能做 hodad（佯装冲浪者），有些人专门做 surfcaster（冲浪预报员），为喜欢冲浪的爱好者提供浪大到可以冲浪的预报和预报地点。一些足球迷为了看足球会在大赛期间请一个 soccer leave（看足球休假）。为了迎合人们对运动场地的需求，美国许多地方也建了一些超大的 soccerplex（巨型足球场地）。美国的高尔夫球场是大众都能消费得起的休闲运动，生意伙伴也会在此谈生意。有些人会在打高尔夫球时故意打得拙劣以取悦于顾客，这种现象为 client golf（顾客高尔夫）。篮球运动中较为出名的新词是 slam dun（灌篮）和 designated hitter（指定击球手）。

值得一提的是 extreme sport。extreme sport 也称为 action sport 或 adventure sport。大多都是近几十年刚刚诞生、方兴未艾的体育项目。由于极限运动有其"融入自然、挑战自我"的"天人合一"的特性，使得极限运动风靡于美国和欧洲。根据季节它可分为夏季和冬季两大类，运动领域涉及"海、陆、空"多维空间。极限运动主要有：rock climbing（攀岩），paragliding on skis（高山滑翔伞速降滑雪），water skiing（滑水），kayat slalom（激流皮划艇），water scooter（水上摩托），bunjee jumping（蹦极跳），extreme ironing（极限熨烫），extreme tourism（极限旅游），black-water rafting（黑水漂流），glacier walk（冰川健走），parahawking（滑翔驯鹰）等。

另外一种受欢迎的运动是 yoga。越来越多的美国人开始练习瑜伽，尤其是婴儿潮一代，他们已经成为中老年人，不能进行剧烈运动。于是 zen house（瑜伽屋）成为他们和一些美国人的新宠。yoga mat（瑜伽垫），yoga room，yoga studio 颇受大众欢迎。为了适应大众需求，健身界推出 urban yoga（传统瑜伽加上配乐有氧运动），使得瑜伽运动在美国大放异彩。

当前，体育运动已成为美国人最热衷的休闲方式。据一项调查显示，约 6/10 的美国人认为休闲时间最好从事某项有具体目的的体育运动。许多美国城市在城建规划中都对体育设施分布作了明确的规定，市政府必须在预算中投入资金兴建体育场馆和体育设施。美国城市的每一个街区几乎都有一座小型的体育场所，免费向公众开放。

在美国，人们为了健康寻求各种沐浴疗法，这些疗法包括 vinotherapy（葡萄酒浴），forest bathing（森林浴），preatharian（空气疗法）。还有些人去氧吧吸氧。有些人为了减肥打赌，称作 betdiet，如果减肥不成功，钱就会捐给慈善机构。新娘为了能穿上美丽婚服并展示曼妙身姿在婚前进行 briet（婚前新娘减肥），有些人或明星雇佣 diet cop（减肥监督人）和 health coach（健康教练），监督他们饮食，达到塑身的好效果。

除了体育休闲外，美国人还喜欢短期度假。度假形式花样繁多，衍生出许多相关词汇：staycation（在家度假），daycation（一日游），nano-break（纳米游，只住一晚的假日），microvacation（短期旅游），manca-

tion（全是男性的旅游）, fakation（不像假期的假期）, weather tourism
（观察天气现象的旅游）apple tourism（采摘苹果游）, agritourism（农家
院）, haycation（农场游）, architourism（建筑观光游）, naycation（不花
钱休假）, barefoot luxury（优雅舒适放松的地点）, black-hole resort（黑
洞旅游地, 阻断所有通信的旅游地）, dark tourism（黑色旅游, 目的地
充满死亡威胁、恐惧的旅游）。

二 新词语与美国科学技术

（一）环保

在美国，公众的环境意识较强，政府的环境政策完善。environmen-
talism（环境保护主义）已经成为一个广为接受的社会思潮。大多数美
国人都确信自己是一个 environmentalist。20 世纪 90 年代，公众的环境
意识日见浓厚，导致环境保护运动的高涨，这些对政府的行为产生了巨
大的影响。1970 年 4 月 22 日，美国首次举行了声势浩大的 Earth Day
（地球日）活动，这是人类有史以来第一次规模宏大的群众性环境保护
运动。举办"地球日"活动的宗旨是唤起人类爱护地球、保护家园的
意识，促进资源开发与环境保护的协调发展。地球日影响力巨大，目
前，全世界有 170 多个国家在 4 月 22 日庆祝"世界地球日"。到了 20
世纪 80 年代，地球变暖和其他气候变化问题引起大众的关注，美国已
有上万多个各种各样的政府和非政府环境保护组织，政府组织有 the
Natural Resources Defense Council and the Environmental Defense Fund, National Wildlife Federation, the Nature Conservancy, The Wilderness Society,
World Wide Fund for Nature, Friends of the Earth, Wyoming Outdoor Council
Wildlife Conservation International。更为激进的组织有 Greenpeace, Earth
First! 和 Earth Liberation Front。

美国联邦环境政策的法律框架建立于 20 世纪 70 年代。由于执政党
共和党较为重视环境，尼克松签署了 national environmental law（国家环
境法），开创了美国 environment decade（环保十年）。该立法注重空气/
水面/地下水的第一代污染物和固体废物处理。Clean Air Act（清洁空气
法）规定汽车排放标准和最后实现及罚金，极大减少了汽车带来的污
染。在此期间，尼克松创建了环境保护局，使其成为一个独立的实体。

EPA（环保局）是由联邦法律授权对国家的土地、空气质量和水资源系统进行保护的联邦机构。它一方面代表政府实施国家的大部分环保法规，另一方面以联邦政府名义采取各种措施来实现国家的环保目标。它提倡使用先进的科学和技术来预防和治理污染。由环保局领导组织的一系列项目非常成功。例如《气候行动方案》，节能照明的"绿灯计划"，1993 年 9 月由克林顿总统发起的"绿色汽车计划"。

克林顿政府在环境保护方面取得了一些进展。副总统 Al Gore 与环保局的 Bruno 都是环保主义者。他们都认为环保与经济发展是可以兼容的。克林顿政府增加了环境保护局的预算经费，美国许多自然资源，尤其是湿地得到了保护。

值得一提的是 Al Gore，他在推动环境保护方面功不可没。他为了鼓励能源效率和燃料多元化积极推动 carbon tax（碳税）的执行。促成规定发达国家承担削减温室气体排放的《京都协议书》这一国际性条约。后来他又以《难以忽视的真相》一书，于 2007 年获得诺贝尔和平奖。

在这一期间，苏联共产主义消失，美国消费主义受到挑战。环境保护主义反对消费主义的做法和观念，他们呼吁减少空气污染，批判大量生产 SUV 汽车，要求提高汽车里程碑，限制在公园和娱乐场所使用雪上汽车、游艇、越野沙滩车和助动车，反对开建折扣商店等。

美国国会迄今为止已颁布了多个联邦环境法规，按年份分类主要有以下几种：

1970—Clean Air Act（Extension）

1970—Environmental Quality Improvement Act

1972—Federal Water Pollution Control Amendments of 1972

1972—Federal Insecticide, Fungicide, and Rodenticide Act

1972—Marine Protection, Research, and Sanctuaries Act of 1972

1973—Endangered Species Act

1974—Safe Drinking Water Act

1976—Resource Conservation and Recovery Act（RCRA）

1976—Toxic Substances Control Act（TSCA）

1977—Surface Mining Control and Reclamation Act

1978—National Energy Conservation Policy Act

1980—Comprehensive Environmental Response, Compensation, and Liability Act（CERCLA）

1980—Fish and Wildlife Conservation Act

1982—Nuclear Waste Policy Act

1989—Basel Convention

1990—Clean Air Act Amendments of 1990

1990—Oil Pollution Act of 1990

1992—Residential Lead-Based Paint Hazard Reduction Act

1994—Executive Order 12898 on Environmental Justice

1996—Mercury-Containing and Rechargeable Battery Management Act（P. L. 104 – 19）

1996—Safe Drinking Water Act Amendments of 1996

1998—Transportation Equity Act for the 21st Century（TEA – 21）

2005—Energy Policy Act of 2005

2005—Safe, Accountable, Flexible, Efficient Transportation Equity Act: A Legacy for Users（SAFETEA）

联邦政府大力支持清洁煤技术开发项目，促进 solar energy（太阳能）和 wind power（风能）技术的开发和应用，征收天然产品发展税旨在保护某些因人类活动而减少的自然产品的发展。例如康涅狄格州的牡蛎发展税。推出汽车行动计划。如企业购买或租用供集体上下班的轿车，该项计划则为其提供30%的财政优惠。美国政府在 1996 年出台了"美国国家可持续发展战略——可持续的美国和新的共识"，责成两个专门机构负责实施这一战略计划。green office, green furniture, green plane 等可持续发展理念深入到了美国人的生活中。绿色办公楼一天只开 11 小时空调，绿色办公家具均是二手旧家具，绿色飞机使用 biofuel（生物燃料）。

美国研究组织在记录和理解地球空气、土壤、大气、动植物等环境方面起到极大的作用。促进了国际性全球工作项目的出台。如世界气候研究计划、国际地圈—生物圈计划、国际人类空间和全球变化计划等。

美国鼓励公众积极参与法规的实施。个人或团体可以起诉执法失职的政府机构和造成环境破坏的企业。法案允许企业根据环保条例自行选择最佳环保途径以便获得最佳成本效益的条款。对减少机动车造成的污染也有规定。它要求使用对空气污染更少的燃料、汽车、卡车及其他机动车，规定机动车定期检查尾气排放，并对减少交通污染企业给予优惠政策。

由于气候变暖、大气污染等原因，越来越多的美国人注重环保，人们纷纷选择健康的生活方式。鉴于此，新版牛津大词典收录了新词 locavore（土食者），hypermiler（超级省油），carrot mob（支持环保商店并购尽所有产品的活动），green collar（绿领），green urbanism（绿色城市化），carbon footprint（碳足迹），green audit（绿色审计），aquascape（水景）。《新牛津美语词典》在每年圣诞假期前都会宣布年度新词。2006 年的年度新词为 carbon neutral（碳中和）。warmist（气候变暖者）唾弃那些 SUV Democrat（宣传环保，但拥有并使用 SUV、破坏环保的民主党人士）。环保人士积极应对 global dimming（全球灰暗化）和 white pollution（白色污染）。明星和政治名人等热衷于 carbon neutral（碳中和）并使用 biodiesel（生化柴油），同情 climatee refugee（气候难民），支持 green GDP（绿色 GDP）。即使是找对象也要看对方有没有 ecosexual（环保性趋向）。吃饭要考虑 food mile（食物运输里程），尽量吃当地产的食物，做一个 locavore（土食主义者）。喝水是污水处理过后的 new water（新水），看的不再是 p-book（纸质书籍），提倡 upcycling（变废为宝）和 free-cycling（免费回收），freeganism（不消费主义），pay as you throw（按垃圾量收费的政治计划）。

在北美，100 miles menu（100 英里内菜单）掀起了一种生活方式浪潮，它倡导人们计算运输食物的 food mile（食物英里），重视本地生长的有机食物。而这些食材，则全部来自餐厅 100 英里范围内的农场，它们都是在原始自然状态下、适应动植物本性自然生长。烹饪用料就地取材，减少 cookprint（烹饪足迹），食物更加新鲜时令，同时达到 carbon offset（抵消因长途运输带来的碳排放污染）效果。

在春秋两季，充满杂草树叶的园林垃圾数量庞大，但是易于降解。从 1993 年开始，美国政府就已颁布法令禁止填埋城市园林垃圾，也很少使用燃烧方法处理。取而代之的是 composting（堆肥处理）和 grasscycling（草坪循环处理）等有机处理方式。堆肥处理是指利用自然界的细菌、放线菌、真菌等微生物，有控制地利用降解作用，将城市园林垃圾中的有机废物转化为腐殖质的生物化学处理技术。市政工人在园林修剪完毕后，将园林垃圾堆积在长、宽、高各三英尺的堆肥处理装置里，使这些有机废物自然降解。grasscycling 是将剪下的碎草留在草坪上。这种专门针对大型草坪碎草的处理方法可以节约处理剩余碎草的时间、费用及人力成本。草坪上割下的碎草可提供氮，这样就可节省气肥（碳酸氢铵）。

目前，奥巴马在环保问题上采取了较为积极的态度，他曾经明确提出，"美国在新能源和环保问题上重新领导世界"。在他的推动下，美国制定了绿色能源法案。该法案由 green energy（绿色能源），energy efficiency（能源效率），gas emission of green house（温室气体减排），low carbon economy（低碳经济）四个部分组成。法案明确规定，美国的电力公司、石油企业和大型制造业企业必须设定减排目标，进行减排量交易。美国应以 2005 年为基准年度到 2012 年使温室气体减排 3%，到 2020 年减排 20%，到 2030 年减排 42%，到 2050 年减排 83%。该法案构成了美国向低碳化经济转型的法律框架。Recyclable energy（可循环利用能源），CO_2 回收与储藏，low carbon traffic（低碳交通），intelligent grid（智能电网）、生物能和地热等成为企业、公众和媒体的热门词语。

（二）计算机

随着电脑的普及和因特网的飞速发展，网络英语进入人们的生活，并迅速发展。因特网的蓬勃发展为人们提供了解信息的最佳途径，人们渴望了解世界大事件和周围的新闻。网民队伍日益壮大，形成了不可忽视的 netizen（网民）群体。他们创造出新词新语并使之传播，形成这个群体的语言标识。如：hypertext（超文本），cybersurf（网络漫游），antivirus（抗病毒的），shareware（共享软件），telecom（远程通信），download（下载），online（在线），preset（预置），prescan（预扫描），preprocessor（预处理程序），password（口令），hyperlink（超链接），upload（上传），login（登录），logoff（注销），backup（备份），onhook（挂机），subdomain（子域），subnet（子网），subprogram（子程序），freeware（免费软件）。一些网络电子词汇已成为使用者表达思想时不可或缺的词语。如：microsoft（微软），micromoney（网络微型货币），microsurf（沉溺于网络），cyberspace（网络空间），cyberfood（电脑食品），cyberfraud（网络诈骗），cybercafé（网际咖啡屋），cybermouse

（三维鼠、遥控鼠），cyberphobia（电脑恐惧症），cyberpunk（网际浪人），cyber sales（网际行销），cybersex/cyberporn/cybersmut/cyberslut（网际色情）。netspeak（网络语言），netsurf（网络漫游），netizen（网民），netiquette（网络礼节），netpreneur（网络企业家），netspionage（网上间谍活动），webpage（网页），website（网址），webcam（网上摄像机），webisode（网络片断），webnomics（网络经济），webucation（网络教育），webzine（网络杂志），teleconferencing（远程会议），telemarketing（电子购物），internaut（网上漫游者），e-trade（电子贸易），e-money（电子货币），e-commerce（电子商务），e-wallet（电子钱包）。

生活节奏加快，要求人们使用缩略语和特殊符号来提高网上实时交流效率。具有时尚、简洁、灵活等特点的网络英语词汇逐渐形成，它们大多使用缩略语和符号。如用 BTW 代替 by the way，WWW 表示 World Wide Web，IP 表示 Internet Protoco（因特网传输协议），ISP 表示 Internet Service Provider（网络服务商），PPP 表示 Point to Point Protocol（点对点的传输协议）。R 等于 are，4 表示 four，B4 表示 Before，F2F 表示 Face-to-Face，B2B 表示 Business to Business，luk 4 表示 look for。YTTT? 表示 You Telling The Truth? IAC 表示 In Any Case，LU4E 表示 love you forever，pls 表示 please，BF 表示 Boyfriend，GF 表示 girl friend，AFAIK 表示 as far as I know，BBL 表示 be back later，TY 表示 Thank you，VG 表示 Very good，DLTM 表示 Don't lie to me，HAND 表示 Have a nice day，KIT 表示 Keep In Touch，YHBT 表示 You have been trolled（你上当了），YHL 表示 You have lost，CU 表示 see you，OIC 表示 Oh, I see，ICQ 表示 I seek you，2B or not 2B 表示 to be or not to be，B4N 表示 bye for now，Good 9 表示 Good Night。

emoticon（表情符号）也成为人们，尤其是年轻人喜欢使用的符号。表示肢体语言的形象符号有 "T－T" 代表流泪，"□_ □" 代表欢呼，":" 表示高兴，嘴巴向上翘着笑，": ( )" 表示不开心，嘴巴向下弯着，等等。"｛｝" 或者 "［］" 表示拥抱，"3" 表示 kiss 接吻，"R" 表示献上一朵玫瑰，"G" 表示送上一份礼物，". ：－e" 表示 disappointed，")" 表示 wink，": － @" 表示 screaming，". ：－S" 表示 confused，"^" 表示 thumbs up（竖大拇指），". ：8 －)" 表示 wear glasses（戴眼镜），"－O" 表示 shocked 或 surprised（惊讶）。

Social network（社交网站）指用户基于共同的兴趣、爱好、活动在网络平台上构建的一种社会关系网络，这种网络服务以"实名交友"为基础，融入了各种娱乐内容，让交流变成了熟人之间的娱乐，使游戏变成了朋友之间的沟通。在美国，Blog，Facebook，Twitter 是最为著名和有影响力的社交网站。与此有关的新词大量出现。如：social swarming（社交聚会），social networking（社交网络交流），social notworking（工作时间浏览社交网络），social networking fatigue（社交网络疲劳），socially produced（合作创建的网络），social book marking（网址收藏夹），selfie（社交网络自我拍照）等。

Blog 全名为 Web log，中文意思是"网络日志"，后来缩写为 Blog。它是继 Email、BBS、IM 之后出现的第四种网络交流方式，是网络时代的个人"读者文摘"，Blog 以网络作为载体，使用者迅速便捷地发布自己的心得，及时有效轻松地与他人进行交流，是集丰富多彩的个性化展示于一体的综合性平台。它的出现和发展催生了许多新词。如：audioblog（音频博客），blog book（博客书），nanopublishing（网络发行，用博客技术出版发行），blogebrity（名人博主），celeblog（名人博客），flog（假博客，公司主办的博客），sock puppet（假名），splog（垃圾博客），microblogging（微博客），peep culture（窥视文化），social media（社交媒体），vlog（视频博客），vodcasting（视频广播），wiki（维基百科），word of blog（博客交流），egocasting（灵魂传输，看、读、听符合自己思想信条的媒体节目），mindcasting（发布自己思想、观点的博客），podcasting（播客）等。

Facebook 是一个社交网络服务网站，于 2004 年 2 月 4 日上线。Facebook 是美国排名第一的照片分享站点，每天上载 850 万张照片。随着用户数量增加，Facebook 的目标已经指向其他一些领域，如互联网搜索、音乐下载等。

Twitter（推特）是即时信息的一个变种，是美国的一个社交网络及微博客服务的网站。它利用无线网络、有线网络、通信技术进行即时信息的交流，是一种微博客。它允许用户将自己的最新动态和想法以短信形式发送给手机和个性化网站群或个人。由于它的纪实性和简短性，受到各种年龄段人群的喜欢。它的大量使用催生许多新词。如：bashtag（标签破坏），death tweet（死亡威胁），defriend（删除好友），friend

（加为好友），diarrhearist（过多分享个人信息），fakester（社交网站发布虚假信息的人），FOMO（被忘恐惧症），meformer（发布个人信息者），Mososo（移动社交软件），sololo（社交本地移动），tweeterverse（社交网络空间），twitchfork（愤怒、挑衅帖子），tweet up（网友见面），tweet seats（剧院推特专位，专供观众上网发微博的座位）等。

Wireless Local Area Networks（WLAN，无线局域网络）是相当便利的数据传输系统，它利用 Radio Frequency（射频）的技术，取代旧式碍手碍脚的双绞铜线局域网络，使得无线局域网络能利用简单的存取架构让用户透过它，达到信息随身化的理想境界。不管人们在办公室的哪个角落，只要有无线局域网络产品，就能随意地发电子邮件、分享档案及网络浏览。与无线网络有关的新词有 digital normad（无线网络游民），piggybacker（非法使用无线网络），Wifi（无线上网），Spim（通过 Instant Messaging 来传播的垃圾信息），whack（非法使用无线网络数据），telematics（电脑数据长距离通信），workshifting（灵活办公），wifi squatter（非法使用无线网络连接者）。

20 世纪末期，随着科技发展，人们造出更多全新的网络词汇：interpedia（因特网全书），netiquette（网络礼仪），newbie（电脑新手），knowbie（大侠，网络高手），cyber vigilantism（网络义务警察，人肉搜索），distance work（远程上班），flashmob（快闪族），fleshmeet（网友见面），phishing（网络钓鱼），zombie computer（僵尸电脑），mousetrapping（捕鼠陷阱），encipter（加密，译成密码），encode（锁码、加密），encryption（加密）。以 web 为首的词更是不计其数：webnomics（网络经济），webbug（网虫），webcast wedding（网播婚礼），web cramming（网络阻塞），webisode（网络剧），weblish（网语），web rage（网络愤怒），webrarian（网络相片管理员），websumer（网络获取信息者），webzine（网络杂志）。与此有关的以 cyber 为前缀而构成的新词也很多。如：cybercasting（网播），cyber Monday（网络星期一），cyber bullying（网络欺凌），cyberslacking（网络偷懒，上班时在网络上干私事），cybersquatting（域名抢注），cyber myth（网络秘密），cybermall（网络商场），cyberpet（电子宠物），cyberphobia（计算机恐惧症），cyberstyle（网络写作风格），cyberpun（计算机科幻小说）。以 google 构成的新词也颇受欢迎。如 google bombing（谷歌搜索炸弹，不同的网页与网站链接，使该网站

在搜索结果显示中始终处于前列），googleganger（谷歌同名的人），
googlejuice（谷歌搜索引擎能力），googleverse（谷歌天地，谷歌产品、
服务、网页），gootube（谷歌 youtube），ungoogleable（谷歌搜索不到
的），discomgooglation（谷歌依赖症）。以维基网站一词催生的新词有
wikiality（维基现实），wikifiction（网站变成维基网），wikigroaning（维
基呻吟，在维基网上有两个同题文章，分别为好和劣质文章）。其他新
词还有 guru site（权威网站），multiple-channel shopping（多渠道购物），
info-channel（信息频道），Apple iPod（以音乐播放器听音乐的行人），
internot（网盲，拒绝使用互联网的人），nerd bird（往来于硅谷等科技
中心的航班），technosexual（科技美型男），alpha geek（阿尔法奇客），
digital native（生长在电子数码产品环境中的），nerdistan（高科技园），
dog food（使用自己公司开发的产品），information pollution（信息污
染），collaboratory（联网合作项目）等。

（三）交通与交通工具

美国高速公路称作 speed highway，基本上不收费。全国 8.9 万公里
的高速公路，只有大约 8000 公里是收费路段。总体来说，最高级别的
高速路是 expressway，freeway 基本上不收费。在美国，如果经常走收
费高速路，司机们可以购买一张高速路充值卡，然后就得到一个条码，贴
在车的前挡风玻璃上。每次经过收费站，走专门的 E-pass 通道（电子
收费通道），司机不用停车，相应的设备会扫一下条码，把钱划走，频
繁使用高速路的还能得到折扣。这些公路具有国防功能，并且横跨数
州，因而称为 interstate highway（州际公路）。收费公路称为 turnpike 或
tollway。在美国中西部地区，绝大多数公路甚至连收费站都没有。因为
这种原因，道路利用率非常高。美国第三大城市洛杉矶的交通部门做过
统计，洛杉矶市每天光行驶在高速公路上的汽车就达 400 万辆。有名的
圣塔莫尼卡 10 号高速公路堪称世界上最忙碌的高速公路，这条路共有
双向 10 个车道，每天有 34 万辆汽车通过。

美国被称为轮子上的国家。家家有车，户户出行选择驾车。一些人
以车为家，被称为 carcoon（车茧），人们在车里安装娱乐设施，可以看
电视、无线上网，甚至吃住在车里，有些人还会买 recreational vehicle
（房车）进行居住或旅游。有些人上班没时间吃饭，只好买些 one hand-

ed food（手指食物）在车里食用，这类食物被称为 dashboard dining（仪表盘食物）或 cup-holder cuisine。car schooling（在车中教育孩子）更是司空见惯的事情。还有一些人边坐车边工作，这些时间被称为 windshield time（驾车上班时间）。鉴于汽车的影响力，人们用 In the driver's seat 表示"对某事负有责任、控制权或决定权，处于支配地位和优势位置"，而 backseat driver 则是"坐在汽车后排，却不停地对前面开车的人指手画脚的人"。

名车种类繁多，豪华名贵，促使许多犯罪分子以身试法，他们偷车贩卖，获取高额赃款，这种行为被称作 twoc（偷车事件）。还有一些人把自己的车进行 car cloning（汽车克隆），从事犯罪活动。有些犯罪分子开车在马路上 cut and shut（碰瓷），一些人把偷来的车子车牌号涂掉 re-VIN（改装所盗车子）并卖掉，有些犯罪分子制造 phantom accident（虚假车祸），骗取车险。这使得警察把自己的车进行装扮，成为 bait car（诱饵汽车），诱捕犯罪分子。尽管都知道"酒后不开车、开车不喝酒"，但是 DWI（酒后驾车），DWY（开车打电话）却屡禁不止，有些人常常 velocitize（习惯快速行驶），对此习以为常。汽车公司为此推出了 alcolock（酒精锁），nanny car（配置电脑设施以防范事故的车）。如果 DWI，或者 DWY，你可能会遭受 ding in a fender-bender（刚蹭中被撞瘪）或者是 crunched rear-ender（挡泥板压瘪）。更严重的会是 fatals（致命车祸），车也会 totaled（毁掉）。如果因非法停车收到许多罚款单但却不去受罚，就会被 Denver Boot（钳锁非法停放车辆的丹佛锁箍）锁住，不能开动。公路管理处为了防止高速行驶设置 speed bump（减速坡），mobile speed bump（流动减速坡）和 pickade（设路桩），在车道变窄或是车进路口时，采取 zipper merge（拉链并道）措施，车辆按拉链方式，左一辆右一辆顺次进入，不争不抢。然而，无论如何，人们还是要 keep on trucking（继续前行）或 move on。美国也会有 panhandler（马路乞讨者）敲打车窗讨要钱财，有些人甚至以马路乞讨为由进行抢劫。road rage 出现于 20 世纪 80 年代，表示"路怒族"。这类人因为在路上开车不满于其他驾驶员而愤怒、咒骂甚至是杀人。

美国人用 lemon car 表示"出厂后问题百出的次品车"，并且延续此称呼，制定了 Lemon Law。柠檬法是美国保护汽车消费者权益的法律。各州法律有明确规定，如果消费者买到出厂即出现问题的新车，有权利要求汽车生产厂家对这种 lemon car 负责。

20 世纪 70 年代末，美国人开始意识到汽车是 gas guzzler（油老虎），一些人开始购买 NEV（电动小轿车）或 economy car（经济型轿车），convertible（敞篷车）让位于 fastback（长坡度车顶车）。超大豪华车被大众怀疑为 pimpmobile（拉皮条豪华定制车）。到了 21 世纪初，出现了更加关心环保的开车人士，他们注重 ecodriving（生态驾车），hypermiler（超级惜油者）努力将一加仑的汽油多行驶一些里程。政府也会给予那些使用节能轿车的车主 feebate（节能补助）。孩子上学、回家组成的 walking bus（健走校车）不仅有助于环保，也有助于健身。然而，一些人依然是 automania（汽车狂），他们有些人宠爱 cuddle tech（大众车新车技术），成为 beetlemania（甲壳虫车迷）。vanners 喜欢开箱式货车，有些人吃住在 motor homes 里，露营者们开着 tent trailers（篷式拖车）shunpiking（走支路行驶）行驶在乡间小路上。这些人为自己的 vanity plates（虚荣性车牌，个性车牌）而骄傲炫耀。为满足各类人的需求，获取很大利润，汽车生产商推出各种各样的汽车类型，sport utility vehicle（运动型多功能汽车），MPV（多用途家庭轿车），SRV（小型休闲车），CR－V（城市休闲车），HRV（两厢轿跑车），Crossover（跨界车）不一而足。根据车的性能，美国人分别用它们指代各种各样的人。中年男人虽然有钱，但是到了中年后患上 menoporsche（保时捷更年期综合征）。变老的焦虑和沮丧驱使他们豪掷千金买名车，或者搭上一名年轻美貌女子。口谈节约能源但是自己却拥有并使用费油的、多用途跑车的民主党政坛人是 SUV Democrat（多用途车民主党）。受过良好教育、比较富裕、思想开明、住在郊区的白人专业人员是 Volvo Democrat（沃尔沃民主党人），Volvoid 则是"白人富裕自由党专业人士"，Lexus liberal 表示"在言行上是自由党但是实际不是自由党人士"。

有车一族为了节省费用，以保护环境为目的，共同使用一辆车上班、旅游、参会及听音乐会，这种现象称为 carpool（拼车）。拼车使用的车道称为 carpool lanes（多人用车道），commuter lanes（通勤车道），diamond lanes（钻石车道）。它供车内包括驾驶员在内共有两人或以上的人使用。多人用车道在美国和加拿大常用钻石形标志。卡车、只有驾驶员一人的车辆禁止行驶。slugging 是华盛顿特区、旧金山和匹茨堡等大城市特有的一种通勤方式，也称为 Instant Carpooling 或 Casual Carpooling，翻译为"随便搭车或即时拼车"。从郊区住所到市中心上班的驾车者，为了达到能在 HOV 专用车道行驶的条件，在公共汽车站停下，招徕至少两位陌生的 sluggers（即时拼车者），以便达到多人用专用车道的行驶条件。然而如果是富人即使没有多人乘车，如果交纳一定数额的银子，也可以使用 HOV 车道，所以 HOV 车道也被人们戏称为 Lexus lane（凌志车、富人车车道）。还有一些家庭为了达到 HOV 规定，共乘一辆轿车，这种现象被称为 fampool（家人拼车）。cruise（漫游炫车）是美国加拿大年轻人间的一种社交行为。许多青年人刚刚获得驾照，为了表达刚刚获得的这种自由，他们按着约定地点在周末聚集在一起。然后沿着某条路线慢速行驶，穿城而过，唯一的目的是交友炫车。

A drive-through, drive-thru 通常是 drive through bank（汽车银行），drive through restaurant（汽车饭店），drive through cuisine（汽车点餐），drive through cinema（汽车影院），drive through café（汽车咖啡馆），drive through wedding（汽车婚礼）的统称。顾客乘车通过这些地点，使用麦克风或窗口接受服务。根据这种构词结构，人们又造出 drive-by spamming（经主动大量传送驱动），drive-by download（路过式下载使用），drive-by shooting（驾车射击），drive-by editing（捕风捉影新闻编辑），drive-by VC（路过风险资金，无技术但有资金支持）等新词。

在美国由于家家有车，50% 左右的家庭选择自驾车出行。停车成为令人头痛的问题。尤其是到市区，常常会兜几圈也找不到车位。市中心停车位大约为 10—20 美元 1 小时，路边的停车位需要每 90 分钟向 o-dometer（停车表）内投币一次，否则就会被拖车拖走。大型的停车场每小时收费 1—2 美元，月费 100 多美元。在购物中心周围，经常可以看到大的停车场供顾客免费使用。一到节假日，形形色色的车辆包括摩托车停在外边。顾客可以悠闲地在商业中心里尽情消遣，不用计算着停车时间，买完东西可以推着购物车来到自己的车前，慢慢地把大包小包商品往里放。即使是地下或者楼层式的停车场，也只需在进门之前按自动仪表拿一张停车卡。商场里面自动收费机用现金或者信用卡交费。

2009 年，美国政府推出了"旧车换现金计划"，英文是 Cash for Clunkers。旨在鼓励车主将耗油量大、废气污染严重的 clunker（旧车）换成更节能的新款汽车。旧车换现金计划或旧车换新节能补贴计划可以扶持本国汽车制造业，同时又益于环保。另外，当车主报废自己的旧车并购买环保新车时，还能获得 3500—4500 美元的补贴，因而美国民众掀起了贴换热潮。

（四）手机电话

美国的手机运营商主要有四家：AT&T，Verizon，Sprint 和 T-Mobile。网络提供商们通常都会在其公司网站上公布其 coverage（网络覆盖图）。通过在这些网站中输入邮政编码，用户可以找到任何特定地方的各公司信号覆盖范围。一般来说，Verizon 和 AT&T 信号覆盖更广更密。因为 ATT 的广告到处都是，网点也很密集，但它们的 plan（套餐，计划）会相对贵一些。而且 Verizon 使用的是 CDMA 制式的通信网络，它的手机没有 SIM 卡。因而如果选择了 Verizon 的服务，就必须使用 Verizon 销售的手机。T-mobile 自称是掉线最少的网络，用户也很多。T-mobile 用的是 GSM 网络，3G 以上的手机可以使用。这里的手机许多都是免费的。它拥有最多品牌的手机，用户有更大的选择权，所以很多年轻人会选这个品牌。

美国电话公司竞争非常激烈，因此都尽可能地想留住更多的用户，所以一般都会跟用户签订 1—2 年的协议，协议期越长，手机越便宜。

美国手机话费大致有这样几个特点。首先是选择很多，单向收费。各移动运营商提供的话费套餐种类很多。例如，AT&T 的手机服务分个人和家庭两大类计划。个人计划月费为 39.99 美元，美国境内通话时间为 450 分钟。当月如果 450 分钟没有用完，可以累积到以后使用。Family plan（家庭套餐）最常用的是两部手机两个号码。如果选择最低的通话时间 550 分钟，月费为 59.99 美元，700 分钟则为 69.99 美元，无限通话是 119.99 美元。每增加一部手机和电话号码，月费增加 9.99 美元。家庭套餐的时间也可以积累顺延使用。此外，美国手机话费有免费时间。各运营商都提供网内互打免费的服务，许多话费套餐规定，从晚 9 点到早 7 点、周末和节假日，各网络之间也免费。至于国际长途则需要 mobile access fee（入网费）和 pre-paid phone card（预付手机卡）。

如果只是 texting（发短信）的话，200 条短信月费 5 美元，1500 条 15 美元，无限制收发短信月费 20 美元。对 3G/4G 手机或 3G 手提电脑，3G 网络数据传输容量 3GB 月费为 35 美元，5GB 容量月费 60 美元。

　　Smartphone（智能手机）像个人电脑一样，具有独立的操作系统，可以由用户自行安装软件、游戏等第三方服务商提供的程序，通过此类程序来不断对手机的功能进行扩充，并可以通过移动通信网络来实现无线网络接入。

　　目前手机采用 GSM（移动通信全球系统），手机功能有 voice prompt（语音提示），roaming service（漫游服务），color screen（彩屏），polyphonic ringtone（彩铃），chord music ringtone（和弦铃声），walkie-talkie（对讲机），sms（短信息服务），mms（多媒体信息服务）。手机分为 flip phone（翻盖手机），bar phone（直板手机），slide phone（滑盖手机），touch screen phone（触屏手机）。

　　人们在生活中手机不离身，手机屏是除了电视、电脑外的第三种屏，被称为 third screen，它是 thumbable（可用拇指的），被称作 thum culture（拇指操作文化）。人们用手机进行 proximeeting（手机约会），有着 location awareness（手机位置意识）。有些人 smexting（吸烟发信息）。一些人在饭店或剧间休息时迫不及待地对着手机 cell yell（叫嚷），有的人受手机打扰睡眠质量低，被称作 junk sleep（垃圾睡眠），半夜睡觉被 butt call（误拨电话，无意电话）扰醒，尤为烦恼。有些人患上 phantom vibration（手机震动幻觉症），nomophobia（无手机恐惧症），phone neck（手机脖），ringxiety（铃声焦虑症），text message injury（过多发送信息而患上拇指痛症）。还有些人用手机进行各种活动，如 drunk dial（酒后拨打电话），sexting（发送性信息），传送 microblogging（微博），发送 mobisode（移动手机短节目），sideloading（侧载）。一些人痛恨手机，公司也不希望员工在班上使用手机，于是推出 magnetic wood（磁木，阻挡手机信号的绝缘木）。自从苹果发布系列产品之后，针对它进行的犯罪频发，出现 apple picking（抢劫苹果手机、iPad 等行为）。bluejacking（手机诈骗），phone phishing（手机钓鱼），smishing（手机信息诈骗）更是司空见惯。

三　新词语与美国政治

（一）总统竞选新词语

　　美国两大政党为民主党（大政府）与共和党（小政府）。民主党和共和党两党长期轮流执政。美国政党除两大党外，还有其他一些政党，但它们都无法影响两大党轮流执政的地位。Divided government（分掌政府）指白宫由一个政党控制（即总统是这个党的成员），而国会参、众两院中的至少一院由对立派政党控制（即其成员占多数）的局面。分掌政权是美国政体的常见现象，它有利于避免激进的变化，并促使两党政治家在立法提案问题上做出妥协。Electoral College（选举团）是一组"选举人"的总称，他们由各州党员在州内提名产生。在大选日，选民把票投给承诺支持某位总统候选人的"选举人"。如果某位候选人赢得的选民票数最多，支持这位候选人的"选举人"就将作为这个州的代表，于 12 月分别在各州州府举行的总统和副总统选举中投票。总统候选人必须在全国获得至少 270 张选票方可当选。Federal Election Commission（联邦选举委员会）是负责贯彻和监督执行联邦竞选财务法的独立管理机构。Third party（第三党）是除共和党和民主党这两个主导美国 20 世纪政治生活的政党以外的任何其他政党。Green Party（美国绿党）是美国两党以外的主要在野党，在 20 世纪 80 年代开始活跃。1996 年和 2000 年绿党成员参与美国总统大选后使得它备受瞩目。近年来美国最成功的另外一个党派就是美国 Reform Party（改革党）。还有一个表现不俗的小党派是 US Libertarian Party（美国自由党），它目前在全国拥有超过 400 个选举出的官职。另外一个颇有影响的政党是 Tea Party（茶党），它主张政府要减小规模、缩减开支、降低税收、弱化监管，发起了一场反对奥巴马政府的经济刺激计划和医疗改革方案运动。示威者打出的口号是 Taxed Enough Already（税收已经太多了），而它的首字母组合在一起正是单词"TEA"（茶）。

总统候选过程需要两年，大致分为四个阶段：春季候选人声明竞选；夏天至 12 月进行 Primary and caucus debates（预选和预选会议辩论）；7—9 月举行 Nominating conventions（命名大会）；第二年 9 月和 10 月为 Presidential election debates（总统竞选辩论）；11 月为 Election Day（竞选日）；12 月选举人投票，1 月份议会计票；1 月 20 号 Inauguration Day（就职）。

在美国，选举是公民管理国事和监督政府的最重要的手段。因此，选举在美国政府生活中是十分重要的。美国英语发展了不少与之相关的语汇。

在 psephocracy（选举政治）和 psephology（选举学）中，primary（预选）是美国选举制度独特的选举方式。primary 在美国的政治术语中，就是指产生各级公职候选人的选举。它包括在国会议员、州和地方公职的选举中，由两大党（民主和共和）的选民直接投票确定该政党提名的候选人。预选指的就是由选民直接投票产生两党全国代表大会的代表。美国有的州采用 closed primary（封闭式预选），即选民必须是一党成员，才能参加该党预选。有一些州采用 open primary（开放式预选），即选民无须进行党派登记就可以按照自己的意愿在任何一个政党的预选中投票。选民也还可以进行 blanket primary（大开放预选），不必宣布自己的政党倾向就可以在一个以上的政党预选中投票。许多州约定的在三月的第二个星期二进行的预选叫作 super primary（超级预选）或 super Tuesday（超级星期二）。如果第一次预选中没有任何候选人获得过半数选票，就要在得票最多的两名候选人之间举行 run-off primary（决胜预选），即第二次预选。

Federal Election Commission（联邦选举委员会）是负责贯彻和监督执行联邦竞选财务法的独立管理机构。Caucus（预选会议）是指在提名总统候选人的过程中，党的地方活动人士举行的会议。总统大选中，候选人前往各地巡回造势，利用自己的声望给本党其他候选人增加胜选机会的能力，被称为 Coattails（燕尾提举力）。共和党支持率较高的州在大选地图上用红色标示，被称为 red state，而 blue state 则代表支持民主党的州。

在竞选中出现了各种竞选人，如 best man（最佳总统候选人），candidate potential（呼声很高的候选人），shoo-in（稳操胜券的候选人），point（领先的候选人），front-runner（领先者），standard-bearer（获得党代会提名视作本党的总统候选人），favorite son（得到本州代表支持的总统候选人）。有些人则非常尴尬，被人称为 long shot（呼声不大的候选人），parachute candidate（外来候选人），perennial candidate（反复竞选的候选人），robot candidate（机器人似的候选人），shoo-out（肯定会落选的候选人），sore head/ sore loser（输不起的候选人），stampede（为赶浪而仓促决定倒向某一胜利在望者的候选人），stealth candidate（不公开表示竞选的候选人），stalking horse（为掩护主要候选人而推出的候选人），San Diego model（以悄悄活动的方式推出候选人）。还有 surrogate candidate（候选人的代言人），baby kisser（到处笼络人心的人），good loser（输得起的候选人）。

竞选激烈是美国总统大选最鲜明的特点。大选中每一位总统候选人用尽各种各样的策略与手段。他们指责对手的政治立场、曝光个人隐私，惯用手段和伎俩有 sleaze（散布私生活丑闻），mudslinging（抹黑），go negative（搞臭对手），hogwash（把对手攻击说成是喂猪的泔水），horse trading（赤裸裸的政治交易），low road（小人式的竞选），negative campaign（反面竞选），come out swinging（互相攻击），character fragging（人身攻击），debategate（辩论丑闻），negative ads（丑化对方的负面广告），wolfsoup（竞选人的空头诺言），corral vote（拉选票），electioralism（拉票术），ring doorbells（逐门逐户拉票），walking around money（拉票的小费），attack line（攻讦性言论），black advance（闹场，用肮脏的手段破坏政治对手的竞选活动），cemetery vote（将死人充数的选票，死人票），gerrymander（不公正地划分选区），pork barrel（政治恩惠），push-poll（在选举前关键时刻向选民提一些有损对手的推离式民意调查），rat fucking（用种种伎俩秘密地破坏或阻挠对手竞选），rigged election（舞弊的选举），steal an election（靠舞弊取得的选举胜利），vote fraud（选举舞弊），wedge issue（制造分裂的问题）等。

由于竞选是对候选人的一次严峻考验，竞选人采取各种手段从选民手中拉票。这类词有 dropby（短暂造访），go on the stump（游历各地做政治演说），swing around the circle（旅行演讲），sell candidate like soap（大肆宣传候选人），snipe（竞选海报），tarmac（乘飞机做竞选游说）。sound bite（电视上竞选演讲），stump speech（竞选演说）。他们做 boom-let（短暂的大吹大擂的宣传活动），talk-show campaign（谈话式竞选活动），TV blitz（电视闪电式宣传战）。每一位候选人为赢得选票而四处奔波，采取各种手段从选民手中拉票。他们乘 battlebus（流动竞选车）进行 buscapade（大客车竞选活动），bandwagon（乘宣传车演讲）。竞选形式花样繁多，如：barnstorm（巡回竞选），campaignathon（马拉松式竞选），teledemocracy（电视竞选），flatout（开足马力竞选），free ride（不影响现任官职的竞选），positive campaign（正面竞选活动），run scared（战战兢兢地竞选），bracket（反宣传），telelection（电视选举），front-porch campaign（家门口或本选区竞选）。其他还有 on the campaign

47

trail（在竞选旅程中），oprahbate（奥普拉访谈式竞选辩论），oprahfica-tion（访谈式竞选），pack the galleries（竞选造声势），full dinner pail（竞选口号）。

政治竞技场上的厮杀不仅胜负难料，而且代价高昂。出现了黑金选举和选举病态现象。拉选票，买断电视时间、报纸杂志版面，包租专机和旅馆，拉拢关系等都需要大笔金钱。可以说美国政治是金钱政治，没有金钱，要想在竞选中获胜是根本不可能的。Political Action Committee（政治行动委员会）是由公司、工会、专业组织或其他利益集团从事游说、捐款的多家机构。好莱坞影人和商人是主要的 political fund-raiser（竞选捐款人），被称为 fat cat（在竞选中慷慨捐款的大佬）。tobacco money（烟草商或烟草公司的竞选捐款）更是总统竞选人不可或缺的雄厚资金。各种竞选专款名目繁多，不一而足：campaign contribution（竞选献金）或 victory fund（竞选专款），frog hair（用于竞选使用的资金），political contribution（政治献金），tobacco moneywar chest（竞选专款），hard money（硬币，从个人或 PAC 募集到的捐款），soft money（软币，不受联邦选举法管制的任何竞选活动捐款）

选民分为 swing voter（无党派选民），switcher/ crossover（跨党投票者），teletorate（电视选民），ticket-splitting voter（投票分散的选民），twilight zoner（态度不明朗的选民）。选票有 absentee ballot（海外选票），blackball/ negative vote（反对票），bullet vote（只投一位候选人的选票），butterfly ballots（蝶式选票），candle-box returns（假选票），clothes-pin vote（无可奈何的投票），couch potato vote（沙发土豆的投票），Mas-sachusetts ballot（麻州式选票），proxy（代理投票），punch out computer cards（打卡投票），rolling-pin vote（家庭妇女的选票），secret ballot（无记名投票），short ballot（候选人名单很短的选票）。

此外还有一些与总统竞选有关的词汇，Oprahbate（访谈式竞选辩论）是由在场的选民提出问题，美国总统候选人就此展开的辩论，尤指1992 年布什和克林顿之间进行的第二次辩论。Oprah 是美国家喻户晓的"名人访谈节目"或"谈话节目"主持人，全名为 Oprah Winfrey。克林顿夫人、美国国务卿 Hillary 是一位成功且自信的女人，受到美国人的欢迎，以她的名字构成的新词也颇为常见。如 Hillary Factor（希拉里因素）比喻成功女性咄咄逼人的支配倾向。

（二）以总统命名的新词语

在美国历史上，许多词汇以总统名字命名，而且影响巨大。这些词有政治趋向中庸的 Nixon（尼克松）词汇。如：Nixologism（尼克松惯用语），Nixonian（尼克松的），Nixonization（尼克松化），Nixonomics（尼克松经济政策）。Watergate scandal（水门丑闻）揭露出尼克松说谎，使得他成为美国历史上第一位辞职的总统。

老布什执政时用过 New World Order（世界新秩序）这个政治口号，意为非西方国家必须按美国意志行事。Bushie 为"布什的支持者"。

1980 年 1 月，卡特总统向国会发表国情咨文。他在咨文中警告：任何企图控制波斯湾地区的外来力量的尝试将被视为对美国重大利益的侵犯，美国会采取一切必要的手段，包括动用军事力量加以回击。这就是后来的 Carter Doctrine（卡特主义）。Carterism（卡特主义）指卡特在国内推行的一套自由派或中间偏左的政策。此外还有 Carterite（卡特的支持者），Carterize（使卡特化，使总统优柔寡断）。

在 1980 年总统竞选辩论前卡特的竞选资料被窃，里根的竞选班子搞到了一份卡特辩论的底本，因而使里根在辩论中占了上风，被称为 Debategate（辩论材料丑闻）。里根在任期间，根据幕僚与顾问的建议，独创了一套经济政策，被称为 Reaganomics（里根经济学），其主要思想就是以减税来刺激供给。Reaganism（里根主义）指里根提出的如减税、小政府、自由企业、控制货币供应等的经济政策。他在执政期间执行的是 New Conservatism（新保守主义）。与 Reaganomics 一同出现的美国政治词汇还有：Reagan Democrat（里根民主派），Reaganite（里根主义分子），Reaganology（里根政策研究），Reaganaut（里根宇航计划的支持者）和 Reagonesque（里根式的）等。里根执政期间，美国向伊朗非法出售武器，并用所得款项资助尼加拉瓜反政府游击队，这一事件被称为 Irangate（伊朗门事件）。

1993—2001 年 Clinton（克林顿）执政。他在执政过程中走了一条"中间道路"。克林顿本人属于民主党的温和派，但是他淡化民主党的自由主义立场，把共和党受人欢迎的一些思想接过来，作为自己的政策目标，成为民主党温和派。在此期间多数选民从国家经济发展中得到实惠，他们认可 Clintonomics（克林顿的经济政策或主张）。New Partnership

（新伙伴关系），New Covenant（新契约）以及 New Economics（新经济学），是克林顿提出的施政纲领。Clinton Doctrine（克林顿主义）的核心则是公开宣扬人权高于主权，打着维护人权的幌子干涉别国内政。File-gate（档案丑闻）指的是"克林顿秘密建立潜在共和党政敌档案的丑闻"。Nannygate（保姆门）是克林顿上任后在任命女性司法部长时爆出的丑闻。Pardongate（特赦丑闻）则指"克林顿卸任前的特赦丑闻"。Whitewatergate（白水事件）是白水开发有限公司事件与克林顿夫妇间的经济案件。Monicagate（莫妮卡丑闻）则是克林顿与前白宫实习生 Monica Lewinsky 的桃色事件。Monicagate 使克林顿处于极为尴尬的境地。但克林顿的支持率一直保持在 60% 以上。他的名字变得家喻户晓，在美语中出现了不少 Clinton 的派生词，例如：Clintonian（与克林顿政策有关的或克林顿政策的支持者），Clintonspeak 表示"闪烁其词、犹抱琵琶半遮面的说话方式"。此外还有 Clintonize（使克林顿化，使适合或适应克林顿的政策），Clintonmania（克林顿热），Clintonite（克林顿派的），Clinton-lingo（克林顿官话），Clintonism（克林顿主义，指克林顿在竞选中和执政之初提出对国内经济进行改革的主张）。

至于 Bushism（布什主义）则含有浓厚的单边主义色彩。在经历了单边主义、"9·11"事件、阿富汗战争和伊拉克战争之后，the Bush administration（布什领导政权）从共和党保守主义和现实主义思想出发，以反恐为重点、单边主义为核心，追求国家利益和绝对安全。这一思想被称为 Bush Doctrine（布什主义）。布什政府误导和欺骗了美国及国际社会，欺骗了美国人民，发动了不应该有的战争。

美国总统奥巴马作为争议颇多的第一位黑人总统，也是颇受欢迎的一个美国总统，给语言带来了一系列新鲜词汇。2008 年 9 月位于美国加州圣地亚哥的全球语言监测机构 Global Language Monitor 的一项研究显示，在过去一年中，ObamaSpeak（奥巴马派生词）成为美国电视媒体中的第二大高频词。Obamacize 表示"像奥巴马那样去做事"。Obamania 被用来表示"奥巴马狂"。Obamanomics 一词是由 Barack Obama 中的 Obama 一词加上后缀-nomics 派生而成的，表示"奥巴马经济政策"。Obamafy 表示"具有奥巴马特征、色彩"。另外还有 Obamanation（奥巴马王国、奥巴马集团），Barackstar（奥巴马的气质），Barackstar Shirts（奥巴马衬衫），Obama berry（奥巴马用黑莓手机），Obama beer（奥巴

马啤酒，奥巴马式举杯释嫌），Obama agenda（奥巴马议事日程），
Obama administration（奥巴马政府），Obama black（奥巴马式黑色），
Obama Biden administration（奥巴马拜登政府），Obama mess（奥巴马一
团糟），Obamabot（对奥巴马盲目崇拜的选民），Obamamentum（奥巴马
的竞选），Obamican（奥巴马的拥护者）。刚刚宣布奥巴马当选为美国
第 56 届总统时所出生的婴儿或在其当选期间出生的婴儿被称为 Obama
baby（奥巴马婴儿）。人们用 Obama 表示"酷、祝福、问候"。例如，
You're so Obama 或 It's Baracking Cool 表示"你真酷"，What's up, my
Obama? 意为过得怎样，希望得到神的祝福可以说 Barack you!（祝好
运!），而 Barack's in the White House 则表示"你要认真做"。

（三）战争新词语

近几十年来，美国军队参与了海湾战争、科索沃战争、阿富汗战
争、伊拉克战争。打击并参与制裁利比亚、叙利亚、伊朗等国的联合行
动。各种与战争有关的新词语源源不断地出现。如：9·11，AOS（即
时战争游戏），asymmetric warfare（非对称战争），belligerati（好战分
子），bioterrorist（生化武器恐怖者），blood diamonds（血色钻石），chick-
en hawk（逃兵），dark biology（生化武器研究），de-alert（断绝核武
器），decapitation strike（斩首行动，军士打击敌方头目，使得部队倒
戈），de-conflict（化解冲突），de-proliferate（数目急剧减少），exfiltration
（逐渗），flat daddy（真人爸爸相），fourth generation warfare（基地组织推
崇的非政府军力），killology（杀人学），Iraqphobia（伊拉克恐惧症），re-
gime change（权力过渡、变化），embed（随军记者），militainment（报
道战争电视节目），information warfare（信息战），information superiority
（信息优势），imperial overstretch（帝国扩张），MOUT（城市区域中的军
事设施），trauma pod（外科医生控制的机器人手术），VBIED（汽车炸
弹），warfighter（战士），weaponize（挂武器导弹），a-geographic（无疆
域），jihobbyist（同情支持极端伊斯兰教者）。

在巴基斯坦，hard-line Islamists（强硬派伊斯兰教徒）并不同意政府
完全支持美国军事打击 Taliban militia（塔利班民兵），示威民众燃烧美
国国旗，表示要拿起武器支持拉登。syndicate of terror（恐怖集团）与
extremist（极端分子）使用 car bombing, bicycle bombing, motorcycle

bombing, homicide bombing, shoetic bombing, suicide bombing, roadside explosives 等各种路边炸弹手段进行 reprisal attack（报复行动），并且使用 cyberterrorism（网络恐怖主义）进行 jihad（圣战，伊斯兰教徒对异教徒的战争）。Ground zero 被用来表示常规导弹瞄准的目标或核设备爆炸点。"9·11"悲剧后，美国总统布什曾称，美国 want Bin Laden dead or alive（本·拉登是死是活，美国都要将其缉拿）。呼吁国际社会加强合作，共同打击恐怖主义，进行 anti-terror campaign（反恐斗争）。美国对阿富汗塔利班发动进攻之后，出现了神秘的疾病—anthrax（炭疽热）。这使得美国政府怀疑是遭到了生物细菌武器的袭击。美国使用 face-mapping software（面部识别软件）实施 manhunt（追捕）。对基地组织进行 aerial bombardment（空袭），airborne attack（空降袭击），carpet bomb（地毯式轰炸），pound（猛烈轰炸），dronebombing（无人机轰炸）。然后集结 military buildup（军事集结）打击敌方。奥巴马上台后，致力于反恐打击。依靠 commando（突击队），counterterrorism professionals（反恐专家），counter-terrorism unit（反恐部队），special forces（特种部队），elite troops（精英部队）于 2012 年 5 月 1 日将 Al Qaeda（基地组织）领导人、terrorist mastermind（恐怖大亨）本·拉登击毙，重创基地组织。国际社会认为本·拉登之死是国际反恐斗争的重要成果。

以英美军队为主的 coalition force（联军）在 2003 年 3 月 20 日对伊拉克发动军事行动。美国国务院 10 月 4 日发表声明称，美国武器核查人员已经在伊拉克境内找到了一瓶活体 botulin toxin（肉毒杆菌），这种生物物质属于 weapons of mass destruction（大规模杀伤性武器）之列。美国以伊拉克藏有大规模杀伤性武器和 chemical and biological weapons（生化武器）并暗中支持恐怖分子为由，对伊拉克实施军事打击。并将伊拉克等多个国家列入 Axis of Evil（邪恶轴心国）。实施了代号为 Decapitation Strike（斩首行动）和 shock and awe（震慑行动）的大规模空袭和地面攻势。布什在战争打响后向全国发表电视讲话，强调战争将"速战速决"并采取 preemptive strategy（先发制人战略）。在这一阶段，美英联军猛烈轰炸，先后向巴格达、巴士拉等十余座城市和港口投掷了多种炸弹和导弹，包括 precision-guided bomb（精确制导炸弹），cluster bombs（集束炸弹），satellite-guided bomb（卫星制导炸弹）。attack missile（攻击性导弹）包括 Patriot missile（爱国者导弹），Tomahawk cruise missile（战斧航导弹），surface-to-air-missile（地对空导弹）。另外还发射了几千枚 global positioning satellite（全球卫星定位系统）制导的 Joint Direct Attack Munition（联合直接攻击弹药）。其他攻击武器还包括 stealth fighter（隐形战斗机），tanks and armored vehicles（坦克和装甲车辆），aircraft carrier（航空母舰），apache helicopter（阿帕奇直升机）。

与此同时，伊拉克武装分子发动了游击战。他们使用迫击炮、Scud missile（飞毛腿导弹）、suicide attack（自杀攻击）、狙击手、简易爆炸装置、汽车炸弹和 RPG（火箭筒）进行反击，战争最终以萨达姆被围捕、处决而告终。

利比亚战争始于第二大城市班加西，示威抗议逐渐蔓延全国，民众要求已经上台统治长达 42 年的革命领导人穆阿迈尔·卡扎菲上校下台并进行民主变革。反对卡扎菲的势力组成"全国过渡委员会"，宗旨是推翻卡扎菲的独裁统治和建立民主政体。2011 年 2 月 26 日，联合国安理会通过首项决议，冻结卡扎菲资产，并把事件交由国际刑事法院处理。美国对利比亚进行 ground blocade（地面封锁）和 air blocade（空中封锁）。3 月初，卡扎菲军队进攻反对派在东部的据点班加西。

8 月，反对派在西部发起进攻，夺取首都的黎波里，"全国过渡委员会"逐渐得到国际和联合国承认。穆阿迈尔·卡扎菲一度逃避追捕，直至 2011 年 10 月 20 日在苏尔特被杀。2011 年 10 月 23 日"全国过渡委员会"宣告全国解放，战斗结束。

四　新词语与美国经济

美国是一个富裕的大国，自然资源极为丰富。它是世界上第三大石油原产国，第二大天然气生产国。它还是世界最大的经济实体。2012 年它的 GDP 约为 15.7 万亿美元，是全球 nominal global GDP（名义 GDP）的 1/4。美国经济属于 mixed economy（混合经济），它的 GDP 增长稳定，失业率适度，研究水平较高，资本投资极高。它的最大贸易伙伴分别是加拿大、中国、墨西哥、日本和德国。美国还是世界上最大的制造国，占世界产量的 1/5。在世界 500 强企业中，有 132 个总部设在美国。美国具有世界上最大最有影响力的金融市场。全球约 2/3 货币是 currency reserves（美元储蓄）。New York Stock Exchange（纽约股票交易所）在 market capitalization（市场资金）方面是世界上最大的股票交易市场。Foreign investments（外国在美国的投资）高达 2.4 万亿美元，是其他国家的两倍多。

Consumer spending（消费力）在 2013 年占美国经济的 71%，The labor market（劳动力市场）吸引了世界各地的移民，移民率为世界最高。美国在竞争力指数上占世界第一。纽约的 Broadway theatre（百老汇剧院）在表演艺术界具有最高水平的经济效益。而 Hollywood（好莱坞）在电影界具有最高的影响和经济回报。

（一）GDP

美国经济在 1946—1973 年的增长率是 3.8%，家庭年收入增长为 2.1%。1973 年遭遇通货膨胀、高利率及失业率，至此之后，经济增长变慢，平均为 2.7%，生活水平处于停滞状态，家庭收入年增长率仅为 0.3%。在这一期间，由于其他一些国家制造成本低利润高，美国把制造业转移至一些发展中国家。逐渐地这些国家学会制造、管理和服务技术，成为 emerging countries（新兴国家），它们在这些方面迎头赶上美国，导致美国收入增长减慢。1973 年美国出现石油危机，GDP 下降了 3.1%。1981—1982 年经济萧条时，GDP 下降了 2.9%。1990—1991 年美国遭遇 downturn（经济下滑），产能下降 1.3%；2001 经济萧条，GDP 下滑 0.3%；2001 年 downturn 持续八个月；GDP 从 2008 年春到 2009 年秋季下降了 50%。美国经济增长最具活力的时期是 1961—1969 年，那时的年增长率是 5.1%；1982—1990 年中期，增长率为 4%；1991 年中期到 2000 年后期年增长率为 3.8%。2008 年，美国出现 financial crisis（经济危机），失业率处于历史最高，2010 年，公共及私有债务达到 50.2 万亿美元。到了 2012 年，公共债务是 GDP 的一倍多。2013 年，美国经济依然处于 economic downturn（经济滑坡），失业率达到 7.6%，家庭收入持续下降，联邦预算减少。

2008 年 12 月，NBER 宣布美国进入经济萧条。经济萧条导致 trade deficit（贸易赤字）减少，从 2006 年的 8.4 千亿降至 2009 年的 5 千亿。个人存款率从 2008 年的 1% 增加到 2009 和 2010 年的 5%。美国公债在 1980 年为 909 万亿，是美国（GDP）的 1/3。而到了 2010 年 1 月，美国公债达到 14.3 万亿。美国财政部于 2012 年 3 月 15 日公布的国际资本流动报告（TIC）数据显示，2012 年 1 月份国际资本对美国股票、债券及其他金融资产的国际需求有所增长，主要购买品种为美国国债。报告显示国外私人投资者和各国政府 1 月份对美国长期股票、票据和债券的净买入总额为 1010 亿美元，中国仍是持有 treasury bonds（美国国债）最多的国家，1 月份中国持有美国国债 1.16 万亿美元；日本仍为美国的第二大债权国，为 1.08 万亿美元。

　　美国是自由经济国家。政府较少监督和介入私有企业。它拥有 2.96 千万小企业。电脑网络科技的迅猛发展催生许多 IT 精英，使它们成为亿万富翁，这些人被冠为 millionerd，two commas，affluenza，Dellionaire，sneaker millionaire，get-rich-click。

　　在世界 500 强企业中，美国就占到 139 个。自从独立以来，它崇尚科学和发明创新。在列入大英百科全书中的 321 个伟大发明中，有 161 项由美国人发明。例如飞机、因特网、冰箱、芯片、个人电脑、空调、流水线、超市、条形码、LCD、LED、电动车、ATM 等。

　　美国劳动力数量和他们的生产力对于美国经济起到巨大作用。Consumer spending（消费力）在 1960 年为 62%，这种消费力一直持续到 1981 年，到 2013 年达到 71%。20 世纪时美国移民大多来自欧洲，成为主要劳动力，还有一些是非洲奴隶后代。20 世纪后期，拉丁美洲人移民到美国，之后许多亚洲人来到美国，成为劳动力大军。仅仅在 20 世纪 90 年代就有 1300 万人入境到美国。劳动力大军及生产力决定了美国经济的健康发展。

（二）就业

　　目前美国有 1.544 亿的受雇职工，政府是最大的聘用部门，拥有 2000 多万雇员。小企业雇佣的职员占美国劳动力大军的 53%。大企业雇佣的员工占劳动力大军的 38%。总体来说，美国私有企业雇佣了 91% 的美国人。政府聘用了 8% 的工作人员。99% 的组织和单位是企业。在大企业中，世界较为著名且规模巨大的企业为 Walmart，它在世界各地拥有 200 多万雇员。

　　2013 年，美国人口为 3.15 亿人，1.55 亿为在职职工。美国的 unemployment rate（失业率）是 7.7%，相当于 1.2 千万人。在 1955 年，55% 的美国人工作在服务岗位，30%—35% 服务于工业，10%—15% 从事农业。到了 1980 年，65% 受雇于服务业，25%—30% 从事工业，5% 从事农业。就业率较高的部门为 retail trade（10%），accommodation and food services（8%），professional and technical services（6%），administrative and waste service（5%），local education（5%），ambulatory health care services（4%），finance and insurance（4%），construction（4%），wholesale trade（4%），hospital（3%），transportation and warehousing（3%），non-durable goods manufacturing（3%），educational services（3%）。男性失业率持续高于女性失业率（2009 年为 9.8% 比 7.5%）。白人失业率持续比非裔美国人低（2009 年为 8.5% 比 15.8%）。青年失业率在 2009 年为 18.5%，青年非裔美国人失业率是 34.5%。鉴于失业率的攀升，人们创出许多失业的委婉语。例如 99er, boomerang, brightsizing, capsizing, career-change opportunity, cashier, corporate anorexia, downaging, dumbsizing, exit memo, flexicurity, funemployment, ghost work, inshoring, layoff lust, mancession, nearshoring, offshorable, pink-slip party, precariat, presenteeism, regime change, RIF, rightshoring, rightsizing, smartsizing, uninstalled, upstaff, warm-chair attrition, worklessness。

（三）美国农牧业

美国是世界上重要的农业国家之一。美国的农场每年生产价值 900 亿美元的农产品。美国生产占世界 50% 的玉米、20% 的燕麦，以及 15% 的鸡肉、猪肉、棉花和小麦。1850 年，美国差不多有 3/5 的工作人口是以农为生。但是当今，只有 5%（约 425 万）的人在务农。美国约有 90% 的农民拥有自己的土地，其他的人则租用别人的土地耕种。他们采用 agrimation（农业自动化），如牵引机、播种机、耕耘机、收割机耕种。使用科学的耕种方法，如改良肥料，使用抗病毒植物和作物轮耕，使得人力更加节省。美国的农产品节日多种多样，仅加州就有节日 Watermelon Festival, International Avocado Day（国际洋蓟节），Pumpkin Festival, Tomato Fest 等。台上有明星表演娱乐节目，台下人们品尝各种美味菜肴及上好的葡萄酒，举行以相应的水果为主题的比赛活动。鉴于经济危机带来的负面影响，有些城市居民开始回归自给自足的农耕生活方式，他们食用 food forest（种植食用植物的花园）的食物和 garden to fork, 100 – foot diet（自家花园种植的食物）。他们还创出了与植物有关的新词，如 green skeleton（城市绿化带），forest bathing（森林浴）。

乳牛与肉牛是美国农场里最重要的家畜。中西部的农场及西部大丘陵区的农耕者饲养肉牛；美国南部，从新英格兰向明尼苏达州是饲养乳牛的地区。大部分的猪饲养于中西部的玉米带。许多地区的农耕者饲养肉用鸡或蛋用鸡。地域的广大，物种的繁多，使得动物联想词层出不穷。例如 cold turkey（吸毒），social butterfly（交际花），unturkey（感恩节不食火鸡），turducken（火鸡鸭鸡），tofurkey（豆腐火鸡），turkey farm（火鸡农场，碌碌无用的政府人员），lame duck（跛脚鸭），dogsit, environpig（环境友好转基因猪），ape diet（类猿素食）等。

（四）美国工业

美国是世界最大的制造商，工业产值在 2009 年为 2.33 万亿美元，它的工业产值是德国、法国、印度、巴西的总和。主要工业包括石油、钢、汽车、建筑机械、航空、农业机械、通信、化学、电子、食品加工、木材等。美国是世界上第一大生产国，其工厂每年所生产的货品价值，比世界第二大生产国日本多出了将近 500 亿美元。就工业基本金属钢铁来说，美国产量占世界的 1/5，汽车产量占世界的 1/4，铝生产占世界的 1/3。在乳酪、衣服、化学品、纸张、纸板、纺织品及其他许多制造品上，美国都居世界领先地位。在印刷业与出版业上，美国也是首屈一指的国家。其最大的生产工业首推机械制造，其次是食品制造业。其他占领导地位的制造工业包括运输装备、化学品、电器与电子器材、基本金属、印刷业、出版业、纸张制造业以及金属产品制造业等。底特律是著名的汽车城，芝加哥是该地区的金融和商业中心。东南部以医药研究、旅游业和建材业为主要产业。美国公司如 Boeing, Cessna, Lockheed Martin 和 General Dynamics 生产制造世界大部分民用和军用飞机。

（五）著名公司和市场

2011 年，以市场资本计算，世界十大公司就有四个在美国，分别是 Exxon Mobil, Apple Inc., Chevron Corporation 和 Microsoft。根据 Fortune Global 500（全球财富 500 强）2011 年的统计，美国最大雇主分别是

Walmart, U. S. Postal Service, IBM, UPS, McDonald's, Target Corporation, Kroger, The Home Depot, General Electric, and Sears Holdings。

Apple, Google, IBM, McDonald's, and Microsof 被 Millward Brown 列为世界上最具价值的五大品牌。2012 年，根据税收被 Forbes（福布斯）列为美国十大公司的有 Exxon Mobil（能源），Wal-Mart（零售商），Chevron（能源），Conoco Phillips（能源），General Motors（汽车），General Electric（多样化），Berkshire Hathaway（多样化），Fannie Mae（金融），Ford Motor（汽车），Hewlett-Packard（电脑）。而 Amazon. com 则是世界上最大的网上零售商。由于大企业实体影响力无所不在，以它们名字构成的新词纷纷出现。如 Walmart effect（沃尔玛效应），CNN effect（CNN 在全球政治上的影响力），Coca-Colanization（可口可乐化，全球化或文化殖民），LUV recovery（全球慢速、中速、快速不同形式的经济复苏），Goldilocks economy（金发女孩经济，温和经济）。

（六）金融

美国经济被认为是世界上最大也是最重要的经济体。美国经济高度发达，全球多个国家的货币与美元挂钩，而美国的证券市场被认为是世界经济的晴雨表。

纽约的华尔街，是一条举足轻重的金融街。它的波动可以影响世界。高度发达的美国经济，使世界各地许多国家与美元挂钩，因此，也使得美元相对较稳定。

以资产计算，美国前十大银行分别是 JP Morgan Chase, Bank of America, Citigroup, Wells Fargo, Goldman Sachs, Morgan Stanley, U. S. Bancorp, Bank of NY Mellon, HSBC North American Holdings, Capital One Financial。

2008 年，mortgage mills（贷款工厂）无视买房人贷款资质，过度贷款，美国 real estate bubble（房地产泡沫）越吹越大，遭遇了由 derivatives market（金融衍生市场），subprime mortgage crisis（次贷危机）和 declining dollar value（美元贬值）导致的经济危机。the housing bubble busting（房地产泡沫破灭）。结果是，房贷人成为 homedebtor，遭遇银行的 foreclosure（房屋没收拍卖），贷方没有能力支付月供，银行收回用于出售的房产。还有些人无法偿还贷款本金，成为只能偿还利息费用的

zombie debtor（僵尸债务人）。与此同时，出现了 zombie bank（僵尸银行，负净资产但在政府支持下偿付债务并保持运营的银行）。

为了表示中美已走入经济共生时代，最大消费国美国和最大储蓄国中国构成利益的共同体，并对全世界经济产生很大影响。美媒体称之为 Chimerica（中美共同体），中国和印度关系称为 Chindia（中国印度）。中国与他国政治经济关系被誉为 BRICs（金砖四国），Chermany（中德关系），Chindonesia（中印尼）。其他如 hyper-power（超级大国），Enronomics，Eurogeddon（欧洲末日），PIIGS（欧猪五国），Grexit（希腊脱欧），以及 Abenomics（安倍经济学）等经济术语更是频现于媒体广播中。中国新一代政府执政后，Barclays Capital（巴克莱资本）创造了一个新词 Likonomics（李克强经济学），用来指代李克强为中国制订的经济增长计划。

2013 年，Bitcoin（比特币）大为流行，成为流行词。人们用它来套现，买进各国的货币，也可以使用比特币购买现实生活当中的物品。在美国小型商户中，比特币颇为走俏。人们可以在这些商店中使用比特币，免除了用信用卡交易所支付的手续费，同时商家还可以吸引更多的消费者。那什么是比特币呢？比特币是一种由开源的 Peer to Peer（P2P）软件产生的虚拟数字货币。2009 年，Satoshi Nakamoto 提出 BitCoin 这一概念，这是根据他的思路设计发布的开源软件以及建构其上的 Peer to Peer 网络。比特币不依赖特定的中央发行机构，而是使用遍布整个 P2P 网络节点的分布式数据库来记录货币的交易，并使用密码学的设计来确保货币流通各个环节的安全性。与比特币有关的词汇如 bitcent（比特分），milli-bitcoin（毫比特），micro-coin（微比特）从此也进入美语，成为金融新词汇。

（七）国际贸易

美国具有世界上最大的贸易量，而国内贸易量又比国际贸易量高出许多。将近 1800 万的美国人是以批发业或零售业为生，操纵这些贸易的商人上自批发商、百货公司，下至地方杂货店。美国每一个地区都生产该地最需要的产品，销售剩余的物资再运到其他需要的地区去销售。美国每年的国内贸易额，批发上约达 5800 亿美元，而零售方面则达 6450 亿美元之多。

20 世纪 70 年代中期，美国每年由国外输入价值 1200 亿美元的货品，输出价值 1150 亿美元的货品。美国最重要的贸易对象毫无疑问是加拿大。美国将 1/5 的输出品运到加拿大，而加拿大也以 1/5 的输出品回报美国。美国最大的贸易伙伴分别是毗邻的加拿大（19%）、中国（12%）、墨西哥（11%）和日本（8%）紧随其后，每天大约有价值高达 11 亿美元的产品流经美加的国界。美国经济被认为是世界上最大也是最重要的经济体。

在全球金融危机不断加剧的形势下，美国人的钱包变得越来越瘪，英语语言却逆行而上，呈现出越来越丰富的态势。据美国广播公司报道，金融危机催生了许多新的英语单词，如 recessionista（衰退达人），shovel ready（获得资金支持后立即上马的项目），staycation（经济拮据而在家中或附近度假），mancession（男人衰退），pop-up store（突现突消的小商店）。经济方面的新词还有 debit card（借记卡），alpha earner（主要挣钱者，养家太太），lipstick effect（口红效应，口红销售量在经济萧条前或萧条期间陡然大增现象），lipstick indicator（口红指数），incubator（孵化器）. glass ceiling（玻璃天花板），glass cliff（玻璃悬崖），mass consumerization（适合每个大众消费），bling bling（闪亮衣饰），cash mob（现金族，同时闪现于某个商店购买食品一族），latte factor（拿铁效应），womenomics（女性经济学）等。

（八）电子商务

E-commerce 或 E-business（电子商务）也称网上零售，是指在因特网上发生的企业与消费者之间的交易行为，这种模式着重于以网上直销取代传统零售业的中间环节。电子商务起源于美国，代表是著名的 Amazon（亚马逊书店）。1995 年成立以来，已有员工 10 万名，净利润约为 4000 万，从最初的网上书店已经发展成为多种经营的 e-tailer 或 netco（网上零售商）。它的市场份额巨大，amazon 这个词已经成为动词，变成"抢占实体店份额"的代名词。例如：The biggest fear that packaged goods companies have is that they are going to get Amazoned.（包装产品公司最大的恐惧是被网店抢占份额）。

在它的带动下，美国出现了众多的网上商店，像雅虎、美国在线等知名的网站开展网上零售业务。传统的零售商如美国第一大零售业连锁企业沃尔玛，第二大连锁企业西尔斯，不但进行零售业务和目录册销售，还开展了网上零售业务。据统计，美国有 3 亿人口，2 亿人上网，截止到 2008 年，美国有 2/3 的网民喜欢在网上购物。

电子商务的主要平台有 B2B、B2C、B2G、C2C 和 M-Commerce。B2B 是 Business-to-Business 的简写，是公司间的电子商务，它占电子商务的 80%。B2C 表示 Business-to-Consumer，是公司与消费者的商务活动，消费者在此收集信息、购买物品，占电子商务活动第二位。B2G 是 Bisiness-to-Government 的缩写，是公司与政府间的电子商务活动。C2C 是 Consumer-to-Consumer 的缩写，表示个体消费者间的电子商务活动，具体表现在电子市场的发展和网上拍卖活动，具有巨大的潜力。M-Commerce 代表 Mobile Commerce，是通过无限技术，如手机和个人数码设备进行的货物买卖和服务交易。由于无线设备具有安全、快捷等特点，这种移动电子商务将会超过有线电子商务，为人们进行数码商务交易提供了一个丰富的选择。T-Commerce（电视商务）是当今新的潮流，是电子与电视结合的商务活动，尤其受到商务网站的推崇。

因特网对于美国人影响深远，人们已经将因特网融入于日常生活。人们借助互联网的力量寻求搜索信息。由此网络搜索系统也应运而生。互联网将广告与支付系统组成一体，人们可以进行网上购物、交易、免费或有偿下载资源，网络可以提供网上服务和网络分析服务等。

目前美国网络商店风靡，人们在家里进行 couch commerce（沙发商务）活动。他们所要做的就是选好商品，通过 the third-party payment（第三方付款）或信用卡付款购买物品。不仅如此，他们还可以根据自己的想法去定制商品，如人们可以订购自己喜好的 T-shirt、海报和邮票。顾客挑选要印在 T-shirt 或海报上的图像，并选定一句话做广告词，很快就可以拿到订货。JC Penney 是全美最大的连锁百货公司，在美国及波多黎各共有 1074 家百货分店，JCP. com 是最大的网上服装及家庭饰品零售商。Amazon 是全球最大的电子商务网站。Walmart 是全球最大的零售商，也在进行网上零售业务。另外一大网上零售商是 Costco，它采取的是会员制度。Groupon 是美国最大的团购网站。Staples Inc. 是美国最大的办公用品销售网站。Netflix Inc. 是最大的电影租赁网站，提供包月的视频播放。美国最大的珠宝首饰购物网站是 Blue Nile Inc.。美国最大的电子产品、计算机配件购物网站为 Newegg，它的总部设在洛杉矶。出售维修、维护工具的最大网站是 Grainer，它有 200 万的用户，每个月的访问量就超过 800 万次。Drugstore 是美国最大的化妆品、医药用品购物网站。汽车零件销售网站是 Auto Parts Warehouse。Petsmart 是美国最大的网上宠物用品连锁商店，它不但提供宠物培训课程，还提供宠物医疗服务。Etsy 是最大的工艺品交易网站。1—800 – flowers 是美国最大的鲜花礼品购物网站。

近些年，贴近人们生活的社区网站相继出现，如 www. craigslist. org 网站就是其中之一，现已在 450 个城市设有站点，居民可在网站上免费张贴自家的售物分类广告，从而对自家闲置、多余的东西进行网上拍卖，受到美国居民的欢迎。该网站上还可免费张贴广告，自行推销美容、美发、电器修理等服务。Over Stock 销售各种打折产品，产品种类超过 60 万。eBay 是美国最大的网上拍卖网站。

网上搜索引擎使得因特网变成了万能词典和顾问，人们几乎可以利用网络搜索引擎搜索到任何需要的信息，近来很受人们青睐的搜索引擎，主要由 Google、Yahoo 和 Microsoft 等公司提供。网络地图和手机、无线移动设备有机结合，使得驾车者搜索到快捷、方便和迅速的行车路径，有效缩短了人们找寻道路的时间。如 Sprint-Nextel 的手机和 Black-Berry（黑莓移动装置）都已开始提供定位和邻近街区地图指引服务，用户也可用短信方式告诉亲友或家人自己的具体位置。

Google、Web Trends、Click Tracks、Omniture 公司推出网络分析服务，出版商、行销商使用这些服务就能透彻了解访问者对自己网站的互动情况，并可统计出对网络流量模式与广告宣传效果的直观数据。这项网络分析工具被 google 称为 Google Analytics。另外，有些公司专门提供美国购物网站的评价和新闻，供消费者参考和借鉴，如 Internet E-retailer 和 Consumer Report。还有一些公司获取个人信息出卖给其他公司但保存个人信息隐私，被称为 infomediary（信息中介公司）。

Microsoft 和 Google 等网络巨头纷纷推出网上图书服务。Google 率先推出纽约市图书馆和斯坦福大学、哈佛大学、密歇根大学、牛津大学图书馆的无版权藏书扫描网站，免费供人上网阅读。同时，美国网上图书服务也提供有偿服务，有偿网上图书的支付模式可以让读者支付几美分，购买图书的单页或部分章节，还可以让读者付出约 1/10 的书价，购得该书的永久阅读权。网上图书的出租或购买都是在图书搜索引擎指引下进行，操作非常方便快捷，因此网上图书业务很受人们的青睐。

电子商务发展迅猛，新科技股频频上市，new chip（新科技股票）受到华尔街和大众推崇，而在这之前，blue chips（蓝筹股）是大众青睐的对象。电子商务的巨大发展造就大量的富翁，他们被称为 get-rich-click（因成立网络公司变富）。

随着数字移动化技术的发展，越来越多的人拿着智能手机在实体店看货、网上购买货物，这种现象被称为 showrooming（展厅现象）。消费者走入一家零售商店，如沃尔玛或百思买，如果对某件商品感兴趣，就掏出手机扫描商品二维码或者条形码，然后利用比价软件进行比价，或者登陆亚马逊等电子商务网站进行比价，然后在电子商务网站上购买物品。

出于省时、简便和价格因素，顾客采用 showrooming 方式的购物。这种购物的方法多种多样。消费者会在实体商店内扫描二维码和条形码，浏览产品评论、比较价格，还会把商品照片和求助帖发到社交媒体上，给朋友打电话咨询意见等。

据 ComScore 的研究显示，智能手机用户进行"商品展厅"式购物的几率很高。美国有 46% 的智能手机用户曾经使用过这种购物方式，他们通过 showrooming 方式购买电子产品、服装和衣帽服饰类产品、图书等商品。

据报道，美国大型超市店内看货然后网上购买的人群比例超出全部进店人数的 30%，IDC 数据表明，2015 年将有 7800 万美国消费者使用 showrooming 的购物方式。下面是 showroom 的使用方式：

Bob：Dude this Apple Iphone looks amazing but I really want to see how it feels in the hands.（Bob：哇！这个苹果手机看起来太棒了，但是我想看一下拿在手中的手感）。

Tiffany：Why not go showrooming at Best Buy and if we like it we can order one on Amazon for a cheaper price.（Tiffany：为什么不去百思买？如果我们喜欢可以在亚马逊以更便宜的价格买一个）。

进行网上购物最基本的条件是有一张可以网上支付的卡。在网站上选好物品，checkout（结账）时候就需要填写 Billing Address（账单地址）。按确认键当天或第二天就可收到货物。

美国的信用卡大都提供 Fraud Protection（欺诈保护），如果有非授权的交易（信用卡被盗用或遭遇网上诈骗），不必承担任何损失，信用卡公司会去追回这笔钱。有些信用卡公司提供 Virtual Account Number（虚拟账号）的功能，可以通过他们的软件自己生成很多 Virtual Account Number。在网上购物时替代真实的信用卡号码，这些号码只在当月有效，在有效期内使用这个 Virtual Account Number 进行网上消费时所付的金额从顾客卡里刨掉。

除了信用卡和 Debit Card 直接来实现网上支付以外，现在很多网站还支持 PayPal 或 Google Checkout 等安全的支付方式。PayPal 在 2002 年被 eBay 收购，现在 PayPal 已经被很多购物网站广泛使用。

但是电子商务也会带来一些负效应。消费者与销售者之间存在一道鸿沟，原因是网络并不能与现实相比，网络提供的只是一小部分的信息，经常是买的商品与网上的描述或图片不符；还有些商品是假冒伪劣产品，cyber fraud（网络欺诈），bait and switch（诱饵推销法）时有发生，导致消费者与销售者间的矛盾。cyber safety（网购的安全性）也让人担心，支付的安全性受到黑客的威胁；由于电子商务的交易活动是在没有固定场所的国际信息网络环境下进行，电子商务没有征收税金，使得国家难以控制和收取电子商务的税金。

Skype（讯佳普）被认为是全球最受欢迎、最好用的网络通信工具，它是一款网络即时语音沟通工具，人们可以进行视频聊天、多人语音会议、多人聊天、传送文件、文字聊天等活动。人们可以免费与其他用户语音对话，也可以拨打国内国际电话。但是它采用了 Freemium model（免费增值商业模式）。即用免费服务吸引用户，然后通过增值服务，将部分免费用户转化为收费用户，实现网站的收入。美国著名网络数码杂志《连线》曾经这样报道过：Rather than bragging about how insanely great its VoIP products are, Skype makes its users insanely productive by letting them talk with any other user worldwide for free. The company makes money by charging users for connecting to phone systems outside of its network. It's a freemium model.（讯佳普没有大肆宣传网络电话产品多么了不起，相反，它允许用户免费与世界其他用户交谈而变得高效。公司通过向用户收取连接网外电话系统费用方式赚钱。这是免费增值模式）。

五　新词语与美国艺术教育

（一）影视

美国电视节目的类型可以划分为两大类，即信息性节目和娱乐性节目。信息性节目以新闻为主，包括新闻杂志和一些纪录性作品。除了特别事件和重大活动的纪录片 The Special Documentary 外，The Investigative Documentary（调查性纪录片）在美国哥伦比亚广播公司的推动下，对已经发生但内情尚未详尽披露的重大事件以及现实社会问题的纪录受到大众欢迎。在此之后，The Mini Documentary（微型纪录片），shockumentary（事故与暴力事件电视），stalkumentary（寻人纪录片），rockumentary（摇滚乐纪录片），web documentary（网络纪录片），mockumentary（仿纪录片）相继而出。而娱乐性节目更是种类繁多，涵盖了黄金时段和非黄金时段的 soap opera（肥皂剧），包括日间肥皂剧、晚间肥皂剧。talk show 有白天脱口秀、晚间脱口秀、资讯脱口秀、新闻娱乐脱口秀。Infotainment（新闻娱乐片）将新闻与娱乐结合在一起，它的主要目的是以提供娱乐为主，但内容是跟新闻与信息相关的节目。例如探索电视公司的 Discovery 系列节目。游戏类节目在电视台与观众之间建立起了强烈的互动关系，吸引广大观众的参与，获得极大成功。如 American Idol（美国偶像）。

自 20 世纪七八十年代开始，美国几大主要商业电视网基本上不再播出好莱坞出品的影院故事片，而在自己的电影时段里专门播出主要由它们自己出资制作的 TV movie（电视电影）。电视电影大多都是两个小时的节目，通常连续播出两三个晚上，这些比较长篇的电视影片被看作 miniseries（微型连续剧）。sitcom（家庭情景剧），comfort TV 或 warmedy（安慰剧，简单家庭剧），zitcom（青少年情景喜剧），kidvid（儿童电视节目），family movies 相继得到推出，观众在笑声中欣赏电视剧情。因特网的高速发展与高科技的突飞猛进使得网上电视电影节目成为大众的新宠：bitcom（网上短小情景喜剧），tele-fusion（因特网娱乐），vodcasting（网上播客传播录像），vlog（录像播客），lifecasting（网上生活播放节目），multipath movie（多途径电影，多情节可选择的网上电影），microcinema（低成本网上发行电影），machinima（引擎电影），Japanimation（日本动漫），forensicanimation（动漫法庭），cerebrility（名人秀节目），reality show（真人秀），Oprahization（奥普拉化，公众场合敞开心扉，讲述所犯错误）等各种影视新词不一而足。科幻片也大行其道，其中就有 hard SF（硬科幻），soft and social SF（软性和社会科幻），Cyber punk（网络朋克），time travel（时间旅行），alternate history（时空穿越），military SF（军事科幻），superhuman（超人），apocalyptic（世界末日剧），space opera（太空剧），space Western（西部太空）。这些节目都有着自己相对固定的制播规则和类型特征。节目类型影响着电视观众的收视心理，也影响着广告商和制片方的市场收益预期。

美国当今有五大电视网，分别为 CNN，ABC，CBS，FOX，CNN，它们成互相抗衡的格局，各具特色。CBS 节目以"主持人崇拜"为特点，占据了行业老大的地位。NBC 则以"栏目创新"和"富有创造性的节目"的优势与前者分庭抗礼。ABC 虽然从 NBC 分离出来，但它依靠"画面动感"和"视觉冲击力"在电视网占有一席之地。20 世纪 70 年代，FOX 和 CNN 后来者居上，FOX 通过将重点放在年轻一代城市观众身上，以新闻节目吸引了大量电视受众者。CNN 以卫星发射有线电视技术并在 20 世纪 90 年代建立新闻频道后来者居上。五大电视网各具特色，思路绝不雷同。

进入 20 世纪 90 年代中期，美国政府不断出台政策打破五大广播公司的垄断，以使其进一步商业化，情况逐渐有所变化。美国家庭不但可以收看 cable TV（有线电视），closed-circuit TV（闭路电视），还可以收看 communication satellite（卫星电视），pay TV（付费电视）。sexploitation（性剥削电影）被分为 soft-core 和 hard-core porn，skin flicks nudies。在遭到社区影院不断反对之后，sexploitation 市场转为 VCR 形式发行，现在 X-rated 三级片也可以在 home screen TV（主屏幕电视）收看。

20 世纪 70 年代，美国电影 Star Wars，Taxi Driver，The Godfather 的成功成就了 blockbuster（大片）。到了 20 世纪 80 年代 home video（家庭视讯）获得巨大发展。Showgirls 和 The Shawshank Redumption 都通过录像市场获得成功，这种电影发行方式改变了美国电影格局。到了 21 世纪，DVD 取代了录像。通过大场面、明星、高生产值、大量广告希望获取更大利润。代表有 Back to the Future，Beverly Hills Cop，Top Gun，Wall Street，Rain Man，Pulp Fiction，Titanic，The Sixth Sense。美国导演詹姆

斯·卡梅隆的科幻大片 *Avatar*（阿凡达）在全球创下超过 10 多亿美元的惊人票房，开启了 3D 电影的新时代，也被称为 blockbuster，即"卖座又成功的电影大片"。对应词 mockbuster 则是"低成本电影"。

与此同时，Studios 推出 independent productions（独立制作）与大片互补。independent productions 为低预算、独立于工作室之外的制作。这类电影注重专业水平，如表演、导演、剧本、创造力等。鉴于它的低成本，独立制作电影获得高利润。21 世纪初，美国主流电影市场之外、处于次要地位的外国电影开始占领市场份额，产生巨大影响。其中包括 Crouching Tiger, Hidden Dragon, Hero, Bowling for Columbine 和纪录片 Super Size Me, March of the Penguins。受亚洲武打电影影响，wirefu（钢丝夫）这个单词取代 gongfu 成为流行词。印度电影效仿好莱坞，制作许多卖座电影，甚至打入美国市场，它的制片工厂被称为 Bollywood（宝莱坞）。spinach cinema（菠菜电影，有教育意义的电影），slow cinema（注重细节情绪不注重叙述的电影），cinema therapy（电影疗伤），Post Potter（后波特效应）都是新时代电影带来的现象。

好莱坞是世界的造梦中心，自然与美国的政治有着千丝万缕的联系。它以总统候选人为直接投资目标。总统大选时，明星们纷纷慷慨解囊，踊跃为支持的民主党或共和党捐款。华盛顿的兴趣所在是好莱坞的捐款，它的生活方式同样吸引着前者。2007 年奥巴马举办了 $2300-a-plate Hollywood gala（2300 美元一盘的好莱坞晚会），募捐了大量款项，这些巨款当然也吸引着政治家。好莱坞同时也影响着华盛顿政治家。影艺界人士里根与施瓦辛格在政治上的成功参选可以说是影星参与政治的典型范例，好莱坞以其魅力和金钱正在影响着华盛顿，但同时华盛顿也影响着好莱坞。明星们为了使大众关注社会问题组织募集慈善捐款的公益活动，被称为 filmanthropy（电影募捐）。

虽然电视走进大众生活，成为人们生活中必不可少的娱乐方式。但是美国大众依然愿意给作家作品 a read（一读）。一些书成为 must read book（必读书），还有一些书虽然是必读书，但是却成为 unread bestseller（只买但是没读的畅销书）。例如 Stephen Hawking 所著的 *A Brief History of Time*，Umberto Eco 的 *The Name of the Rose*，Allan Bloom 的 *The Closing of the American Mind*。21 世纪美国出现了各种新类文学，其中有：chick lit（女性文学），lad lit（青少年文学），misery lit（悲惨题材文学），issue literature（问题文学），Kmart realism（描写工人阶级奋斗的现实主义文学），lad mag（青少年杂志），blog book（博客书籍），fictomercial（植入广告的小说），micro-fiction（微小说），wheredunit（场景侦探小说）。一些美国作家如此著名，以至于他们的名字进入英语新词，成为某种思想或方式的代名词。Orwellian 是《1984 年》的作者，被用来指独裁。Kafkaesque Pinteresque 表示荒谬和可笑。Faulknerian 被用来指福克纳式的冗长且难懂的句子，而 Hemingwayesque 则代表着简洁的句子，macho 是男性阳刚之气。Nabokovian 代表着充满性感的女性。Wildean wit 是智慧和复杂的象征，而 Brechtian 则正好相反，表示严肃和现实主义的。Galbraithian 表示自由经济的，Friedmanite 代表着保守经济。Hicthcockian 是悬念剧的代名词，Disneyesque fantacies 更是动画片的象征。

（二）美国流行音乐

美国音乐囊括了 hiphop + rap（嘻哈饶舌说唱），R&B + soul（节奏布鲁斯和灵魂乐），pop（前卫流行乐），rock & roll（摇滚乐），American country music（乡村音乐），Latin music（拉丁乐），Disco jockey（DJ 电子混音舞曲，属于 hiphop），Punk（朋克，rock 的一种），Funk Music（放荡杰克音乐），CRunk & B（旷课乐），Gothic（歌特音乐），Home（舞曲），Jazz（爵士），Metal（金属乐），Alternative（另类），Raggae（雷鬼）等多元化美国本土以及欧美混合音乐元素。

Hip-hop 是 20 多年前始于美国街头的一种黑人文化，也泛指 rap（说唱乐）。Hip-hop 文化的四种表现方式包括有节奏地说、街舞、玩唱片及唱盘技巧、涂鸦艺术。rap 只是 hip-hop 文化中的一种元素，要加上其他舞蹈、服饰、生活态度等才构成完整的 hip-hop 文化。代表人物是 Jay-Z，他是美国嘻哈音乐艺术家、企业家，被誉为说唱界教父。过去 gangsta rap（匪帮说唱）一直受到企业的推助，歌迷们也迷恋于这种轰动效应。但是，近年来青少年对于世界大事、艺术和生活的差异相对来说持比较温和的态度，conscientious rap（道德责任说唱）中强调的责任和道德受到推崇。除此之外，新生代也很喜欢 poetic rap（诗歌说唱）和 geeksta（电脑奇客表演的音乐）。与此同时，homohop（同性恋表演的嘻哈乐）获得一定知名度，嘻哈同性恋也从过去遮掩状态转而以嘻哈乐形式大胆歌颂同性恋的生活方式和 homohop 艺术。

R&B 的全名是 Rhythm & Blues。早期的摇滚乐就是以 R&B 为基础的，它是由受流行音乐影响的"乡村和西部音乐"发展而来。R&B 不仅仅是在布鲁斯和摇滚乐之间的一种重要的过渡音乐。还是布鲁斯和灵魂乐之间最重要的音乐分支。代表人物有 Mariah Carey。

美国朋克开始于大约 1975—1976 年的 Ramones。朋克在纽约得以繁荣和涌现。类似的音乐在美国路易斯得到蓬勃发展，并且向硬核朋克方向积极发展。20 世纪 80 年代，美国朋克开始枯萎并发展成一种新的形式：硬核摇滚。在 20 世纪 90 年代加利福尼亚州中心依赖 Ramones，又使其成为盛行的音乐。代表乐队有 Green Day，Black Flag，Ramones。

摇滚是一种音乐类型，起源于 20 世纪 40 年代末期的美国，20 世纪 50 年代早期开始流行，迅速风靡全球。摇滚乐以其灵活大胆的表现形式和富有激情的音乐节奏表达情感，受到了全世界年轻人的喜爱。Bill Haley 是摇滚乐之父，也是摇滚乐的创始人。20 世纪 70 年代摇滚艺术家 Bruce Springsteen 一夜成名，他的专辑 Born in America 和 Born to run 深受大众喜欢，其地位不亚于猫王和甲壳虫乐队。他的音乐使人感到猫王英雄般的谦逊和普通人的幽默感，是美国中产阶级发言人。20 世纪 80 年代与之齐名的，甚至成就比之更为辉煌的就是流行音乐之王 Michael Jackson。他的音乐使人感受到猫王般燃烧的性感，福音音乐之根，有时又充斥着令人困扰且矫饰的怪癖。emo（情绪硬核）是一种独立的摇滚风格。是从 Hardcore Punk 中派生出来的一种有着艺术家气派的音乐，但在 20 世纪 90 年代末它成为地下摇滚的一支重要力量，投合了当时的朋克和独立摇滚乐于，最著名的代表人物是 Weezer。摇滚受到大众欢迎，新词不断出现在大众视野中，如 dadrock（老摇滚明星），foprock（只注重华丽衣饰的摇滚）。

乡村音乐是美国人民宝贵的音乐财富之一。它的分布区域广泛，有反映南部山区和少数民族的民歌，中西部拓荒者的生活之歌，西部的牛仔歌，东南部山区伐木之歌以及东部沿海水手的劳动歌曲，等等。这些地区的音乐，都与当地的自然地理环境、历史背景、风土人情有着密不可分的联系，反映了当地人民的生活状态。它所诉说的都是生活中的平常事情，具有亲切感，能够引起听者共鸣，而且曲风清新自然，能够给人们带来恬美与宁静。乡村音乐的曲调，一般都很流畅、动听，曲式结构也比较简单。Taylor Alison Swift 就是乡村音乐女创作歌手，她会用木吉他、钢琴演奏。乡村音乐的代表人物有 John Denver 和 Shania Twain，John Denver 代表作品有 Country Road, Rocky Mountain High, Annie's Song, Sunshine On My Shoulders 等。Shania Jwain 代表作有 What Made You Say That, Any Man of Mine, You're Still the One 等。

随着国际化加速，美国出现一种新的音乐内容，即 country-eastern（乡村亚洲音乐），它把北美西部乡村音乐与中东或亚洲音乐元素结合在一起，成为近些年一种新的乡村音乐形式。

爵士乐的主要风格有：新奥尔良爵士、摇摆乐、比博普、冷爵士、自由爵士、拉丁爵士、融合爵士等。摇摆爵士乐中切分音的频繁运用使旋律产生交错的节奏效果，让听众即兴随音乐"摇摆"。演奏者（特别是独奏时）可以充分即兴发挥。富于爵士魅力和内涵。独特的声音音响的处理方法也是爵士乐风格的重要标准。乐手们通过改变强度、随意升降音高、使用弱音器、爆裂吹奏、突出打击乐等，创造出一片与众不同的音响天地。爵士乐的代表人物是 Louis Armstrong, *The Essential of Satchmo* 唱片中有他著名的 What A Wonderful World, Hello Dolly, La Vie En Rose 等；爵士乐第一夫人 Ella Fitzgerald 的代表作品有 Forever Ella, Summertime Misty, How Deep Is Ocean, I Get Kick Out of You, The Very Thought of You 等。

蓝调，意为在感情上悲伤的意思。发源于 19 世纪的美国，是由非洲被贩卖到美国南部庄园中做奴隶的黑人所哼唱的劳动歌曲、灵歌和田间号子结合而成。其中有一大部分都是描写生离死别之情，抒发忧伤凄惨的内容，是美国黑人音乐中一种典型的曲调。Bessie Smith 是布鲁斯之皇。布鲁斯之王为第一个把布鲁斯写下来并交付出版的 W. H. Handy。布鲁斯的代表人物还有 Lemon Jefferson, B. B. King, John Lee Hooker, Etta Baker, Jimi Hendrix, Junior Wells 和 Buddy Guy。Whitney Houston 在 1990 年出版的专辑《今晚我是你的情人》获得了该年度格莱美最佳节奏布鲁斯专辑奖，奠定了其当代"灵歌女皇"的地位。

（三）美国教育

美国是世界上教育事业最发达的国家之一。当代美国教育分为 elementary（基础教育），secondary（中等教育）和 higher education（高中教育）三级体制。美国学校分为公立、私立两类。公立学校系统规模庞大，由美国政府资助。联邦政府也设有教育部，但美国教育部是教育政策研究和咨询的机构，负责制定教育政策，不参与执行工作，也不监管地方学校。它对于国家的教育素质、教育问题研究、通过教育法案等都起很大的作用。由于公立学校得到州政府和联邦政府的拨款，因此受到各州州政府的监管，并遵守各州议会制定的有关教育的法律。还有一些院校是私立的，最初主要是由教会和其他宗教团体创立的，但当今却不再以宗教教育为主。私立学校基本上不受任何政府的监管，对学校政策有影响力的是家长和教师联合会 PTA（Parent and Teacher Association）。

在美国，6—18 岁是属于中小学义务教育年龄。教育大概分为四个阶段，分别是学前教育、小学、中学及高等教育。美国小学一般指学前一年级至五年级（幼儿园小学），但有一部分小学提供教育到六年级，或是合并中学教育到八年级。Secondary School 为 12—18 岁，包含两年的初中（12—14 岁）和四年的高中（15—18 岁），学生如果顺利完成12 年级的学业，就可以拿到高中文凭了。在高中毕业前是属于通才教育，到高等教育（学院、大学和研究所）才分职业教育和一般教育。学生凭着在校成绩及 SAT/ACT 分数，自行申请大学入学。在美国受义务教育都是免费的，不必缴纳学杂费、课本费。美国所有的中小学都为学生提供免费的课本，多数的课本都是上届学生传给下届学生，一直到不能用为止。

在全美 50 个州中，几乎每个州至少都有一个由州政府或当地出资创办的公立大学，虽然经费来源与私立大学不同，但学制和课程类似。公立学校通常是州立大学或两年制社区学院，主要从所在州获得资助。由于主要资助不是来自州和联邦政府，私立学校一般费用高些。有宗教关系的大学是私立大学，大部分是信基督教的，也有少数犹太教和伊斯兰教。这些学校通常不会干涉学生自己的宗教观点。

私立学校与其他学校的唯一区别是它们是私人拥有的，是赢利的。它们是教育企业，提供与其他学校相似的服务和课程，它们的学习内容倾向于技术和为从事职业做准备的课程学习。

美国现有的院校主要是两年或四年学制。两年制的多为 technical school（技术专科学校）和 community college（社区学院）或 junior colleges（副学士学位），毕业后获得 associate degree（大专）。在成功完成某专科两年全时学习后，颁发准学士学位 Associate of Arts（A. A.）或 Associate of Science（A. S.）。社区学院有两种基本类型，一种是为学生转入四年制学士学位的大学做准备，另一种是提供专门领域的职业培训。大多数社区学院是由州和当地社区支持的，也有私立社区学院，一些私立社区学院是赢利性质的。

Bachelor of Arts（B. A.）或 Bachelor of Science（B. S.）是最常见的学士学位，但还有许多其他名称的学士学位。通常成功完成四年全时学习可获得学士学位，某些专业或学校的学士学位学习超过四年。正规四年制的学校主要为文理学院、独立专业学院和综合性大学。由于 18 岁高中毕业生不需要入学考试就能升入高等院校学习，60% 以上的高中毕业生都能进大学继续深造。教师要在四年制高等学校任教通常必须获得博士学位。他们培养大批高层次的专业人才，并且承担着美国政府的大量高精尖的科研任务。

大学生毕业获得学士学位后就有资格继续攻读硕士学位。攻读医科、法律等专业课程必须在大学毕业后，进行相关考试，才可申请。学位体制采用五级制，即：准学士、学士、硕士、博士和第一专业学位。其中，硕士学位分为两种：一种必须撰写学位论文，另一种不要求写论文，但要进行口试和笔试。硕士学位学制通常为两年，博士学位为两到三年。博士研究生由几名专家和教授组成的指导小组负责指导，专业考试合格通过博士论文签办后获得学位。

美国高等教育学校通过多种途径为大学生提供各类经济资助，如奖学金、助学金、低息贷款、联邦政府勤工俭学计划、学校内外兼职工作和打工等。现在几乎所有的美国高校都是 coeducational 或者是 co-ed（男女混合）。教职员工、管理层在任何学校都是有男有女的。

美国虽然经济发达，生活优越，但是青少年问题多多，校园问题也无处不在。在美国，校园欺凌现象司空见惯，在美国俄克拉荷马州一所中学，一名学生因不堪长期被欺辱，在校园举枪自尽，这种行为被称为 bullycide（霸凌自杀）。随着网络盛行，美国青少年之间 cyberbullying（网络霸凌）行为已经取代以往的校园暴力，2010 年，年仅 15 岁的少女菲比·普林斯因不堪在学校受同学欺负和网络上遭遇语言暴力在家中上吊自杀。美国近期出现多起同性恋青少年无法忍受校园欺辱和网络霸凌而自杀，这让校园霸凌现象得到了全美关注。马萨诸塞州议会通过了菲比·普林斯反霸凌法。当地法院对六名南哈德利高中学生提出强奸、侵害民权、骚扰和跟踪等多项重罪指控。据统计，还有 1000 多所学校中一半多的学生不能毕业，这些学校被称为 dropout factories（辍学工厂）。有些青年人既不工作，也不上学，更不参加培训，被称作 Neet。美国公司裁员频繁，雇佣新的职员越来越少，新的毕业生很难找到工作，这些人被称作 sad grads（可悲的毕业生）。鉴于此，毕业生们开始进行 just in time learning（即时学习）。

大学附近的居民区由于学生租户的增加变得拥挤脏乱，使得居民怨声载道，这种居民区学生化被称为 studentification。美国的学历造假现象屡禁不止，顾客花 50 美元就会买到 fake diploma 或 novelty degrees（伪造学位证书）。鉴于许多学校培养 I-shaped people（专攻自己的专业不熟悉其他学科的人才）或 hyphen-shaped people（涉猎广但不精的人才），美国教育界开始倡导培养 T-shaped people，即术业有专攻又涉猎广泛的有多方面潜质的人才。

21 世纪，MOOCs（慕课）开始成为教育新潮流。MOOCs 是 massive open online courses（大规模网络公开课）的缩写，是面向全世界的免费网络课程。开设课程的主要是顶尖大学或大学附属机构。例如斯坦福、加州伯克利、哈佛和哥伦比亚。课程的范围不仅覆盖了广泛的科技学科，比如数学、统计、计算机科学，也包括社会科学和人文学科。慕课课程正吸引着成千上万的学生，具有巨大的规模和潜力。

（四）当代美国文学

当代美国小说，在形式和内容上既有对传统的继承，也有推陈出新的实验特征。最令人瞩目的是其所呈现出的多元特征，20 世纪 60 年代的民权运动、女权运动、反战示威、刺杀、水门事件等重大的社会事件震荡着社会，也影响到文坛，使美国进入一个大众文化时代，postmodernism（后现代小说）在 20 世纪 60 年代达到顶峰。20 世纪 70 年代之后，美国社会局势趋向平稳，种族冲突得到缓解，少数族裔的生存状况得到改善，美国小说重新呈现出对于现实主义的回归。Ethnic literature（少数族裔文学）如 African American literature，Asian American literature 异军突起，lesbian and gay literature（同性恋文学）也在这一时期逐渐出现在文坛。20 世纪 80 年代末以苏联解体为标志的冷战结束，20 世纪

90 年代初的海湾战争进一步确立了美国在世界上的霸主地位。社会运动与文化变革，也在很大程度上影响了文学的发展。

美国南方文学在 20 世纪末方兴未艾。Ellen Gilchrist 于 1984 年出版了著名作品 *Victory Over Japan*，Anne Tyler 在 1982 年发表畅销小说 *Dinner at the Homesick Restaurant*，Peter Taylor 于 1986 年发表 *A Summonsto Memphis*。Larry Brown 发表了代表作有 *Bid Bad Love* 和 *Dirty Work* 等，他所创造的文学作品被称为 grit lit（粗粝文学），大多描写被贫困、婚姻问题、暴力、酗酒、虐待等困扰的南方农村底层人物。

犹太文学在美国文坛中享有盛名，在世纪末的 20 年中仍然焕发着旺盛的活力。Saul Bellow 的 *The Dean's December*（1982）有着浓厚的世纪末色彩，揭示了现代人的精神危机。Philip Rose 的 *The Anatomy Lessen*（1983）描写了犹太人的反叛精神。Cynthia Ozick 关注于美国犹太人的生存困境，Paul Auster 以超现实的手法描绘一个噩梦般的荒诞世界，代表作品是 *The Country of Last Things*（1987）等。

20 世纪 70—80 年代非裔美国作家大放异彩。Toni Morrison 获得诺贝尔文学奖，著名作品有 *The Blue Eyes*（1970），*Song of Solomon*（1977），*Beloved*（1987）等。Alice Walker 以她的 *The Color Purple*（1982）开创美国 Womanism（美国妇女主义）先河。Ishmael Reed 的反现实小说、Clarence Major 的实验性元小说、John Edgar Wideman 的历史元小说、Toni Cade Bambara 的新现实主义小说都在美国文坛上散发出流光溢彩。

华裔小说也在 20 世纪 70 年代末进入公共视线。这些小说表现了华裔身份与美国文化交融的希望，探讨了种族、跨文化冲突、文化错位等问题，弘扬宣传积极形象。汤亭亭在 1976 年出版了 *The Woman Warrior*、*Tripmaster Monkey*：*His Fake Book*，Amy Tan 于 1989 年发表了 *The Joy Luck Club*。赵健秀于 20 世纪 70 年代曾因发表剧作而风靡美国文坛，于 1991 年和 1994 年分别发表小说 *Donald Duck* 和 *Gunga Din Highway*，伍慧明于 1993 年发表小说 *Bone*。

第一位获得普利策奖的印第安土著作家 N. Scott Momaday 著有 *The Ancient Child*（1989），著名拉美裔作家 Oscar Hijuelos 著有 *The Mambo Kings Play Song of Love*（1989），西班牙裔女作家 Elena Castedo 的著名作品有 *Paradise*（1990），日裔作家 Karen Tei Yamashita 以 *Through the Arc of the Rain Forest*（1990）轰动文坛。

Isaac Asimov 为当代美国最著名的科幻小说家之一，一生撰写无数部作品，1987 年因其在科幻小说领域的巨大成就获得 SFWA Grand Master Award。代表作有 *Foundation Series*，*Galactic Empire*，*Robot Series* 等。William Gibson 率先将电脑语言引入科幻小说，被视为 cyber punk（网络朋克）小说的鼻祖。代表作是 *Neuromancer*。

在当代美国小说领域，多元性已经成为其最引人注目的特征。这种特征首先表现在美国少数族裔文学的蓬勃发展，种族、阶级、性别等都与其有着密切联系。此外，这种多元性还表现在小说的创作模式、叙事手法、体裁等诸多写作手法方面。

六　新词语与美国亚文化群体

亚文化群体为了牢固他们团体的团结和凝聚力，或者为了表现他们的身份，都有着他们自己的俚语和行话。语言是亚文化群体区别各自身份的一个最大特征。很多原本来源于亚文化群体的俚语，由于其成员和普通人密切的接触，这些俚语也逐渐变成了一般人的口头词汇了。美国亚文化群体包括青少年、士兵、吸毒者、信教者、音乐家、大学教授等等，这些群体都属于俚语起源的典型的亚文化群体。了解亚文化群体这一文化现象和他们使用的词语能够帮助我们深刻理解美国社会的全貌及文化。下面讨论的是较为典型的规模较大的亚文化群体。

（一）青少年和大学生群体

青少年的文化是西方文明的一个典型特征。广义来讲，teenagers 在美国包括中学生和大学生，他们个性鲜明，追求独立自主，思想活跃激进。在成长过程中创造了很多新的俚语词汇，也催生了各类亚文化群体。他们创造出新词，描绘一个人的品质好坏、食物饮食和各类关系等。经常用于形容男学生的俚语词汇有：nerd（学霸），a class act（一个优秀的人），flamer（在男同性恋中扮演女角的人）、bf（boyfriend），school hunk（校草），barney（长得帅的男生），buster（busta）和 chat（一个比较衰的人），hot carl（一个有魅力的男性），pansy（性格懦弱的男生，表现得愚蠢，而且还女人气），pussy-boy（娈童）。经常用于形容女学生的俚语词汇有 peach（皮肤白里透红的女孩），hood-rat（低俗邋遢的女人），foxy（性感的女生），bitch（非常粗俗，吝啬自私的人，尤指女性），chick（性感，漂亮女朋友），school babe 或 campus belle（校花），bimbo（漂亮无脑的年轻女性）。既可形容男学生也可形容女学生的词汇有：combo（双性恋的人），airhead（没脑子的人），player（花花公子），hepcat（指某人很时尚，走在时代的前沿），baller（能够吸引很多异性的人），bopper（任何时候都想吸引异性的人），candy（非常漂亮或者非常帅气的女生或男生）。这些新词语反映了美国年轻人的生活、思想以及他们对待社会的态度，为青年文化和新词增加了鲜明的色彩。

（二）音乐人群体

Jazz，blues，hiphop 等音乐大多由黑人群体创建。很多年以来，这些音乐已经成为美国主流流行音乐的一部分。从一开始，这些群体就有自己的语言和术语，如 hip，cat，daddy-o 这些俚语词汇使爵士更增添了一丝神秘性，常用的词语有：blow（指演奏任何乐器），cats（玩爵士音乐的人），bling bling，cans（耳机）、head or head arrangement（一组歌曲的编排，没有写下来，但是由乐队的成员记在心里，通常用于即兴表演的时候），Jazz Box（爵士吉他），skins player（鼓手），heavy metal（重金属），等等。组成美国俚语的一大部分是黑人俚语，这些由爵士音乐人使用的俚语词汇也展现出美国黑人群体的生活和文化。

（三）政治亚文化群体

美国老百姓把在政府里工作的人称为 G-man（Government man），或者 garbage man，因为他们认为政府是无能的。他们称卷入政治活动中的演员为 actorvist（演员兼社会活动积极分子），发生在幕后的或是没有通过正常渠道而办成的事情为 backchannels（衬托型反馈形式），如果他们举行一系列的政治选举活动，他们就开始进入了 campaign mode（竞选模式）。在选举活动中，阐述选举政策或是相关规定的行为称为 issue positioning，再如 ugly season 指竞选候选人为了打倒对方不惜牺牲对方利益或者揭露对方不光彩的过去，以获得大众支持的竞选初期阶段。在这段时间里，任何有关竞选日程的猜测或是走漏的信息都称为 a dope story

（内幕消息），如果哪方是出乎意料地赢得这场竞选，该方就被称为 a dark horse。一个在政治圈里不守纪律、不受约束的人，被称为 cowboy，强势有力的候选人有着 strong muscle（通常指有很强的臂膀、背景或者参与了什么政治阴谋），分裂竞选对方势力的行为被同行称为 rat-fuck-ing。当竞选人被成功地选为总统，他一般都会做一些小型的演讲，被称为 Rose Garden rubbish——因为这些演讲通常是在美国白宫的玫瑰园举行。如果某位总统以后有了什么政治丑闻，如与性有关的丑闻，就被人称为 sexgate，或者被称为 Velcro president，即指绯闻、争议缠身的总统。

（四）犯罪和吸毒者群体

黑社会群体为了逃避警察的追捕把一些平常的单词赋予特殊的含义，使圈外人不知道他们话语的含义。例如 to blot out someone（干掉某人），out of town（入狱），knock-over（抢劫），eagle（警察），put the claw on somebody（被警察抓到），cut up the touches（瓜分赃物），bush parole（从监狱里出逃），set（帮派分支），set tripping（帮派内斗），smoke（杀人），soldier（没有案底的帮派分子），toa（帮派间的义气），thug（身无长物的人，恶棍），up north trip（被送往监狱）。

贩毒能带来巨大利润，有些人会不惜以身试法。贩卖毒品是违法行为，从事贩卖毒品的人就必须说暗语。使用这些俚语暗号为的是辨别贩毒团伙成员的身份，如果使用错误便不能识别团伙成员和交易对手，甚至有可能进入监狱。因此他们就用 grass 代替 hashish 和 mainline（静脉注射毒品），primo，turbo 或 zootie 指代掺了可卡因的大麻，slab 或 snow 指代可卡因，angel dust（天使尘）指代被非法当作迷幻药使用的麻醉剂。Cred cocaine 是哥伦比亚贩毒集团利用新技术所制造的一种辛可卡因，可以逃避检测。dosia（大麻）还被称为 marijuana，weed，pot。rush 为神仙水。Ecstasy（快乐丸）与 ice 被称为 designer drug，即上流社会毒品。head waggling pill 是摇头丸，Liquid X 是液态快乐丸，也被称为 GHB，其他俗称还有 Goop，George home boy，gamma-oh。yaba 是泰国本土性的冰毒，吸毒者吸食毒品会产生 acid trip（服用 LSD 所引起的幻觉）。其他吸毒词汇还有 Poppy（罂粟），smacked（药效发作），through（嗑药的兴奋状态），triple beam（称量毒品的秤），skins 和 zig zags（卷大麻烟的纸），sherm stick（浸泡过精油的大麻烟），roll（卷一管大麻），zooted（抽大麻），spliff（牙买加产的大麻烟），Vegas（卖大麻烟的厂商）。贩卖毒品为 push，slang，trap。贩卖毒品的人被称为 watermelon man，candyman 或 madhatter，他们在专门的毒品交易地方见面，这类地方被称为 greenhouse 或者 jam house。Pitch 作为动词表示"在街头贩卖毒品"。Entrepot 和 transit 都表示"毒品转运站"，transit route 为运毒路线。trafficker（drug smuggler）是毒枭。drug trafficking 或 drug smuggling 是毒品走私。rock star 是吸毒上瘾的人，boofer（美俚）是买毒品的人，drug cartel 统指贩毒集团。body-pack 是将毒品等藏在体内的运毒方法，如将毒品装进橡皮袋塞进肛门内等。

（五）同性恋群体

同性恋人群里有很多受过高等教育的人，他们聪明严谨或很时髦，他们影响美语语言。同性恋使用自己的暗语，帮助其群体成员表达他们的身份，暗指他们是什么人，保护他们免受外界的伤害，自由表达自己的观点和思想。在美国有些大城市会有 gay bar（同性恋酒吧），gay street（同性恋街区），同性恋者会光顾这些地方，一个圈外人去同性恋酒吧，听不懂在那里说的语言。同性恋俚语包含了很多的描绘各种性角色和性行为的词汇，如：baby doll（长得很俊美的男人或男孩），career-boy（以卖淫为职业的男孩），daisy（男性同性恋，像女人般懦弱），dirt（俊美的男性，被警察用来做诱饵吸引在公共场合发生性行为的同性恋），mama's boy（非常女气的男孩或者男人，对他的母亲过度的依恋），man friend（同性恋爱人中年龄较长资助较年轻的同性恋爱人或者朋友的人），out of cabinet 或 lancer（宣布出柜的人），escort service（用电话来找寻男妓或妓女的地方），frame（指吸引同性恋的异性恋男士），fresh meat（没有性经验的同性恋），knock off a piece（指发生性行为），Queen Bee（与很多年轻的同性恋男子交往的有钱女人），shirtlifter（男性同性恋），lesbian（女同），gay（男同），lipstick lesbian（女同中扮演女性角色的女性），butch lesbian（女同中扮演男性角色的）等。

（六）美国的 generation

美国人常以某一特定称谓泛指某一时代出生的、有着许多共性和广泛影响的人群。Generation 就是一个最好的证明。年龄在 40 岁以下的公司创始人、所有者被称为 Generation E（Generation Entrepreneur）。GI Generation（Government Issue）指美国"军人一代"或"大兵一代"。原意是"政府所颁"（士兵的装备等），后来被用来指（美国）军人、大兵。肯尼迪、约翰逊、尼克松、福特、卡特、里根、老布什七位总统都属于 GI Generation。Sandwich Generation 被称为"夹心层一代"，他们上有老，下有小，要同时照顾父母和孩子。20 世纪 60 年代中期到 70 年代后期继婴儿潮后，美国生育史上出现了低谷期，生育低谷期出生的人在美语中称为 baby busters，Babybust Generation 是"低谷潮一代"。由于这一代人出生在婴儿潮一代之后，所以又称为 Posters（后婴儿潮一代）。Generation Jones（愚蠢的一代）是指 1954—1965 年出生的一代人，他们介于婴儿潮一代和 X 一代之间，学校总体平均成绩最低，他们比其他时代的人更愿意看电视而不是学习，且青年吸毒者较多。在这一代人出生时，美国社会出现了很多离婚家庭，吸毒者剧增。Jones 有吸毒之意，这代人被称为"愚蠢的一代"。Beat Generation（垮掉的一代）指美国 20 世纪 50—60 年代对社会不满的部分青年，大多是小资产阶级及知识分子。在文学上它还指一种文学思潮或流派，其成员被称为 Beat，也作 beatnik。Beat Generation 放荡不羁、不满现实、反叛传统、我行我素。1976 年，美国作家 Tom Wolf 把那些昧着良心、追求自我幸福、对政治和国家大事持冷漠态度的青年称为 Me Generation（自我一代）。Me Generation 奉行处处为我思想。美国 1776 年成立至 20 世纪 60 年代共经历了 13 代人，因此 20 世纪 60 年代至 70 年代末出生的 Generation X 这代人亦被称为 The Thirteenth Generation（第十三代）。Generation X（X 一代）指出生于 20 世纪 60 年代中期至 70 年代末的一代人。他们当时面临许多社会问题，有着明显的消极悲观色彩，这些人愤世嫉俗，以自我为中心。但是其中有些人锐意进取，学有所长，十年后事业有成。有些人成为政界要人，如奥巴马、小布什，还有些人投资股票债券，成为商界精英，被称为 Generation Nadaq。Generation Y（Y 一代）是 20 世纪 80 年代后至 21 世纪初出生的美国年轻人，人数超过 7600 万。Generation Y 不但乐观自信，执着坦率，而且有主见，知识面广，求新，求变，时尚且聪明。他们借助互联网成长，靠互联网创业。Generation Z（Z 一代）通常指那些在 1996 年以后出生的孩子；是生于 20 世纪 60 年代中期至 70 年代末的 Generation X 的儿女。Generation Z 尚未出生就成了网络注册用户，被认为是 digital native 的一代。肥胖一代被婉称为 Generation XL。20 世纪 80 年代至 2000 年出生的美国人被称为 Millennial Generation（千禧年一代），占美国人口的 1/4。他们的特点是，投票率远远低于全体年龄层，不太热衷于政治。但是 2001 年发生的"9·11"事件改变了年轻人的态度，政治成了他们生活中的重要部分。在之后的 2004 年和 2008 年两次美国大选中，他们的参与程度非常高。年轻人的选票已经成为美国大选的关键因素。

焦虑和恐惧是现代社会的流行病。越来越多的年轻人被恐惧、缺乏安全感、自我封闭等现象所困扰，这就是 Generation F（F 一代）。他们由于焦虑、工作、学业等原因，承受力有限，经常光顾心理诊所，抑郁感增加。

在 2008 年的美国总统大选中，美国 18—29 岁的选民投票率创下了 36 年来的最高纪录，2/3 的年轻选民选举奥巴马。因此，这一代被称作 Generation O（奥巴马一代）。美国的年轻人认为奥巴马是他们这一代的马丁·路德·金和约翰·肯尼迪，Generation O 们对奥巴马抱有很高的期望。Generation Q（Quiet Generation）是"沉静的美国人"，他们沉溺于网络，许多人是宅男或宅女，他们不声不响地实践着自己的理想主义。当今的年轻人要比前辈承担更多的义务，他们增加收入和创造财富的难度也更大了。他们要交纳大学学费，承担更大的风险。领取养老金的老人不断增加，年轻人不得不供养他们并支付他们的医药费。因此，当今这一代年轻人被称为 Ipod Generation（Insecure，Pressured，Overtaxed，Debt-ridden）。被贴上各种标签的人们还有 yippies（易皮士）和 yuppies（雅皮士），luppies（拉丁裔雅皮士），huppies（西班牙裔雅皮士），yettie（年轻有为的技术公司经营者），等等。

BoBos 是由《纽约时报》资深记者戴维·布鲁克斯在其《天堂中的 Bobo 族——新社会精英的崛起》（*BoBos in Paradise*）一书中提出的，BoBos 是 Bourgeois（布尔乔亚）及 Bohemian（波希米亚）两词的合成。意指资本主义的布尔乔亚，并且崇尚自由与解放的波希米亚，20 世纪 70 年代的嬉皮，就是某种波希米亚的延续。20 世纪末，随着科技社会经济飞速发展，全世界范围内出现了一批新兴中产阶层——布波族，他们既具有布尔乔亚赚钱的本事及鉴赏的能力，又有波希米亚对艺术与自然的热爱。Bobos 的生活宣言是：追求自由，挑战自我，实现心灵满足。一个纯粹的 Bobo 族，既懂得享受生活，又不铺张奢靡；既特立独行，又不标榜另类；他们事业有成，却不追名逐利，只试图在生活品质和灵魂自由中寻求到最为超然飘逸的态度。

1984 年美国出版了《雅皮士手册》一书，描写了一对忙着赚钱的夫妇。自此以后，雅皮士即成为"美国年轻的城市专业人员的"代名词。雅皮士从事那些需要受过高等教育才能胜任的工作，如律师、医生、建筑师等。他们没有颓废情绪但不关心政治与社会问题，只在意赚钱。雅皮士是成熟优雅的代名词。他们的工资颇高，大约年薪为 40000 美元以上。雅皮士在自己的专业方面均有所成就，因而他们踌躇满志，盛气凌人。这些人穿的是精品，吃的是美味佳肴，住的是独门独户的房子，乘高级豪华轿车。这些人不留长发钟爱短发，他们不戴珍珠项链却手拿公文包，他们不穿奇装异服，但西装革履。雅皮士的口号是"最高、最好、最舒适"，他们在美国社会发展过程中发挥着至关重要的作用。

第四章 当代美国文化特征

一 美国文化的融合性与包容性

美国被称为 Melting Pot（大熔炉），这是因为美国是一个由来自多个民族移民组成的国度，这些拥有不同文化背景的人在美国形成了一个新的民族——美利坚民族。还有一种理论认为，美国文化是一种 Multiculture（多元文化），这个大熔炉并没有吞噬所有外来文化，外来移民所带来的文化传统以某种方式被不同程度地保留下来。美国文化的包容性体现在对各民族文化的吸收与容纳。

德国文化的特征被德国移民带到了美国。经过几代人以后，美国德裔人的不少文化特征变成了美国生活的一般特征。Lager（淡味啤酒），hamburger, delicatessen（美味），Kipfel（牛角包），Gummi bear（小熊糖），Muesli（早餐麦片），Pretzel（椒盐脆饼干圈），Pumpernickel（酸黑面包），Sauerkraut（酸菜）和 hotdog 已成为美国生活方式的必备之物。

美国华人以中餐馆著名。到 1989 年，全美中餐馆近 19000 家。20 世纪 70 年代后期，美国总统尼克松访华时，品尝过北京烤鸭，对这一美食赞不绝口。不久，北京烤鸭就在美国火起来。Fengshui（风水），acupuncture（针灸），Dim Sum（点心）在美国颇受欢迎，guanxi（关系），wirefu（钢丝夫），sifu（师傅），chengguan（城管），qinghaosu（青蒿素），Xinhua（News Agency）等词也进入美语，成为普通词汇。

美国文化包容了拉美文化。墨西哥文化不断被融入美国社会，墨西哥美国人以他们的建筑、文学、艺术、音乐、戏剧和烹饪法丰富了美国文化，他们的壁画在许多城市的墙壁上随处可见。今天墨西哥美国人仍然过墨西哥传统节日。他们有自己的教堂、足球队、电视台、电台、报纸和杂志。20 世纪 80 年代，讲西班牙语的艺术家在美国不被重视。但到 20 世纪 90 年代初，拉美音乐在美国已有巨大的市场。savvy（有知识的），Lolita（洛莉塔），El Nino（厄尔尼诺现象），silo（导弹发射井），bonanza（繁荣），plaza（广场）已经成为美语日常用语。salsa（汁），fajitas（法吉塔），taco（墨西哥卷饼），ancho（大个芳香辣椒），tortilla（墨西哥玉米煎饼），chipotle（烟熏干红辣椒），habanero（哈瓦那椒）均成为美国大众熟悉并喜欢的食品。

　　阿拉伯文化对于美国文化也带来影响。如中东的 hijab（源出阿拉伯语，指穆斯林女子所围的头巾），土耳其的 doner kebab（土耳其烤羊肉），阿富汗的 Taliban 或 Taleban（塔利班），rai（含有阿拉伯和阿尔巴尼亚民间音乐、西方摇滚乐等音乐成分的流行乐），希伯来语中的 challah（犹太教徒在安息日吃的白面包）和 kippa（正统派犹太男教徒所戴的无檐便帽），土耳其语中的 sheshbesh（中东的一种 15 子游戏），gala（狂欢），Alqaida（基地组织）。

　　美国文化也应包括黑人文化，美国黑人在体育和音乐方面为美国赢得大量荣誉。美国黑人在国际体育大赛中屡创佳绩，成绩斐然。在第三届奥运会拳击比赛中，以黑人为主的美国队囊括了七个级别的全部冠军。在奥运会 12 届的篮球比赛中，美国队九次荣登冠军宝座。在第 21 届和 23 届奥运会上美国获得了 31 枚和 13 枚金牌，其中有 2 枚和 12 枚分别为黑人所夺得。美国职业篮球、拳击及国家田径队中，黑人选手占 65%。在田径项目上，黑人运动员更是战绩辉煌。欧文斯在 75 分钟内曾四次破世界纪录，并在第 1 届奥运会上以四枚金牌的战绩轰动世界体坛。卡尔·刘易斯在洛杉矶奥运会上创造了一人独得四枚金牌的奇迹。在跳远比赛中，鲍维尔以 8 米 95 的佳绩打破了保持 23 年之久的世界纪录。美国拳坛几乎被黑人所垄断。荣获"本世界拳王"称号的路易斯、蜚声拳坛的阿里、伦纳德、泰森、霍利菲德尔等人形成了垄断美国拳坛的黑人群体。

　　美国黑人音乐和舞蹈别具一格。Jazz and blues 是黑人青年中流行的一种音乐。rock and roll 诞生于黑人世界中，曾成为通俗音乐的主流，它不仅影响了美国社会进程，而且流传全世界。

　　法国社会文化，与英国的社会文化不断交流融合，使英语不断充实、丰富和完善并传至美国。与流行时尚有关的词语有 BCBG（流行时尚人士，为 bon chic，bon genre 的缩略），partouse（夜总会）。与运动有关的用语有 chef d'équipe（负责日常事务的运动队经理），parkour（跑酷），levade（古典骑术中的前肢起扬），soigneur（自行车队助理教练）。与政治相关的词语有 fonctionnaire（公务员），franc fort（强势法郎政策）。此外还有 ye-ye（爵士音乐的），deja vu（已见过），vis-à-vis（面对面），faux pas（失礼），nouveau riche（新富），touché（讲得好），rentier（靠收租生活的人），jamais vu（旧事如新）等。

美国文化的包容性还表现在，美国文化具有宽容兼纳的一面。以美国宗教和美国的难民政策为例。在美国，宗教主要是基督教。分 Catholicism（天主教）和 Protestant（新教），但以后者为主。虽然它们各自分为若干教派，但几乎是大同小异。它们对人民思想生活的影响很大。美国的启蒙运动对美国的民族特性和文化产生了极为深刻的影响。它向人们灌输一个普遍化的梦想。各种宗教信仰总是声称适合于所有的人，但同时又强调彼此之间的差异。许多美国人认为，民族特性和文化背后的神的力量可以呈现出各种各样的表现形式，并且为众信徒们以不同的方式所领会。

政治体制多元化也是美国文化包容性的体现。美国两大政党为民主党（大政府）与共和党（小政府）。民主党和共和党两党长期轮流执政。但第三党甚至第四党的势力一直存在，在政治信仰上，尽管多数美国人敌视共产主义，但美国共产党却可以长期安全存在。Green Party（绿党）是美国两党政治以外的主要在野党，自 20 世纪 80 年代开始活跃。1996 年和 2000 年绿党成员参与美国总统大选后使得它备受瞩目。近年来美国另外一个最成功的党派就是美国 Reform Party（改革党）。还有一个表现不俗的小党派是 US Libertarian Party（美国自由党），它目前在全国拥有超过 400 个选举出的官职。Tea Party（茶党）在美国异军突起。

美国是世界上接纳难民最多的国家。1946—1986 年，美国共接纳了 260 万难民，其中有的是持有移民签证的难民，有的是被"临时准入"的难民，有的是以"入境者"身份入美的难民。美国出于冷战外交考虑，对难民的接纳和重新安置，具有一定的人道主义色彩。总的来说，虽然美国没有始终一致地在难民问题上表现出人道主义精神，但美国的难民政策体现了慷慨和仁慈，因此，从美国的外交文化来看，它具有宽容性的一面。

美国文化的包容表现在种族文化的互相融合。白人文化通常指WASP文化，即白人男性中产阶级文化。美国的主流文化就是以欧洲白人移民为核心的文化，而土著印第安人、黑人和亚裔黄种人都是作为边缘文化而存在的。白种人、黄种人和黑种人各自拥有完全不同的文化背景，现实中也具有各自的文化习惯。在美国白人中，持有种族主义思想的人今天大有人在，歧视黑人和黄种人的现象和事件不断发生，出现许多与此有关的新词，如 glass ceiling, racial discrimination, segregation 等。可以说，经过300多年的磨合与斗争，包括 sit-in（静坐）等反抗运动，黑人和黄种人正在逐渐与白人文化相接近，甚至有相融合的表现，出现了 mixed marriage, salt and pepper family（黑白人通婚家庭），但现代美国仍然是以白人为主流的社会。随着社会的发展和进步，那种明显的阶级偏见和种族歧视受到越来越多的谴责和唾弃，反映本阶级或本种族利益的文化思潮也在收缩，美国的阶级文化和种族文化在慢慢相互融合。

20世纪初期以后，以下层民众为主体的消费观念、娱乐兴趣和自我实现的思想成为流行文化，被称为大众文化。大众文化亦被称为 pop culture（通俗文化），low culture（下层文化）或 folk culture（民间文化）。它流行于普通民众中间并反映下层阶级社会生活。上层文化被称为 high culture（高雅文化）或 elite culture（精英文化），是被服务于统治阶级的知识分子所归纳、提炼和记载下来的。由于各个国家和民族的统治者与普通民众之间从来都存在着一条难以逾越的鸿沟，反映在历史写作与研究中，就成为精英文化与大众文化的差别，美国政府的实权从来都是控制在一少部分社会精英手中。美国各界的头面人物也大都是社会精英人物。然而，自19世纪末以来，美国大众文化，如 hippies，hiphop + rap（嘻哈饶舌说唱），R&B + soul（节奏布鲁斯和灵魂乐），pop（前卫流行）开始逐步取代精英文化，成为美国文化的突出代表，它们不但在美国社会逐渐取得主导地位，还以其特殊的魅力和效用，感染着本国人和全世界各国人民。

二　美国文化的个人主义

美国人把处理一切事物——包括家庭关系、个人与社会其他成员的关系——的基本准则都纳入个人的范畴，都从个人的认识出发。美国的个人主义是要强调个性解放和个人意识的不可侵犯。个人主义不意味着个人利益高于一切，而仅仅要求一切都属于个人的。个人的责任感、义务感、罪过感、悔过感、自豪感、爱国感、民族感等等，都可以看成一种个人主义。

美国民族主义可以从两个角度来看：一个是世俗观念中的美国优越论；一个是宗教观念中的"使命感"。二者相辅相成、不可分割。从移民始祖到北美创建 A City upon A Hill（山巅之城）开始，美国人从来都把自己看成是上帝选定的民族，这个民族肩负的不仅仅是美国民族本身的使命，同时她还是世界其他民族的楷模，她还要履行与上帝的契约拯救其他民族。人们希望能发展自己的个性，从而使自己看起来与众不同。这不是个人主义，而只是希望通过自己的经历和所拥有的东西来使自己具有个性。人们越来越喜欢订阅比较专业的杂志，参加任务特定的小团体。各种形式的俱乐部、组织比比皆是。如 fitness club, golf club, sports bar, yoga club, country club, Autograph club, Childhood secret club, Fan club, Network of After School Film Clubs, Garden club, Probus Clubs（cater for the interests of retired or semi-retired professional or business people）。人们购买有特色的衣服、汽车和化妆品。仅婚礼就有各种与众不同的个性化婚礼形式。如：sponsored wedding（赞助婚礼），drive up marrriage（开汽车快速办理结婚手续的结婚形式），brokeback marriage（断背婚姻），common-law marriage（习惯法婚姻），green wedding（绿色婚姻），starter marriage（不指望白头偕老的婚姻），elderweds（晚年结婚），destination marriage（目的地结婚）等。

三 美国文化的开放性

文化开放是历史发展的趋势。所谓文化开放，是指世界各国精神产品的交流和交换，是各国文化的相互影响、吸收、融合以及矛盾和斗争。在人类发展的历史进程中，各民族都有自己的精神产品。一个善于吸收其他民族优秀文明成果的民族，其发展也很迅速，文明程度更高，其文化也就丰富多彩。17—20 世纪的西方文化之所以独领风骚，重要原因是它吸收了东方各民族的精华。进入现代社会，交通、科技的发展，信息技术的广泛使用，把人类的文化开放带进了一个崭新的信息时代，正是这种革命性的变化，使得文化开放成为不以人的意志为转移的大趋势。美国文化开放的基本途径有以下几种：首先，通过人员流动而实现的文化交流。当今，美国与其他国家之间包括教师、科研人员、医务工作者、体育工作者、新闻工作者以及政府官员、社会团体组织人员等的交流频繁。在美学习的外国学生不断增多。目前，在美国接受高等教育的外国学生有 57% 来自亚洲。其次，报刊、印刷品和音像制品是进行文化交流的最普遍的形式。美国的国会图书馆是世界文化开放的中心，世界各国的学者到此进行思想交流。美国图书馆的藏书之丰富、设备之先进、使用之方便，在世界上是闻名的。美国图书馆大体上分为三种类型：academic library（学术图书馆），professional library（专业图书馆）和 public library（公共图书馆）。20 世纪 60 年代初，美国一些政府和商业部门开始使用电子计算机。进入 20 世纪 70 年代后，越来越多的图书馆运用计算机进行图书检索、分类和借阅等工序，使图书馆事业进入了一个新的阶段，webrarian 成为新的现象。50 多年来，美国图书馆事业突飞猛进，各种类型图书馆密布全国各地。美国不仅图书馆事业发达，报刊在国外发行量之大也是其他国家所不及的。据 1986 年统计，*Time* 在国外发行量为 133.6 万份；*Newsweek* 100.7 万份；*Reader's Digest* 1240 万份。美国现在约有 1.8 万种杂志，其中消费类杂志占 50%—60%，其余的是专业杂志。美国的电台和电视广播业在世界上首屈一指，拥有最多的电台和最多的电视台。据统计，美国现有广播电台 1.1 万多家，各类电视台 1300 家。这是美国实现义化交流的重要途径。最后，计算机网络、卫星通信系统、电话的广泛运用成为文化开放的最有发展前途的形式。自 1973 年出现超级计算机以来，美国一直垄断着超级计算机的研究、生产和销售，其巨型机占国际市场的 90% 以上。1975 年商业微机问世，美国微机产业迅速发展，连续九年不衰。1965 年 4 月 5 日，美国发射第一颗国际通信卫星。它为北美与欧洲之间提供通信服务。目前，美国已经发射 400 多颗不同性能的 communication satellite（通信卫星）。

　　民族特色文化的开放。民族特色文化是各民族在历史发展中形成的民族习惯、风土人情、社会风尚等独有的特点。如美国人喜欢相互直呼其名，体现一种亲近和无拘无束的个性。美国人穿衣追求与众不同。在美国，人们可以着各种奇装异服招摇过市，即或是只穿 bikini（比基尼）也不会引来太多惊奇的目光，因为美国人对此司空见惯，不以为奇。

思想道德文化的开放。在这一层次上，文化开放的内涵极其复杂，它应包括该民族所信奉的世界观、政治意识形态、道德规范、社会价值和社会理想等精神产品的相互关系和相互影响。越来越多的人希望能使社会在教育、道德和环境方面更有责任感。人们组成各种团体来促使公司和其他机构承担更多的社会责任。希望汽车公司能收回 lemon（劣质产品）并给他们退款；他们会阅读 Consumer Report（消费者报告）；会参加 MADD（反对酒后驾车母亲协会）；会购买 green product（绿色产品）和具有社会责任感的公司的产品，抵制那些无责任感的公司的产品；许多人支持 Good Samaritan Law，并且做一个 Good Samaritan（见义勇为者）。

四 美国文化的进取性

美国人的进取精神，是美国得以成功的动力所在。企业家的冒险精神对美国新经济具有独特的贡献。美国充满了旺盛的创业家精神，风险企业不断地出现。这些企业在股票市场上，积极调动研究开发、设备投资、扩大专利权等的资金。美国的投资风险虽然很大，但是投资者决心也很大。

进取性的第二个层面是，美国人对权利和优越的追求。美国人对 civil rights（民权）的追求，反映了美国文化的进取性。20 世纪美国公民权利扩展的一个重要特征是对民权和社会经济权利的强调。美国人对"美国梦"的追寻和开发西部是"乐观进取"精神最生动的体现。它是对自由、平等、宽容、进取和成功进行不懈追求的理想主义信念，是对机会均等、人人都有成功的希望和创造奇迹的可能性的乐观自信。追求更多更好，是美国人的永久希望。有不少中国人尤其是新华人留在美国，是为了实现 self worth（个人价值），也是为了寻求 American Dream（美国梦），即人人可以当总统、成富豪。

美国人推崇进取精神有几个原因：首先，美国得天独厚的自然条件，对培育乐观进取精神起了特殊的作用；其次，新教价值观的影响，

"被上帝选中"的加尔文教义使得美国早期移民乐观进取，去开发这些资源；再次，美国没有封建传统，这种美国文化中独特的现象，培养了美国人乐观进取的处世生活态度；最后，美国平等、自由的原则影响了美国人的进取精神。

美国人的进取精神造就了许多著名企业。2011 年，以市场资本计算，世界十大公司就有四个在美国，分别是 Exxon Mobil, Apple Inc. Chevron Corporation 和 Microsoft。根据 Fortune Global 500（全球财富 500强）在 2011 年的统计，美国的最大雇主分别是 Walmart, U. S. Postal Service, IBM, UPS, McDonald's, Target Corporation, Kroger, The Home Depot, General Electric, 和 Sears Holdings。

美国人民的进取精神使得美国科学技术突飞猛进，社会经济迅猛发展，而反映不断出现的新发明、新事物、新概念的科学技术新词应运而生。例如 nerd bird（往来于硅谷等科技中心的航班），technosexual（科技美型男），alpha geek（阿尔法奇客），digital native（生长在电子数码产品环境中的），nerdistan（高科技园），dog food（使用自己公司开发的产品），information pollution（信息污染），collaboratory（联网合作项目），tobacco industry（备受歧视的科学及工业），ringtone（手机铃音）等。

美国由一个依赖英国的殖民地发展成为强国，靠的就是主动进取和兢兢业业的工作精神。美国人在前进的道路上也会碰到困难，甚至艰难险阻，但是他们不放弃必胜的信念，他们的未来是光明的。

五　美国文化的创新性

美国创新创业服务机构众多、专业化程度高。比如，剑桥创新中心（CIC）孕育了 1230 多家包括谷歌、亚马逊等在内的新兴企业，被称为"全球最富有创新活力的一平方英里"。旧金山 Greenstart 公司通过自有基金和引入风投资金，支持具有成长潜力的创新型企业创业，只要众多项目中的其中几项获得成功，就能在股权分成中获得巨大投资回报。

为了建设创新型社会，美国教育在教学内容、学校种类和学校管理等方面做出了重大改革。美国公立的中小学大多采用统一大纲、实行统一考试。在教育改革中通过高标准、严要求达到高质量的做法已经得到普遍认可。在此基础上，以统一教学大纲为指导的学校网在全美各地逐渐兴起。多数学校网都设有一个对学校教学进行监督并为其提供必要技术服务的监管组织。美国设有公立和私立学校，还有 charter schools（特许学校），school choice（择校就学）和 home school（家庭学校）等多种就学途径，为学生选择适当的学习场所，开发其潜力和创造力创造了必要条件。

美国注重创新教育，各级各类学校在加强基础知识和基本理论教学的同时，高度重视学生创新能力的培养。美国的中小学共 12 个年级，除了将创新能力的培养贯穿在整个教学活动之中，使所有学生都有机会提高其创新能力外，还设立专门的天才班级和天才学校。

中小学教育在创新人才培养方面的具体做法和特点是：教学内容丰富，重视培养学生的实际动手能力；学校与社区密切联系，强调学生的社会责任感；师生平等交流，鼓励学生的参与意识；课堂教学活动除教师以外，还有同学互教、小组讨论或团队协作等形式；教师通常作为协调人和协作人的角色出现在课堂；学生不仅是为了教师而且是为了教师以外的现实社会而完成作业；课内外活动丰富多彩，为激发学生开发和发挥其想象力和创造力提供机会；强调理解并掌握新知识，坚持重温所学内容；实行定期或不定期测试与评估。

大学教育中，教师引导学生有效获取已有知识，鼓励学生通过与教师或同学的合作，积极创建新的知识，努力开发创新能力。具体做法和特点包括：在教师的指导下，学生自己发现、重组和创造知识；教师的作用是开发学生的能力和天赋；大学教育是一种人际交往过程，是一种学生之间和师生之间的交流过程，因此，良好的人际关系在这种学习环境中非常重要；创新人才的成长需要一个合作的学习环境，因为激烈竞争的学习环境不利于发展良好的人际关系，对相互合作和积极创新都有负面影响；教学是一个应用理论和研究的复杂过程，它需要教师具备足够的训练，不断更新知识和改进教学技巧。

美国国际金融危机爆发以来，美国抓住新一轮科技革命带来的机遇，瞄准新能源、生物、信息、新材料、航天等新兴产业领域，加大政府投入，扶持前沿技术创新，着力培育未来竞争新优势。美国之所以能够长期处于全球技术领先地位，很大程度上归因于它拥有一个包括企业、政府和社会在内的比较完备的创新生态系统。如奥巴马政府在其创新战略中明确提出，美国公共和私人的研发投资要达到 GDP 的 3% 以上，达到历史最高水平。联邦政府每年对麻省理工学院等五所大学生物技术的研发支出相当于英国一年的 R&D（研发）投入总数。在预算分配中将民用研发投入的 50% 投向生物技术（包括健康和农业等领域）。人才培养方面，鼓励个性化发展和个人创造发明，制定有利于吸引人才的奖学金政策和移民政策。美国还有大量基金会，以及风险投资、商业贷款和企业投资支持创新。比如，少数富有且具有冒险精神的个人直接进行 angel investment（天使基金）等资本类的创业投资；有一定资本实力和实业投资经验的大型企业设立附属创业投资机构等。

第三篇
美语新词语的构成方式
和构成趋势

第五章　美语新词语的构成方式

英语这种全球语言不断地演变和发展。根据《巴恩哈特词典伴侣》（*The Barnhart Dictionary Companion*）杂志的统计，每年进入他们的计算机数据库的新词和新义达到 1500—1600 个。新词语中最为典型的语言随着社会文化的发展而发展。在发展过程中，新生事物层出不穷，各种概念不断产生。为了表达这些新生事物和概念，人们根据各种方法创造出新词语。可以说，英语新词语的产生与构成具有一定的规律可循。英语新词语的构成主要分为复合法（compound words）、缩略法（short forms or clippedwords）、类比法（analogy）、派生法（affixations）、旧词新意、转换法（conversion）、外来语（loan words）、逆成法（back formation）等。美语新词语的构成也遵循这样的规律。

一　复合法

复合词是一种构词形式，它可被简单地定义为：由两个或两个以上的根词（base）构成的一个词。英语中的复合新词语常根据构成复合词的词性分为四类：名词复合新词语、形容词复合新词语、动词复合新词语和功能词复合新词语。还可按复合新词成分之间存在的语法关系进行分类：并列复合新词语，主从复合新词语，属性或转意复合新词语及合成复合新词语。在语义上，复合新词语有着固定的语意。词的组成部分之间的语义关系呈多样化。如 soft power, phone neck（长时间夹电话患上的颈部痛），airdash（快速飞行），water bus（水上汽车），fat free（无脂）。有的是第一部分限定第二部分，有的相反。但是每个复合新词语的意义基本不会被理解错。复合新词语还使用隐喻、换喻和提喻等手段构成。例如：turkey farm 被用来指那些"无用的"人，使得用词上显得生动形象。

由于复合词具有简洁、明了等特点，其使用范围较为广泛。英语中出现了大量的复合新词语，例如 glass ceiling, grass ceiling, bamboo ceiling。复合词的生成能力大大高于其他类型的构词，而且近年有逐年增加的趋势。鉴于复合词极强的构词能力和重要性，将会在下章进行详细讨论。

二　派生法

派生法也称为词缀法。在一个词根前或后加上一个词缀，变成一个新词语。可以说，词根是派生词的基础，而英语词缀（affix）是英语形态构词中的一种粘附语素（bound morpheme），它既不能单独存在，也不能独立使用。它常常附在自由语素（free morpheme）的前面或后面或嵌在其他语素中间，只表示附加意义和语法意义，而不表示词汇意义。

英语词缀的构词能力强且灵活性大，是构成新词语的强有力的一种手段。派生词以其独特的方式，不断地扩充英语词汇，从而丰富英语的表现力。例如随着中国的崛起，中国经济政治及文化在世界起到很大作用。出现了以 chi-为前缀的新词语。Chinology（中国学），Chimerica，Chindia，Chimerny，Chinglish 等。出于各种原因，人们患上各种-phobia，有 hoplophobia（持枪械恐惧症），Iraqphobia（伊拉克恐惧症），Sinophobia（中国恐惧症），Japanophobia（恐日症），Anglophobia（恐英症）。据多个网站统计，以此为后缀的词汇就有 500 多个。

此外还有以-xual 结尾的 ecosexual, metrosexual, retrosexual, technosexual, ubersexual；以-rexia 结尾的 drunkorexia（节食以便喝更多酒），orthorexia（食用健康食物的欲望），anorexia（厌食）；以-vore 为后缀的 oppotunivore（吃垃圾族），vegivore（只吃蔬菜者），locavore（土食者），faunavore（食叶动物），photovore（感光机器人），planktivore（吃浮生物者），piscivore（食鱼者）等。

三　类比法

类比是英语中较多且实用的一种构词方式。特点为以某个词为参照物，在词素上进行替换，在语义上进行联想，构出形式上与意义上类似的新词。如由 landscape（陆上风景）类推出如由 scape 构成的 cityscape（城市风景），moonscape（月面风景），Netscape（网景浏览器），river-scape（江河风景），roofscape（屋顶风景），waterscape（水景），seascape（海景），streetscape（街景）等；由 hijack（拦路抢劫）类比出 skyjack（空中劫持），seajack（海上劫持）等词。这种构词法将在下章进行详细讨论。

四　旧词新意

随着科学技术的发展，社会的进步，各种新概念也应运而生，为此需要大量新词语来表达。表达一个新概念不一定非创新词不可，人们可以利用语言中现有的词汇材料，赋予它们新的含义，这样就有了语义性新词语。

20 世纪 60 年代以来，美国社会发生巨大变化，科学技术迅猛发展，各种思潮丛生，各种活动十分活跃，各种风尚变化不断。民权运动、妇女解放运动、群居群婚、领养热潮、同性恋爱、另类约会无奇不有。美国英语的表达方式随之推陈出新，朝着生动活泼、简洁的方向发展。除了大量新奇醒目的新词语外，许多现有的"旧"词也纷纷通过词义的转借和引申而有了新的含义，内容涉及美国社会生活各个方面。

（一）科技环保

bail out 来自法语的 baille，意为"水桶"。当人们舀水时也会说 bail it out of water。但是当人们从飞机跳出也可以说 bail out。原因是美国是最早发明飞机的国家，飞机事故频发不足为奇。当飞行员在空中发现汽油不足时或是机器出现了故障，就不得不使用降落伞，以保生命安全。飞行员认为，把船上的积水舀出与避免飞机出事故具有相似之处，二者都有把负面的东西解决掉的含义。后来人们又引申出"通过给予经济上的帮助使得他人摆脱麻烦"的含义。例如：President Obama said the government will recover all the taxpayer money his administration provided to bail out the auto industry last year. In an interview aired Thursday on the ABC daytime talk show "the View", Obama said the auto industry "tells a good story"

97

of his administration' efforts to rescue the economy. （奥巴马总统说，在他当政期间，政府将收回纳税人用于救助汽车工业的资金。在周四美国广播公司的日间访谈节目——"观点"访谈中，奥巴马说，汽车工业讲述了一个政府努力救助汽车经济的成功故事）。

柠檬不能作为主食，只能作为调料，用来调制饮料、菜肴、化妆品和药品。由于柠檬味道极酸，吃上一口就会感觉龇牙咧嘴，于是人们买了东西感觉不对时，这种东西就可能被称为 a lemon。这种感觉就像是吃了柠檬一样，在嘴里留下酸味且不舒服。美国经济学家、加州大学伯克利分校的乔治·阿克罗夫教授在 20 世纪 70 年代发表了论文《柠檬市场：质量的不确定性和市场机制》，对于二手车市场的影响机制进行了探讨。在论文中，阿克罗夫用不同的水果代表不同特性的二手车，以香甜的樱桃与水蜜桃来比喻车况优良的二手车，而用酸涩的柠檬来比喻状况不佳的二手车商品。后来人们延续他的用法，以 lemon 表示"出厂后问题百出的次品车"，并且延续至今。

表示拼车的 carpool 于 20 世纪 70 年代中期出现于美国。有车一族为了节省费用，以保护环境为目的，共同使用一辆车上班、旅游、参会及听音乐会。

footprint 曾经被用来指"（航天器、卫星残骸的）预定着落地带或者落轨道区"。到了 20 世纪 70 年代，它以另外一种含义出现于一些文章中。人们又把这个含义引申为"（交通车辆的）轨迹、（通信卫星信号的）覆盖区"等。而到了 20 世纪 80 年代初，随着个人电脑和其他微型计算机的开发和利用，footprint 一词又有了新的含义，表示"台面面积"。近来人们用 carbon footprint 表示人们产生或排放的碳足迹。

这类旧词新意还有 plastic（信用卡、借方卡），green food（绿色健康食品），go green（过环保健康生活）等。

（二）日常用语

语言是文化的载体，它的使用受制于该种语言所属文化的各种因素。一个民族的历史条件、地理环境、价值观念、思维方式、生活情趣、风俗习惯等对该民族语言的形成和发展起着十分重要的作用。例如，生活在北极圈内的爱斯基摩人（the Eskimos）可以用丰富的词语来表示各种各样的雪，因为他们长年生活在冰天雪地里，他们的生存状况时刻都与冰雪联系在一起；比如说 graze 一词的原义是"（牛、羊等）啃食牧草""放牧""以草为食""作为牧地"。虽然它是一个人们已经使用了几百年的"旧"词，但是 20 世纪 80 年代初，它在美国却成了男女老少争相使用的时髦词。它被用来比喻人们"（不按时吃三餐）每天吃零食、点心、快餐"或"（在超市、购物中心）顺口品尝、吃架上还未购买的食品"的行为。其比喻义非常形象、生动、幽默，充分展示了美国人开朗活泼的特性和敢于推陈出新的机智。

美国人对糖和甜食喜爱有加，因而创造出 eye candy 和与之有关的短语和词汇。最早这个词汇表示"某些人和东西只能用来养眼，但拿不来或不属于自己"，后来人们用 eye candy 指那些"非常性感、吸引人的女性"。例如：When I was walking the mall I scoped out some nice eye candy.（我在购物中心闲逛时发现了几个美女）。20 世纪 90 年代美国又出现了 arm candy 和 ear candy 两个新词。ear candy 是指那些"听起来非常悦耳但没有什么意义的流行音乐和轻音乐"。而 arm candy 则是指那些陪伴名流和富人甚至是普通人出入社交场合，但没有实质性感情的男女。

cold 最早是一个中性词或贬义词，表示"bad"。例如在体育竞技赛中，如果说"He was cold"，那就表示他赛前没有进行充分的热身，所以不能取胜。如果说"Uta has cold climate"，则表示犹他州气候恶劣，相当于 harsh。而当一个人受到欺负发泄不满时，则可以说"That was cold"，这时这里的 cold 表示卑鄙。cold 的这种用法也是随着时间的推移逐渐演变过来的。cold 现在受到越来越多的美国年轻人的喜欢，表示酷极了。例如："Those new Nike shoes are cold, I'd die for a pair."（这些耐克鞋真的很酷，我太想有一双这样的鞋了）。

Dude 这个词起源于美国。早期的 dude 表示 old rags，相当于"稻草人"（scarecrow）。19 世纪 70 年代美国的城里人开始去西部度假，被当地人称为 dude，意为"花花公子"（dandy）。还有一种说法是，它来自 Yankee Doodle 这首歌中的"Doodle"。20 世纪 30—40 年代期间，dude 又从原有的意思转变为 cool。20 世纪 60 年代随着民权运动的兴起，更多的黑人角色出现在电视、电影中，这些人物频繁地使用这个词语。不仅如此，黑人社会中男男女女也对它情有独钟。到了 20 世纪 80 年代，dude 最终被大众接受，成为颇受欢迎的一个流行词。

根据颇具权威的 free dictionary.com 解释，dude 表示"哥们儿、家伙、兄弟"。它表示的是年轻男性间的友谊,使用它的人试图传达一种言外之意,即我们是朋友,但是互相独立,没有同性恋倾向。近年来女性朋友间也开始以 dude 互称,甚至男性也以 dude 称呼女性好友。

white bread 属于白色食品。在美国不但超市卖白面包,就连廉价药店 Walgreen 柜台上通常都会摆满名为 Wonder 牌的白面包。这种面包是典型的美式面包。平淡无味,比较细腻,容易消化。White bread 成为"普通、平凡"的代名词。随着时间的推移,人们根据白面包的特点,用 white bread 指那些中规中矩、平凡无味、非常直白的美国人。

根据词源字典解释,nut 这一词最早在 19 世纪被用来指头部。后来人们用它来指头脑有问题的人。现在,精神病或脑子有病就被称作"nuts,wing nut,nut job 或 nutty"。美国加州汽车拥有量达到 800 多万辆,而它的人口只有千万。每天上下班时间塞车现象严重。经常听到人们抱怨:"The heavy traffic is driving me nuts."(交通堵塞让我发疯)或"I'm going nuts."(我要疯了)。

glass ceiling 从最早的玻璃天花板转义为"无形的种族或性别歧视阻碍女性和有色人种在事业上获得提升",虽然表面上看来提升之路一片平坦。2008 年,Hilary Clinton 竞争美国总统失败,也没有得到作为奥巴马副总统的提名,但是她却得到许多妇女的尊重与爱戴。竞争对手佩林在接受共和党作为副总统提名演讲时也表示对她的尊敬:"Hilary left 18 million cracks in the highest,hardest glass ceiling in America,but it turns out the women of America are not finished yet and we can shatter that glass ceiling once for all."(希拉里在美国高不可攀、坚硬的玻璃天花板上留下 1.8 千万缝隙,但是美国妇女不会就此罢休,我们最终会永远打破这一天花板)。

更多的例子还有,hoodie 由"卫衣"演变成为"玩世不恭的年轻人",size zero 由"零号"转换为"骨瘦如柴的时装模特",lame 由"跛腿的"变成"糟糕的",dogfood 由"狗食"转换为"试用自己公司销售的产品",kidnap 从"绑架"成为"重划选区形成同党竞争",mafia 从"黑手党"变成了"秘密帮派",burn out 从"烧断、精疲力竭"转换为"枯槁的吸毒者",deep throat 从"低音嗓门"转变成现代的"身居要职匿名揭发政府内部非法活动的人",sweep 从"打扫"转变成"对广播电视节目是否受欢迎而进行的调查",beat 从动词变成形容词,表示"丑陋的"。

（三）计算机词汇

世界正处于科技高度发达的信息时代，计算机与人们的生活息息相关。"旧"词语"新"用的现象在计算机词汇中表现得尤为明显。语言学家、电脑专家们充分利用语言共核中大量的"旧"词传播科技信息。许多现有的"旧"词已被注入科技时代的"新鲜血液"而焕然一新。例如，drive 不是开车的司机，而是磁盘驱动器。bank 不再指银行，而是指内存的库。而 bus 在计算机词汇中则是指总线。此外还有 compiler（编辑者编译程序，编译器），memory（记忆存储，存储器），register（注册寄存器），sink（污水池接收器，转接器），tablet（图形输入板），worm（恶意程序，病虫），smart（由精密传感装置制导的），rip of（扯掉，偷窃，骗取），bump（同意，支持灌水，顶），lurk（潜水，在论坛、聊天室等只浏览不发言的行为）。cookie 原指"小甜饼"，网语指"为响应客户请求而由服务器返回给客户的一块数据"，此外，menu 一词由"菜单"转换为在计算机英语中的"选单"；而 mouse 则一跃从"老鼠"摇身变成了"鼠标"；bounce 由"弹回"变成网络上"退回无法投递的电子邮件"；wicked 由"邪恶的"变成网络聊天中的"好极了"。flood 原指"洪水"，但是在网络用语中指"在实时聊天室中有的人为了不让别人发表意见，故意输入大量的文字使得系统无法正常运作"。bug 原意为昆虫，网络引用为"故障"之意。因为据说最早的一次计算机故障是一只飞蛾引起的，这只小东西飞入一台早期电子管计算机，使这台机器不能正常工作。这些旧词新义现象值得注意，否则稍不留神便会误入歧途，掉进"陷阱"，出现不必要的误解。

五　缩略法

缩略法（shortening）是对原词进行剪裁，缩略其中一部。缩略语是英语日常生活中非常流行的新词语构词法，是因特网语的一种主要的构词手段，它们具有造词简练、使用简便的特点，具有很强的生命力。这些词语的缩略方法主要有首字母缩略法、同音借用法、数字缩略法、截断缩略法、拼缀法。

（一）首字母缩略法（initialism）

开头字母缩略法用每个单词的第一个字母（通常大写）进行组合来取代。有的是一个字母代表整个单词，有的是一个字母代表部分单词的缩略词，还有些词组中主要词的每个字母连成一个新词。如：WAG（wives and girlfriends），LOHAS（lifestyles of health and sustainability），LAT（living apart together），Generation XL，VB6，SPIN（situation + problem + implication + pay off），BANANA（build absolutely nothing anywhere near anything），CHAOs（can't have anyone over syndrome），GPS（global positioning system），SITCOM（single income, two children, oppresissive mortgage），SMUM（smart middle-class, uninvolved mother），TGIM（Thank God it's Monday），TMT（technology, media, telecommunications），UMPC（ultra mobile personal computer），VBIED（vehicle-borne improvised explosive device），VUCA（volatile uncertain complex ambiguous），WMWM（white married working mom），WOMBAT（waste of money brains and time），YIMBY（yes in my backyard），CEO（chief executive officer），DINs（double income no sex），DUPPIE（depressed urban professional），DWT（drinking while texting），FOMO（the fear of missing sth interestingor fun），GOOMBY（get out of my back yard），NIMBY（not in my back yard），HENRY（high earner not rich yet），IMBY（in my back yard），JOOTT（just one of those things），Kipper（kids in parents' pockets eroding retirement savings），LULU（locally unwanted land use），MTBU（maximum time to belly up），SIFI（systematically important financial institution），NEET（not in employment, education or training），NEV（neighbourhood electronic vehicle），NOISE（Netscape, Oracle, IBM, Sun and Everyone else），NOTE（not over there either），BAM（bric and mortar），BHAG（by hairy andacions goal），BIY（buy it yourself），BRICs（Brazil Russia India China），CAVE（citizens against virtually everything）等。

（二）同音借用缩略法

虽然英语是非常重形的语言，但是因特网语重音。根据词汇或句子的读音进行简化改写成为因特网语所特有的一种构词方法。缩略的语句一般为常用的起衔接作用的短语，即使初次触网的人不明白其含义，也不会对理解对方的意图影响太多。这些缩略语通常很快就会被广大网民所接受。如 IC 表示 I see；Y 表示 Why；U 表示 You 等。还有一种就是词组仅按照发音来描述，而不再有一一对应的替代字母。如 ICQ（I seek you）中 seek 的尾音 k 和 you 结合在一起用发音相同的字母 Q 来代替。

（三）截短缩略语

为了方便简洁，人们还会截去词尾、词头或者去掉元音，写出了一些新的缩略词。有的单词截至只剩第一个字母，如 P = Pardon（再说一遍），G = Grin or Giggle（狞笑或咯咯笑）。截词头的如：cause（或 cuz）= because（因为），veg = vegetable。截词头在因特网语中似乎比较少见。去元音是指去掉词语中的元音字母，只保留辅音中发音突出、外形明显的那些字母。如：MSG 表示 MESSAGE（消息），PLS 表示 PLEASE（请），PPL 表示 PEOPLE（人们），THX 表示 THANKS（谢谢）等。

（四）借用数字缩略法

因特网英语中有一种特殊的缩略形式——用数字替代重复字母或同音数字代替某一字母，可以把它称为数字缩略语。这是缩略语的一种新动态，也是因特网英语的新事物。例如：3A（3A 服务，P2P（peer to peer），PLUR（peace, love, unity and respect），AOS（all options stink），B2B（business to business），B2B2C（business-business-to-consumer），B2C（business to customer），2D4（to die for），g2g（got to go），4ever（forever），B4（before），F2F（face to face）。

（五）拼缀法

这种构词法在英语流行新词中日渐增多，富有生命力。拼缀词具有表现力强、结构巧妙的特点，符合现代人快节奏的生活方式。将在下一章进行详细讨论。

六　转换法

现代英语创造新词语的最常用的手段之一就是词类的转换（Conversion），即不依靠词形变化，直接把一个词从一种词类转换成另一种词类。词类的转换因其简便直接和形象生动，自然就成了产生新词语的重要途径。最突出的，也是最多的就是名词转换成动词和动词转换成名词，此外也有一小部分形容词转换成名词。在英语的发展过程中，由于词尾的基本消失，衍生出这种构词法，特点是无须借助词缀就实现词类的转换，名词转化为动词是现代英语中极为普遍的现象。其使用范围日趋广泛，经常出现在不同语体和不同语言环境中。可以说转换法是英语朝着简化方向发展的一种必然结果。例如：google（搜索引擎）→to google（通过使用搜索引擎 Google 在网上搜索信息），text（正文，原文）→to text（发送信息）。

（一）专有名词转换为动词

专有名词转用动词是很常见的，我们熟悉的有 boycott，charleston（跳查尔斯顿舞）等。C&C 1979 也开列了一些较新的词，如 Concorde，TWA，UA，Air California 均为航空公司或飞机型号名，用作不及物动词表示乘坐航空公司的航班飞去之意。Clinton 以及 Lewinsky 之名被美国人用于动词，前者表示说谎，后者表示口交。专有名词转为动词原因是，它们所指称的事物特性和功能同普通事物一样，必定也同一定的动作相联系，此外事物也是在不断变化，由此新的特性不断增加。Titanic 最早只是用来指称一艘巨轮，但是现在却表示"撞在冰山上"之意。Amazon 现在被用来表示"被亚马逊化"。例如：

The canoe Titanicked on the rock in the river.

There are many steps to stop getting Amazoned.

更多的名词转动词的例子还有 blackhole（消失），celeb（使用名人效应），chip（植入芯片），dejunk（清除、打扫），elder（与比自己年轻的人分享知识），friend（加为好友），unfriend（删除好友），lance（宣布出柜），office（办公、打杂），re-anchor（加上主力零售商），text（发送信息），wife（在家做全职太太），veg（窝在家里），bagel（体育竞技中没有得到分），potato（打）。

（二）动词转换为名词

另外一种常用的转化法就是动词转换为名词，通常为了表示原来动词的动作或状态。例如：a dump（堆放垃圾地），a burn（烧伤），a divide（分界线），have a commute to London（通勤到伦敦）等。

（三）形容词转换为动词

形容词转换为动词不如以上两种多见，但是它们简洁易懂，起到生动形象的效果。例如：cold（变冷），rewild（恢复野生物种），regreen（重绿化），to arsen（感染白砷），green（漆绿）等。

（四）形容词转换为名词

1. 在形容词前加定冠词 the，表示一类人。可以从下面例子窥见一斑。The disabled（残疾人），the challenged（残疾人），the weird（怪人），the privileged（有特权的人），the underprivileged（穷人），the well-to-do（富人）等。

2. 在形容词前加入定冠词 the，表示抽象的事物。例如 the mystical（神秘之事），the impossible（不可能的事），the esoteric（秘传的东西），the pragmatic（实用的东西）等。

3. 用于一些惯用法中，例如 at the latest（最迟），for sure（没错）等。

七　外来语

外来语是指语言中的某些词语从一个民族的语言传到另一个民族的语言中。英语中有着大量外来语的存在。随着全球化趋势的日益增强，各国之间在政治、经济、文化、科技等各个领域之间的交流也会日益频繁，在与不同的民族语言文化接触和交流过程中，英语经过语音和文字方面的再创造产生语言与文化的融合物。作为全球第一大交际语言，英语外来词语尤为丰富，语言融合特征非常强。梅益在其撰写的《简明不列颠百科全书》中说道："近代英语词汇约有一半属于日耳曼语族（古英语和斯堪的那维亚语）词汇，一半属罗曼语族（法语和拉丁语）词汇，还有大量的科技方面的词汇是从希腊语言引进的，从荷兰语、意大利语、德语、西班牙语、阿拉伯语以及其他许多语言也借入相当多的词语，此外还有俄语、日语、汉语也越来越多地进入英美社会，成为新词语。"

（一）汉语外来语

汉语外来语进入英语有多种渠道。香港殖民者使英语受到粤语的熏陶，借入许多汉语外来词，例如 cheongsam（长衫）。一些汉语通过日语、韩语、越南语传入英语，成为外来语。例如 ginkgo（银杏），gyoza（饺子）。改革开放以来，中国在经济上获得腾飞，政治、文化方面也取得巨大成功。中国对世界的影响越来越大。反映到语言上就是，越来越多的汉语进入到英语中。例如 wushu, guanxi, Fengshui 等。总而言之，汉语外来语大致分为五类：

1. 与中国传统思想、历史文化等有关的外来词

Fengshui（风水）。它凝聚了古代中国在活人住宅和死人墓地关系方面的集体智慧。风水的整体原则是"趋利避害"，这也是安全生存最起码的信条。近年来，风水在美国红极一时，各种相关书籍充斥市场。其他汉语新词语有：Kungfu（功夫），wirefu，Lao-tzu（老子），Tai-chi（太极拳），Tao（道），koolie（苦力），Yin and Yang（阴阳），Sifu（师傅）。另外，专指有钱有势的商人或者企业家的 Tycoon 是闽粤语的音译，这种称呼近些年流行于英美街巷。

2. 与中国食物有关的外来词

从美国东海岸到西海岸，许多光顾中餐馆的顾客大部分都是美国人，菜单出现的许多汉语单词，已经被美国人接受。如：Chaomein（炒面），Wonton（馄饨），Gongbao Chicken（宫保鸡丁），Tofu（豆腐），Dan Dan Noodle（担担面），Ma Po Tofu（麻婆豆腐），Mushu Pork（木须肉），Chaofan（炒饭），Chopsui（杂碎），Chǎo（炒），General Tso's Chicken（左宗棠鸡），Haosin（海鲜），pekoe（白毫），wok（锅），vitsin（味精）等。Dim Sum 表示中餐里的甜点，包括虾饺粽子等小吃。这个词据说来自闽粤。英语原本有表示蛋糕、点心的词，但英美人却对其情有独钟，Dim Sum 在美国的中餐馆里非常受欢迎，表达了他们与时尚接轨和东方同步的愿望。

3. 与中国语言、货币和计量单位有关的外来词

这些词有 Li（里），Kuai（块），Yuan（元），Ganbei（干杯），Dingho（顶好），lose face（丢脸），yen（瘾）。Gung-ho 表示热情高涨，

极感兴趣。在美语里使用的频率颇高，人们常常把它挂在嘴边。比如：

At first everyone is gung-ho about this idea. But now no-body even talks a-bout it.（刚开始大家对这个想法都抱有极大的兴趣和热情。而现在谁也不提它了）。

4. 与中国国名和地名有关的外来词

这类词有 Shanghai，Beijing，Sichuan，Shaolin，Xinhua（News Agency），Taiwan，Qingdao beer 等。

5. 与中国物产、动植物有关的外来词

这类词有 Bonsai（盆栽），Ginseng（人参），Mulan（magnolia），ginkgo（银杏），egg foo young（芙蓉），qinghaosu（青蒿素）等。

随着中西文化的相互渗透，更多中文词汇进入到英语中，如 peaceful rising（和平崛起），two sessions（两会），one country two systems（一国两制），taikonaut（宇宙飞行员），chengguan（城管）等直接借用汉语拼音。

可以预见，随着中国的和平崛起与国际地位和影响力的提高，汉语词汇将会大量地、更深刻地融入英语中去，为英语语言注入新的活力。

（二）希腊拉丁外来语

拉丁语和希腊语的外来语大多是一些术语或科技词汇，如：abducens nerve（外展神经），candida（念珠菌病），exvivo（来自体外的），realia（实观教具），gyro（皮塔三明治），ultrasaurus（超大型恐龙，指侏罗纪后期一种与长臂龙有关的恐龙，据信为世上最高的动物）等。虽然在英语中早有用作组合词素的 mega（源出希腊语中的 megas），但 mega 单独作为一个词语使用开始于 20 世纪 80 年代，表示"超大"。如 mega house，megasuperstar，megavitamin，megawatt，megavolt，megaton，megastore，megatechnology，等等。

（三）法语外来语

饮食外来语。英法两国地理位置相邻，有着密切关系。英语中的许多菜名都是法语词汇，美语亦是如此。美国至今有些饭店的菜单都是法语写的。这些词有 fromage blanc（软干酪），amusegueule（可口小吃），mesclun（幼嫩叶蔬菜沙拉），nouvelle cuisine（新式烹饪法）等。法国的葡萄酒、香槟和白兰地享誉全球。法国葡萄酒的生产至今已有两千年的历史。大量与葡萄酒有关的词汇涌入英语。如 Beaujolais nouveau（新博若莱葡萄酒），domaine（葡萄园），gueule de bols（宿醉），vendange（法国的葡萄采摘季节）等。

与流行时尚芭蕾有关的词语 BCBG 为 bon chic，bon genre 的缩略，表示"流行时尚人士"，与英国英语中的 Sloane Ranger 相同。partouse 表示"夜总会"。芭蕾对世界影响意义巨大，ballet 来自法语，还有 ballonné（单腿跳跃）等。

还有与运动有关的用语，如 chef d'équipe（负责日常事务的运动队经理），parkour（跑酷），levade（古典骑术中的前肢起），soigneur（自行车队助理教练）。与政治相关的词语有 fonctionnaire（公务员），franc fort（强势法郎政策）。此外还有 ye-ye（爵士音乐的），deja vu（似曾相识的感觉），vis-à-vis（面对面），faux pas（失礼），nouveau riche（新富），touché（擦边球），rentier（食利者），sautee（炒的），jamais vu（旧事如新），aplomb（镇定），barrage（障碍），dossier（卷宗），mirage（海市蜃楼），panache（羽毛饰），élite（精英），lingerie（女内衣裤），armoire（大型衣橱），critique（批评文章），genre（流派），ambiance（气氛），collage（拼贴），plaque（匾），penchant（斜坡），repertoire（保留节目），entourage（随从），terrain（地势），glacier（冰川），debris（残骸），tranche（一期款项），entrepreneur（企业家），toboggan（急剧下降），femme fatale（美女），bête noire（讨厌的人），enfant terrible（可怕的顽童）。法国的社会文化与美国的社会文化不断交流融合，使美国英语不断充实、丰富和完善。

（四）西班牙外来语

墨西哥有许多都是来自西班牙殖民遗留下来的西班牙外来语，最终传入英语，成为外来语。例如：fajitas（法吉塔斯），taco（玉米面卷），ancho（大个芳香辣椒），tortilla（墨西哥玉米煎饼），chipotle（烟熏干红辣椒），habanero（哈瓦那椒），maquiladora（美国人在墨西哥开办的装配工厂），palapa（墨西哥传统的棕榈树叶顶遮阳棚），sinsemilla（无籽大麻），telenovela（电视肥皂剧）和 tomatillo（粘果酸浆）等。另外，从西班牙语进入英语的外来词还有 tonto（笨的，愚蠢的），savvy（有知识的），Lolita（洛丽塔），El Nino（厄尔尼诺现象），silo（导弹发射井），bonanza（繁荣），plaza（广场），salsa（汁），fiesta（派对）。

（五）意大利外来语

与饮食有关的新外来语包括 bresaola（意大利腌晒牛肉），bruschetta（小吃烤三明治），caffèlatte（牛奶咖啡），calzone（有馅比萨饼面团），focaccia（意大利芳草橄榄味面包），mascarpone（淡味奶油干酪），panzanella（以橄榄油和蔬菜制成的面包色拉），radicchio（意大利菊苣），rucola（制作色拉的蔬菜），taleggio（有外皮的半软干酪），confetti（糖果），casino（赌场），concerto（协奏曲），fresco（壁画），gondola（意大利威尼斯小船），lido（海水浴场），mafia（黑手党），malaria（疟疾），zany（小丑），primma donna（首席女高音），mandolin（曼陀林），requatta（赛舟会）。

（六）日语外来语

Garland Cannon 在 1987 年对英语中外来词语的语源分布进行了研究，结果发现 8% 的外来语来自日语（Jacbson et al 2000：42）。这一百分比甚至超过欧洲的许多语言所占的比率，如意大利语与拉丁语各占 7%，德语和希腊语各占 6%。据统计，共有 900 多个汉词进入了英语词库，其中约有 200 个是借助日语进入英语的，而且这些词以双音的词汇居多，可能这和它们比较适合英国人的发音有关，还有一个原因是日本在全球经济中占有重要地位。最新的日语外来语主要涉及饮食、流行文化、经济等方面。有关饮食的词语包括 fugu（河豚），nori（海苔片；紫菜），gyoza（饺子），ginkgo（银杏），ramen（日本的汤面），shabushabu（涮牛肉，涮猪肉），tamari（酱油），teppanyaki（铁板烧），kombu（昆布），matsutake（松茸），sashim（刺身），wakame（裙带菜）。有关流行文化的词语有 anime（动画片），ikabana（插花术），karaoke（卡拉OK），manga（动漫），tamagotchi（电子宠物）。与经济有关的词语包括 kaizen（改进），kanban（看板法），karoshi（过劳死），keiretsu（系列企业集团），tsunami（海啸），zaitech（财术）。此外还有 kamikaze（遥控飞行器），karate（空手），kendo（剑道），sum（相扑），Otaku（indoorsman 宅男）和 Otaku girl（indoorswoman 宅女）等。

（七）德语外来语

饮食方面的德语外来语有 Berliner Weisse（加糖浆酸啤酒），Kir-schwasser（樱桃酒），Hefeweizen（未过滤小麦啤酒），Schnaps（蒸馏啤酒），Tafelwein（普通的德国葡萄酒），Spritzer（苏打白酒饮料），Stein（大酒杯），Pils 或 Pilsner（淡啤酒），Hasenpfeffer（炖兔肉），Lager（淡味啤酒），Biergarten（啤酒花园），Bratwurst 或 brat（香肠），Bundt cake（圆环蛋糕），delicatessen（美味），Kipfel（牛角包），Gummi bear（小熊软糖），Muesli（早餐麦片），Pretzel（椒盐面圈），Pumpernickel（酸黑面包），Rollmops（香料醋鲱鱼卷），Sauerkraut（酸菜）。

与休闲和运动有关的外来语包括 Kletterschuh（登山鞋），Rucksack（背包），Turner（体操运动员），Turnverein（健身俱乐部），Volks-marsch / Volkssport（徒步健身走），blitz（美式足球闪电式进攻）。

其他德语外来词有 Wanderlust（渴望旅游），Wiener（软弱之人），Wunderkind（儿童天才），Zeitgeist（当代精神），Gestalt（格式塔）。Doktorvater（医生顾问），Festschrift（六十周岁庆生纪念册），Privatdo-zent（无薪讲师），Professoriat（教授阶级），gemutlich（舒适宜人的），Fingerspitzengefühl（直觉；机敏），Kaffeeklatsch（喝咖啡聊天），kaput（无序，破裂），Kitsch（路障用以减慢交通），Waldsterben（大气污染引起的森林树木死亡），wrangle（争论），yodel（真假嗓音唱歌），strudel（果实或干乳酪烤点心），schadenfeude（幸灾乐祸）等。

（八）俄罗斯外来语

来自俄罗斯的外来语不是很多。它们有 taimen（一种多见于西伯利亚和东亚的哲罗鱼），cosmonaut（宇航员），intelligentsia（知识界），glasnost（公投），Lunokhod（月球行走），Mir（太空站），Lunik（探月使命），Politburo（政治局），sputnik（人造卫星），icon（标记），mam-moth（庞大），muzhik（真汉子）等。

（九）阿拉伯外来语

来自阿拉伯语的词语有 Nadir（低点），artichoke（洋蓟），arsenal（兵工厂），zenith（顶峰）。中东的 hijab（源出阿拉伯语，指穆斯林女子

所围的头巾），peshmerga（源出库尔德语，指库尔德人的），rai（一种融
合阿拉伯和阿尔巴尼亚民间音乐、西方摇滚乐等音乐成分的流行乐）。
土耳其的 doner kebab（土耳其烤羊肉），imam bayildi（油炒蒜味带馅茄
子），sheshbesh（中东的一种 15 子游戏），gala（狂欢）。巴勒斯坦的
Hamas（哈马斯）。黎巴嫩的 Hezbollah（真主党，一极端什叶派穆斯林组
织：源出阿拉伯语，字面意思为"上帝之党"）。阿富汗的 Taliban 或
Taleban（塔利班）。希伯来语中的 challah（犹太教徒在安息日吃的白面
包），eruv（安息日犹太教徒的活动范围）和 kippa（正统派犹太男教徒
所戴的无檐便帽）。

（十）其他欧洲外来语

欧洲外来语有荷兰语中的 gabba（刺耳、节奏快的浩室音乐），
woonerf（设有减缓交通设备的道路）；丹麦语中的 landnam（为耕种对林
地的清理）；挪威语中的 gravadlax（加了调味品的生三文鱼）；挪威的
springar（挪威乡村舞蹈或舞曲）；葡萄牙语中的 vinho corrente（廉价葡
萄酒）和 vinho verde（葡萄牙新酿葡萄酒）；捷克语中的 kolach（捷克共
和国和斯洛伐克的一种水果馅饼）和 velvetrevolution（天鹅绒革命）；波
兰的 kielbasa（蒜味烟熏红肠）；罗马尼亚的 sarmale（菜叶包加料碎肉）；
波兰的 oberek（比玛祖卡舞节奏更快的波兰民间舞蹈）；来自塞尔维亚
和克罗地亚语的 zurla（肖姆管）。

（十一）其他亚洲外来语

来自亚洲的外来语有：印度的 pakora（油炸面糊蔬菜丁），rogan
josh（咖喱羊肉），dacoit（土匪），loot（抢劫），juggernaut（强大力
量），dinghy（小舟），chutney（酸辣酱），pundit（博学者）；印地语中
的 paneer（凝乳干酪），basmati（印度香米），bandanna（繁荣），chintz
（印花棉布），pukha（好）；泰米尔语中的 kavadi（教徒忏悔时背着的赎
罪架）和 sambar（浓味小扁豆）；旁遮普语中的 bhangra（以旁遮普民乐
与西方摇滚乐融合的流行音乐），dilruba（长颈三弦或四弦琴）；马来西
亚的 nasi goreng（肉炒饭）；越南的 nuoc mam（辛辣鱼酱）；孟加拉语
中的 esraj（带和弦的三弦或四弦琴）；巴基斯坦的 qawwali（穆斯林音
乐）；韩国语中的 chaebol（家族大型集团公司）等。

（十二）来自非洲的外来语

这些外来语包括南非的 koeksister（蘸有糖浆的辫子状炸面圈）；西非的 balafon（类似木琴的乐器），yam（甘薯），tote（手提袋）；中非的 zombie（僵尸）；刚果的 soukous（流行舞曲）；南非的 patha（能刺激性欲的非洲黑人舞蹈或舞曲）；斯瓦希里的 safari（游猎），jukebox（投币式自动唱机）；等等。

（十三）其他语言的外来语

这些外来语有加纳的 kente（一种彩色条纹布料或由此制成的长衫），西班牙的 ETA（埃塔，巴斯克分裂主义组织），冈比亚的 dalasi（达拉西地），圣多美和普林西比的 dobra（多布拉），巴布亚新几内亚的 kina（基那，意为蛤蜊或贻贝），安哥拉的 kwanza（第一的，首要的），秘鲁的 nuevosol（索尔），马来语中的 ikat（扎染布）。

英语语言从外族语言中借词，同时自己的词汇又被不同的外族语言借用。这样的词汇借出和借入无限循环，最终导致不同民族语言词汇的融合而产生英语新词语。目前，现代英语已经发展了一整套与俄语、法语、西班牙语等语种的科技词汇相通的国际科技词汇。在金融领域、政治及大众传媒方面的新词正在逐步接轨。可以预见，这类国际通用词汇也迟早会出现并不断完善。虽然英语语言中融入其他各大语种，如阿拉伯语、俄语、法语、汉语、日语、西班牙语等，但英语良好的使用基础，较强的开放性和改良能力，在各种语言词汇的融合过程中，英语词汇极有可能成为国际通用词汇的主体。

八　逆成法

20 世纪初以来，美语中出现大量逆生新词语，由于逆成构词法的形成起因于过度推广，人们受某种普遍存在的语言模式的影响，不断仿照类推，从而使语法和词汇形式发生变化。这种原本不是英语词汇的新词经人们多次使用后约定俗成，形成逆成词。钱歌川在《英文疑难详解续篇》中（第 291 页）认为，这种构词法是由于文化水平不高的人不知道字源而误用，而后逐渐形成的。例如：人们会错误地把已经存在的较长单词诸如 loafer 中的词缀-er 删掉, 逆序推出较短的动词 loaf, 出现了逆生词现象。

美语在形成过程中受到了很多外来语的影响, 在美国国家的历史发展过程中, 一些外来语早已渗透到生活领域的各个方面, 如宗教、教育、医学、法律、物理学等等。这些外来语的词尾很多都与英语的词缀变化规则十分接近, 因此很容易产生逆生词, 所以逆成构词法在科学、技术、医学等领域运用广泛。如在医学英文词汇中的动词 delir（神智昏迷）是由 delirium 逆生而成; euthanase 由 euthanasia 逆构而来; 物理学中 electrophorese（电泳）是由 electrophoresis（电泳现象）逆构出的词汇。

随着科技的发展及电脑网络等通信设备的普及, 大量新词以逆生构词法涌入美语。很多职业不再限定工作地点, 一些自由职业者在家工作, 他们利用电脑终端远程 telecommuting（在家办公）, 由此逆生出动词 telecommute（利用电脑终端在家办公）。同义词 distance working（远程工作）逆生出动词 distance work。很多信息和科技英语中原有的名词如 information（信息）, hacker（黑客）, aviation, conversation（聊天）, photolurker（网上匿名偷看相册的人）, brainwashing（洗脑）, lie-detector（测谎仪）, computer（电脑）, laser 也逆生出了相应的动词 informate（为……提供信息）, hack（黑客进攻）, aviate（飞行）, converse, photolurk（网上匿名偷看相册）, brainwash（给洗脑）, lie-detect（测谎）, compute（计算）, lase（激光治疗）。

进入 21 世纪人们的生活方式也与以往有极大的不同, 出现各种各样的新生事物, 有 housesitting（代为看家业务）, petsitting（代人看宠物）, 由此逆生出了两个新的动词 housesit（代人看家）和 petsit（代人照顾宠物）。Maffick（狂欢庆祝）由 mafeking（南非地名, 因 1990 年一次狂欢庆祝闻名）逆生而来。sass（无理、粗鲁对待）由 sassy（无礼粗鲁的）逆生而来, moonlighting（月光活动）逆构形成 moonlight（兼职）。

（一）逆成法的构词规律

逆成法（back-formation）是构词法中一种不规则的类型, 即把一个语言中已经存在的较长单词删去想象中的词缀, 由此造出一个较短的单词。逆生词多半属动词，极少数属于其他词类，如名词和形容词，并且逆生词多半是由名词包括复合名词构成，由英语形容词或副词转成的逆生词不多。形成逆生词的原形词可分为以下几类：

1. 以-er，-or，-ar 结尾的名词，例如：

Bartender（酒保）→to bartend（在酒吧当招待）

muck raker（收集并报道丑闻的人）→mukrake（收集并报道丑闻）

loafer（游手好闲者，流荡者）→to loaf（游荡，虚度光阴）

bulldozer（恐吓者，威胁者；推土机）→to bulldoze（恐吓；用推土机推平）

helicopter（直升机）→to helicopt（乘直升机旅行；用直升机运送等）

author（作者）→to auth（创作）

eavesdropper（偷听者）→to eavesdrop（偷听）

ghostwriter（枪手）→to ghostwrite（雇人代为写作）

stargrazer（占星师）→to stargraze（眺望远空，凝视）

windowshopper（逛商店者）→to windowshop（逛商店）

kudos（光荣、荣誉）→to kudo（获得光荣）

2. 删除抽象名词中的后缀，逆生出动词，例如：

One-upmanship（胜人一筹）→to one-upman（占上风）

acculteration（劣货）→to acculterate（掺假）

automation（自动化，自动操作）→to automate（使自动化，自动操作）

cybernation（用电脑进行的控制）→to cybernate（使受电脑控制，使电脑化）

advection（水平对流）→to advect（用平流输送）

transfection（传染）→to transfect（使传染）

banting（减肥疗法）→to bant（节食减肥）

claustrophobia（幽闭症）→to claustrophobe（幽闭）

3. 删除原复合词中的后缀，逆生出动词，例如：

babysitter（临时照看幼儿者）→to babysit（代人临时照看婴儿）

blockbuster（大片；重磅炸弹）→to blockbust（引诱房主低价抛售房地产）

house-sitter（看房人）→to house sit（看房子）

pet-sitter（临时替人照看宠物者）→to pet sit（临时照看宠物）

double-header（由两辆机车牵引的列车）→to double-head（由两辆机车牵引）

mass-production（批量生产）→to mass-produce（成批生产）

eavesdropping（偷听）→to eavesdrop（偷听）

lip-reading（唇读法）→to lip-read（用唇读法观唇辨意）

4. 删除原词中的形容词后缀，逆生出动词。例如：

funky（时髦的；恐慌的）→to funk（因为恐慌而逃避）

sunburned（晒黑的）→to sunburn（晒黑）

flossy（丝棉似的）→to floss（用牙线清洁牙齿）

cosy（舒适的）→to cose（使感到舒适）

drowsy（打盹的）→to drowse（打盹）

calmative（使镇静的）→to calm（使平静，镇静）

hazy（朦胧的）→to haze（变朦胧）

hardboiled（煮老的）→to hardboil（煮老）

tongue-tied（张口结舌的）→to tongue-tie（张口结舌）

5. 删除名词、形容词等以-ling 结尾的后缀，逆生出动词。例如：

moonlighting（月光下活动）→moonlight（兼职）

darkling（暗）→to darkle（变阴暗）

sightseeing（观光游）→to sightsee（观光旅游）

airconditioning（空调）→to air condition（调节温度）

sleepwalking（梦游状态）→to sleepwalk（梦游）

banting（减肥疗法）→to bant（节食减肥）

6. 由复合词去掉两个词尾构成新词。例如：

wishy-washy（淡而无味的）→to wishwash（做淡而无味的饮料）

hotch-potch（大杂烩）→to hot-pot（罐焖土豆烧牛肉）

wishful-thinking（如意算盘）→to wish-think（打如意算盘）

（二）逆生构词法的特点

1. 通过逆生构词法构成的词大多数在词性上有了转变。有的是由名词或复合名词反转成动词或形容词，有的是由形容词逆转成动词或名词等。

2. 从语义角度看，逆生词和原词的词性虽不一致，但含义却是紧密相连。例如：enthusiasm（n. 热情）逆转成动词表示 enthuse（v. 使热情）。

3. 逆生法构成的新词简洁明了。逆生构词法适应了当代英语简洁明了这种大趋势，使得表达的方式去复杂化。例如，倘若没有逆生构词法，要想表现一个类似的思想，就要再造一个动词配合使用，结果会使新事物和新现象越来越多，英语就显得越来越复杂了。

4. 逆生词经常在口语中或非正式场合使用。有些词带有幽默和诙谐色彩。例如：

Who authed this?（auth 由 author 逆生而成）。

第六章 美语新词语构成的趋势

一 复合法

复合词是把两个或两个以上的词按照一定的顺序排列组成一个新词。在英语新词构成中，复合词所占比例最多，也最为常见。它为英语补充了大量新词汇。复合词的构词材料多数由基本词汇提供，许多复合词从字面可以猜出含义。还有些复合词使用连字符构成连字符复合词。近年来，这类构词法呈现大量上升的趋势。

（一）复合词构成方式

复合词主要有复合名词、复合形容词、复合动词等。

1. 复合名词的主要构成方式

（1）名词十名词：veggie libel（素食诽谤），foreclosure mill（止赎），fright mail（恐吓邮件），recession chic（危机时尚达人），Botox party（整形派对），cosmetic underclass（不敢或做不起整形手术的人），cinema therapy（影院治疗法），oxygen bar（氧吧），vinotherapy（红酒理疗），arm candy（蜜糖伴侣），eye candy（养眼美人），scar management（疤痕切割治疗），badge item（徽章暗示），dress correctness（服装正确性），ape diet（类猿餐），heirloom pork（有机猪肉），home meal replacement（家庭取代餐），bird dog（禽肉热狗），bubble tea（泡沫奶茶），candy bar phone（直板手机），cappuccino economy（某一部门经济快速增长而其他部门经济稳定增长），champagne problem（香槟问题，两件绝佳好事之间做抉择的两难境地），Coca-Colanization（可乐殖民化），coffee-spitter（惊恐之事），deprivation cuisine（健康、淡而无味的食物），cookprint（烹饪痕迹），marmalade-dropper（震惊之事），meat tooth（喜肉食

的人），molecular gastronomy（分子美食），latte factor（拿铁因素，每天花出去的小钱），spinach cinema（菠菜电影，尤指有教育意义的电影），food miles（食品英里），relaxation drink（放松饮料），salad dodger（不吃沙拉的人），toy food（玩具食品），window farm（窗口农场），ego wall（个人荣誉墙），Garage Mahal（巨型停车场或车库），celebrity worship syndrome（名人崇拜症），celebrity advocacy（名人代言），decapitation strike（斩首行动），big hair house（巨型房子），monster home（巨大的房屋，尤指与周围环境不符的大房子），paper road（图纸上的路），reno coach（房屋装修顾问），yuppie slum（雅皮士高级社区），telecom hotel（电信大楼），phantom spring（愿景春天），zoo rage（动物园愤怒症），climate canary（气候变化），snake head（蛇头），voice lift（声音整形），yard sale（庭院贱卖），mouse wrist（鼠标腕），mouse potato（鼠标土豆），Kmart realism（凯马特现实主义文学），security mom（安全妈妈），shutter man（卷帘男人，尤指老婆比自己挣得多每天为她卷拉门市门帘的男人），cot potato（婴儿土豆，整天看电视的婴儿），left coast（左海岸，西海岸）等。

（2）形容词＋名词：perma youth（驻颜），one-handed food（手指食物），pharma food（保健食品），pink slime（粉色肉渣），ethical eater（道德食者），extreme beer（极度啤酒），slow food（慢餐），functional food（功能性食物），golden rice（金大米，转基因黄色大米），golden ghetto（城里贫民窟中的富裕区），imperial overstretch（帝国扩张），universal release（全球首映），purple state（紫色州），intellectual tourist（教育目的旅游），talking hairdo（肤浅的电视记者），unread best seller（未读完的畅销书），fat tax（肥胖税），commercial creep（商业侵占），fast-food zoning（快餐食品区），drunk dial（醉酒后打电话），greenprint（宏伟绿图），elder widow（孤寡老人），silver ceiling（银发天花板），late bloomer（大器晚成者），clockless worker（过劳模）等。

（3）动词＋名词/副词：fly-in community（有飞机机场的社区），jingle mail（叮咚邮件，弃掉房子把钥匙邮给债权人），going-away（度蜜月），back-up（备用），sing-song（合唱），mark-up（盈利）等。

（4）名词＋动词-ing：songlifting（歌曲盗版），spear-phishing（鱼叉式网络钓鱼），homicide bombing（自式爆炸），passive overeating（被动

吃多），peanut buttering（把时间、金钱等放在同一件事上，结果却一事无成），car-schooling（车内教育），car pooling（拼车），yarn bombing（针织涂鸦），auto-eating（机械地吃），bet dieting（打赌减肥），drunk driving（醉酒驾车），drive time dining（在车上驾驶吃饭），second hand drinking（二手酒），gold plating（漆金），forest bathing（森林浴），news fasting（新闻斋戒），brain fingerprinting（脑波指纹），car cloning，phone phishing（电话钓鱼），culture jamming（文化反堵），google bombing（谷歌轰炸）等。

（5）-ing + 名词：parking permit（停车证），parking meter（停车表），trailing spouse（随迁配偶），walking bus（健走小队），sunlighting（白天兼职），shopping boyfriend（购物男友）等。

（6）介词/数词 + 名词：third wardrobe（第三衣橱，尤指上班外和休闲以外的装束），100-foot diet（百英尺内食物），by-product（副产品），two commas（百万富翁），third place（第三地，除了家和单位以外的休闲地）等。

2. 复合形容词的主要构成方式

（1）名词 + -ed：Digital native（数码原住民），US proposed（美国提出决议的），US-led（以美国为首的）等。human induced（人类活动引发的），bird witted，book learned（轻浮的），rock-ribbed（顽固的），the market-oriented（市场导向的），exam-oriented（应试为导向），sun-drenched（阳光明媚的），precision-guided（精确制），the Human-Centered（人类为中心的），computer aided（计算机辅助的），value added（增值的），atom-powered（原子动力的），glue-tied（塞满的），export-oriented（出口为导向的），air-borne（空运的），password-protected（受密码保护的），man-made（人造的），hand-made（手工缝制的），state-owned（国有的）等。

（2）名词 + 形容词/：tuition-free（免学费），fault-tolerant（容错），carbon neutral（碳中和），smoke easy（私密吸烟俱乐部，非法吸烟地），duty free（免税）等。

（3）名词 + -ing：time-consuming（耗时的），epoch-making（划时代的）等。

（4）形容词 + -ing/ed：extreme ironing（极限熨烫运动），extreme

119

gardening（极限园艺耕种），fast-paced（快节奏的），ill-humored（缺乏幽默的），black-browed（黑眉毛的），hoary-headed（白头发的），deep-rooted（根深蒂固的），sharp-sighted（眼光锐利的），lighter-skinned（肤色较浅的），red-handed（当场捕获），green-painted（漆成绿色的），high-pitched（尖嗓的），overseas-funded（海外资助的），hot desking（轮流办公），car panning（马路乞讨），car schooling（车内教育）等。

（5）副词＋-ed：newly-elected（新当选的），a newly-built（新建的），fore-sighted（有远见的），under-estimated（低估的），down-hearted（无精打彩的），tightly-packed（被塞得满满），well-bred（有教养的），well-spoken（谈吐优雅的，善于辞令的），well-judged（中肯的），well-turned（恰当的），well-developed（体格健壮的）等。

（6）介词＋名词：in-depth（深度），in-car（车内），in-city（市内），in-college（校内），in-station（值班）等。

3. 复合动词的主要构成方式

（1）副词＋动词：uphold，outweigh，outnumber，offset，cross-question 等。

（2）名词＋动词：window shop，babysit，dog sit，pet sit，house sit，breastfeed（母乳喂养），fibershed（擦亮），carpool，data fast（数码设备持斋），speed date（速配）等。

（3）动词＋动词：cut and shut，make do（凑合用）等。

（4）形容词＋动词：green wash（漂绿），pinkwash（利用乳腺支持项目推销产品），whitewash（粉饰，漂白）等

（二）重叠音节的复合词

这类词由两个发音相似的词组成。有的押头韵，有的押尾韵，比一般的词语鲜明而生动。在描述性的句子中读起来铿锵有力，具有加深印象、加强语义的效果。例如：

1. 押尾韵：nuts and bots（具体细节），huff and puff（虚张声势），nitty-gritty（具体的基本情况），willy-nilly（无论是否愿意），walkie-look-ie（手提式摄像机）等。

2. 押尾韵和头韵：shilly-shally（踌躇不决，支支吾吾），wishy-washy（软弱无力的，淡而无味的），talkee-talkee（对话过多的），tick-tock（腕

表），dilly-dally（拖拖拉拉），riff-raff（不三不四之人），hip hop（嘻哈），niddle-noddle（不断点头）等。

3. 押头韵：Push and pull（牵扯、推动）等。

4. 两个词发音一样的复合词：goody-goody（假殷勤），talkee-talkee（对话过多的），bling-bling（亮晶晶服饰或饰品），yada-yada（等等），hush-hush（私密的），win-win（双赢），go-go（戈戈舞），blabla（等等），slow slow（慢慢地）等。

（三）连字符复合词

新词越来越借助连字符复合词，这种构词法的数量大幅度增加，显出越来越多的趋势。因为连字符复合词巧妙地体现了现代社会的特点，它们大多是旧词间的结合。例如 military-entertainment complex，panda-hugger，fourth-generation，back-channel media，pencil-whip，office-park dad，click-wrap，dog-collar，knee-mail。简便的表现手法更加符合现代英语日趋简洁、明了的趋势。作为英语中一种极为活跃的构词法之一，连字符复合词已经被大众接受，并展现出强大的生命力。那么在什么情况下加连字符呢？下面就是复合词加上连字符的原则：

1. 当副词加上动词过去分词形成形容词作前置定语时，要加上连字符。例如：Well-known（知名的）well-spoken（谈吐优雅的，善于辞令的），well-judged（中肯的），well-turned（恰当的），well-developed（体格健壮的），well-tried（历经磨炼的）等。

2. 构成复合词的前一个词语结尾的字母与后一个词语开头的字母相同时，要加连字符。例如：bell-like（钟形的），still-life（平静生活）等。

3. 由动词加副词或动词加 er 再加副词构成的复合名词。例如：picker-up（采摘），set-back（挫折，后退），play-off（总决赛），turn-out（切断）等。

4. 复合名词的第二部分为副词或介词时，如该复合词已成为一个单独的概念为人们所接受，也可连写。例如：stander-by（旁观者），run-ner-up（亚军），pop-up store（突然出现的商店）等。

5. 用于叠声复合词。例如：goody-goody（假殷勤），wishy-washy（缺乏决心的），talkee-talkee（对话过多的），tick-tock（腕表），bling-

bling（亮晶晶服饰或饰品），yada-yada（等等），hush-hush（私密的），dilly-dally（拖拖拉拉），shilly-shally（浪费时间），flip-flop（左右摇摆，拿不定主意），riff-raff（不三不四之人）等。

6. 用于一身兼两种职务或一物兼两种职能的复合词。例如：actor-producer（演员兼监制人），fight-bomber（战斗轰炸机），city-state（州城），house-boat（船屋）。当复合词中间有两个以上相同元音或有三个相同辅音时加连字符，如 sea-adder，bee-eater，egg-gatherer，secretary-treasurer 等。

7. 由名词加上动词过去分词构成的复合形容词做前置定语时，要用连字符。例如：rock-ribbed（顽固的），the market-oriented（市场导向的），exam-oriented（应试为导向），sun-drenched（阳光明媚的），precision-guided（精确制），the human-centered（以人为中心的），computer-aided（计算机辅助的），air-borne（空运的），man-made（人造的），password-protected（受密码保护的），hand-made（手工缝制的），state-owned（国有的）等。

8. 由三个或三个以上的词构成且含有介词或连词的时候，必须要用连字符。例如：hard-to-operate（难以操作的），life-and-death（生死攸关），garden-to-fork，pay-per-read（按次付费下载），next-war-itis（未来战争冲突计划），do-it-herself（自助），clicks-and-mortar（网店加实体店），get-rich-click，pay-per-listen（按次收费）等。

9. 如果是由句子构成的复合词来做修饰语时，该修饰语词与词之间也必须要用连字符，例如：pick-me-up（兴奋剂），what's-his-name（某某人），man-of-war（战舰）等。

10. 由一个颜色或形状形容词加上名词构成的复合词时，可以用连字符，例如：scarlet-collar，orange-colour，big-box，pink-slip，job-loss，dot-com 等。

11. 专有名词加上名词：Market-Leninism（共产主义市场经济），Coca-colanization（可口可乐化），Cappuccino economy（某一部门经济快速增长而其他部门经济稳定增长）。

12. 名词加上形容词：smoke-easy（私密吸烟俱乐部），friction-free（无摩擦），office-free（无办公室的），tuition-free（免学费），fault-tolerant（容错）等。

二 类比法

类比构词（analogy）是一种仿造原有同类词语的形式创造出与其相对应的新词语的方法。类比构词具有较强的活力，在新词海中俯拾即是。它不但存在于人类生活的方方面面，而且在英美报纸中比比皆是。在现实生活中，客观事物之间具有普遍的联系。这种联系表明同类事物具有共性，即使不同类事物也具有相似性。由于类比构词是将两个语义成分合并，因而产生的词具有简洁凝练、生动形象的特点。这类新词使得人们不需要借助字典就能明白它们的含义，因而深受人们的欢迎。类比构词具有强大的构词力，其基础是与人们的类比心理现实紧密相连的。首先。人类的心理现实是以客观现实为基础的。在客观世界中，事物之间彼此不是孤立的而是具有各种普遍的联系。这种联系不仅表明了同类事物具有共性，还表明了不同类事物往往具有相似性，这是人类长期在与客观世界的交往和接触中形成的一种普遍认识。正是基于这样一种认识：同类事物之间具有共性，不同类事物之间具有相似性，人类的类比才有真实的客观前提。其次，人类在与客观世界的交往与接触中形成了另一种认识，那就是客观事物的普遍联系还表现在任何一个事物的各个属性之间也是相互联系的。再次，类比是人类认识世界和改造世界的重要手段之一。借助类比，人类往往能在生活和工作中做"举一反三"和"触类旁通"式的思维，而且许多科学研究均建立在类比这一创造性思维的基础之上。最后，人类的思维往往是通过已知事物推想未知事物，只要已知事物与未知事物具有某种相似性，人类往往会将对这种相似性的深刻认识投射到未知事物上。Harley 认为，人类往往会在客观世界中寻找一致性，从相邻的事物中寻求相似性，这就是认知世界中的相邻效应。

例如，名词 paparazzi 源自于意大利语，表示"专门追逐名人偷拍照片的摄影者或记者"，人们根据 azzi 或 razzi 创出 snapperazzi（偷拍照片者），stalkerazzi（狗仔队），videorazzi（录像偷拍者）等一系列的新词。从名词 alcoholic 中的词缀 holic 或 aholic，造出 computerholic（计算机迷），spendaholic（嗜花钱者），clothesaholic（讲究穿着的人），shopaholic（购物狂），crediholics（赊账买物成癖的人），teleholic（看电视成瘾的人）, filmholic 或 movie-holic（电影迷）, videoholic（录像迷）, sweet-holic（甜食迷）, beerholic（啤酒迷）, bookholic（读书迷）, playholic（游戏狂人）等新词。

（一）类比构词的形态结构

1. 混合结构类比词

这种结构的类比词结构上是"词基+词缀"，即构成方式是词缀法（affixation）或派生法（derivation），具有同样特点的事物的词都黏附同一个词缀。这种词特点鲜明，结构新颖，使人产生好奇，又容易理解和接受。虽然这种结构的类比词与混合词（blends）结构上相似，但二者是有区别的。混合词是缩略的复合词，而类比法构成的混合词是模仿原有词的结构组成。其中这种类比词的某一成分往往被误认为是语素，而将错就错把它们用作构词成分，构成活跃、生动、易懂的混成结构类比词。例如，由 docudrama（documentary + drama）（文献电视片或电影）类比出 docufantasy（电视文献幻想节目）和 gastrodramas（观众参与吃东西的剧）等词。从 carnivore 类比出 herbivore（食草动物）, informavore（信息消费者）, opportunivore（找到什么吃什么者）, vegivore（食菜者）, omnivore（杂食性动物）等词。从 vacation 类比出 mancation（清一色男士度假）, naycation（不度假）, staycation（在家中度假）等词。

2. 复合结构类比词

这种结构类比词是由两个自由语素构成的。例如：由 babysit（代人照看孩子）类比构成 house sit（代人照看房子）, pet sit, dogsit；由 Watergate（水门事件，政治丑闻）类比构成 oilgate（石油门，指几年前英国一家石油公司不顾联合国关于对南非种族主义政权实行经济制裁的决议，私自将石油卖给他们一事）, cattlegate（牲畜门，指美国密歇根州一家化学公司把剧毒化学品掺入饲料添加剂而造成大批牲畜死亡的严重事故）, debategate（辩论丑闻）, Cartergate（卡特丑闻）, Irangate（伊朗门事件，指为伊朗提供军火事件）, Gospelgate（福音丑闻）, Monicagate（克林顿的绯闻）；由 lost generation 类比出 generation XL, generation 9-11, generation Y, millennial generation, reset generation, sandwich genera-tion, therapy generation；由 road rage 类比出 web rage, work rage, wrap rage, trade rage, gallery rage, checkout-rage（结账时的愤怒）。

（二）类比构词的语义构成

类比构词可分为色彩类比、数字类比、地点空间类比、近似类比和反义类比。新词语类比构词也分为六类。

1. 色彩类比。指通过替换表示颜色的词类比构成新词语。由 white/blue collar（白领／蓝领）类比出了 greycollar（灰领职工，指服务性行业的职工），pink collar（粉领），new collar（新领），gold collar（金领阶层，指高级专业人士），bright collar（亮领阶层，电脑及通信专业人士），green collar（绿领），black collar（黑领），从 whitewash 类比出 pinkwash，greenwash。

2. 类比构成新词。如 3R's 指美国儿童们熟悉的 reading，writing and arithmetic 三种能力。人们据此类比出新词 the Three I's（inflation，interest rate，impeachment，通货膨胀、利率、弹劾）；又根据 First World，Second World，Third World 类比出了 Fourth World（没有资源的最贫穷国家）；由 monopoly（垄断）的构成，类比出 duopoly（双头卖主垄断），globopoly（全球垄断）等词。

3. 反义类比。指用与现有词中的一个成分意义相反的词来替代该成分，以构成新词。例如人们把人才流失叫做 braindrain，又据此词类推出 braingain（人才流入）；从 highrise（现代社会拔地而起的高层建筑）类比出 lowrise（低层建筑）；从 housewife（家庭主妇）类比出 househusband（操持家务的丈夫）；由 upmarket（高档商品市场）类比构成 downmarket（低档商品市场）；由 man Friday（忠仆，得力助手，源出 Daniel Defoe 所著《鲁滨孙漂流记》）类比 girl Friday（得力女助手或秘书）；由 broadcast 构成 narrowcast（小范围播送，指用有线电视播送）；由 sitcom（情景喜剧）类比构成 sit-tragedy（情景悲剧）。

4. 地点类比。指在含有表示地点成分的词中，通过替换该成分构成新词。如由 landscape（陆上风景）类推出 cityscape（城市风景），moonscape（月面风景），Netscape（网景浏览器），riverscape（江河风景），roofscape（屋顶风景），waterscape（水景），seascape（海景），streetscape（街景）等；由 hijack（拦路抢劫）类比出 skyjack（空中劫持）和 seajack（海上劫持）等词。

5. 近似类比。指根据类比词间的近似点由此及彼类比出新词。如

125

由 environmental pollution（环境污染）类比出 noise pollution（噪音污染）
和 cultural pollution（文化污染）。

6. 方式类比。不同的活动方式需要不同的词汇。这些词汇可以借
助类比的方法促使新词的产生。例如由 broadcast（广播）类比出 radio-
cast（无线电广播），newscast（新闻广播），telecast（电视广播）等。

总之，通过类比来构成新词是英语中一种十分活跃的构词方法，它
反映了人们对事物某些特点的认识、比较、联想，显示出人们在创造新
词过程中的想象力和创造力。作为一种有效的构词法，它使大量生动形
象的新词的出现成为可能，令其中许多词语具有鲜明的"流行色"，是
词汇跟上当今人类社会飞速进步的最好构词途径之一。

三　派生法

派生法在英语历史的发展过程中，起着极其重要的作用。随着社会
的发展，科学技术的突飞猛进，人类社会取得巨大进步，英语词缀的构
词能力越来越强且灵活性大，是一种构成新词强有力的手段。派生词以
其独特的方式，不断地扩充英语词汇，从而丰富英语的表现力。

派生法也称为词缀法。在一个词根前或后加上一个词缀，变成一个
新词。可以说，词根是派生词的基础，而英语词缀（affix）是英语形态
构词中的一种粘附语素（bound morpheme），它既不能单独存在，也不能
独立使用。它常常附在自由语素（free morpheme）的前面或后面或嵌在
其他语素间，只表示附加意义和语法意义，而不表示词汇意义。

英语词缀从词形变化角度，可分为屈折词缀（inflectional affix）和
派生词缀（derivational affix）。屈折词缀是指只有语法意义，没有词汇意
义的词缀。屈折词缀在现代英语中屈指可数，例如，表示单数第三人称
一般现在时的-s/-es，表示动词过去式的-ed 和过去分词的-en。

派生词缀是指可以决定词性，有一定语义的词缀。根据其所处的位
置词缀可分为前缀（prefix）、中缀（infix）和后缀（suffix）三种。前缀
是附加在自由语素前的语素，例如 unilateral 中的 un-。后缀是指附加在
自由语素后的语素，例如 togethering 中的-ing。英语中颇为常见的词缀是
前缀和后缀，中缀的作用与其数量都非常有限，本章将不做讨论。

（一）词缀来源

词缀包括英语本族语中的词缀和来自拉丁语、希腊语、法语、意大利语等外来语词缀。

来自本族语词前缀大致有 a-, be-, counter-, fore-, mis-, pro-, re-, over-, under-, off-, out-, un-, up-, with-等。后缀包括-er, -ed, -dom, -fold, -hood, -ing, -less, -like, -ling, -ness, -ship, -some, -th, -ward, -wise等。

来自拉丁语词缀中的前缀有 ab-, ad-, ante-, bene-, circum-, counter-, com-, contra-, de-, deci-, demi-, dis-, en-, ex-, extra-, in-, inter-, infra-, inter-, mal-, milli-, mini-, multi-, non-, ob-, per-, post-, pre-, pro-, re-, semi-, sept-, sub-, super-, trans-, ultra-, uni-, vice-等。后缀有-age, -al, -ance, -ant, -ar, -ary, -ate, -ence, -ent, -ible, -ion, -ive, -ous 等。

希腊语词缀中的前缀有 anti-, archi-, auto-, cata-, di-, dia-, enne-, ge-, hector-, hemi-, hexa-, holo-, homo-, hydro-, hypo-, kilo-, micro, neo-, -mono-, octa-, pan-, para-, peri-, penta-, poly, proto-, pseudo-, psycho-, radio-, syn-, tele-等。后缀有-cracy, -ism, -ist, -ite, -ize, -gy, -graph, -logy, -meter, -graph, -phone, -scope 等。

来自法语外来语的前缀有 kilo-, mal-, sur-等。后缀有-age, -ant, -ee, -ery, -ite, -ory, -ure 等。

（二）常见的英语旧前缀和旧后缀构成的新词语

英语词缀具有语义和语法功能。前缀、后缀的语义和语法功能截然不同，前缀不影响词根的词性及语法范畴，但具有明显的语义，起到修饰和限制词根作用。因而，前缀的作用类似副词。表示程度、向背、时间、地点、否定、反意、贬低、数量等含义。旧词缀由来已久，属于旧有的词缀。美语中通过旧前缀构成新词语并赋予新意俯拾即是。

1. 较为常见的旧前缀构成的新词

（1）表示程度的前缀及构成的新词有

a. over-表示"过分"，如：overvoting（过多投票），overachiever（超级优秀生），overclass（特权阶层），overnighter（小旅行），overstretch

127

（战线过长）等。

b. under-表示"不足、低于"，如：underprivileged（穷人），under-work（少做工作），under-employment（待业），underachiever（低等生），underexcercised（缺少锻炼的）等。

c. ultra-表示"极端、超"，如：ultra-fashionable（超时髦的），ultra-conservative（极端保守的），ultramilitant（极端好战的），ultraviolence（极端暴力）等。

d. mini-表示"小型的"，maxi-表示"超大的"，如：minimalist（极简抽象派艺术的），minisub（小型潜艇），minirecession（小规模衰退）等；maxi series（长篇电视连续剧），maxiskirt（超长裙），maxi-order（超大订单）等。

e. super-表示"超级"，例如：supersize（超大量），superette（小型超级市场），superfly（显眼的），supergene（超级基因），superbug（超级细菌）等。

f. hyper-表示"超级"，如：hypermedia（超级媒体），hyper-local（超本地化），hyperwhite（无白人影响的衣饰），hypermiler（超级省油者），hyperdrive（超光速推进）等。

g. out-表示"外、缺少"，例如：out-enthusiasmed（缺少比赛热情和士气而失败的），outsource（外包），outdoorsman（喜欢野外活动的人），outplace（调职）等。

h. down-表示"剪裁"、"减少"，例如：downsize（裁员），down-shift（调到压力较轻的工作），down-market（低端市场），downdressing（穿便装）等。

i. para-表示"旁、近"，如：parahawking（滑翔驯鹰），paracopy-right（超著作权），parajournalism（非常规新闻写作），parakite（风筝伞）等。

j. mega-表示"大"，如：megadeal（大宗交易），megavitamin（大量维生素），megatrend（社会发展趋势），megamerger（强强联合，举行合并），megaton（百万吨级），megastore（大型商场），megaseller（热门畅销书）等。

k. micro 表示"微、小"，如：micro-donor（微额政治献金），micro-credit（微额贷款），microeconomy（微观经济），micropolis（小型城

市），micropopulation（微生物种群）等。

（2）表示向背的旧前缀及所构成的新词语

a. co-表示"共同、一起"，如：co-opetition（合作竞争），co-parenting（共同抚养子女），copreneur（夫妻企业家），cooperative（合作公寓）等。

b. counter-表示"反、逆"，如：counter cruising（反巡航），counterforce（军事打击力量），counterculture（反文化）等。

c. pro-表示"支持、赞成"，如 pro-ana（益肠），probiotics（益生菌），prosumer（体验性消费者），prolife（益生），pro-democratic（推进民主的）等。

d. anti-表示"反对"，如：anti-terrorist（反恐怖主义活动的），anti-pollution（防止环境污染），anticipointment（大失所望），anti-rail（反铁道建设的）等。

（3）表示时间的旧前缀及新词语

a. post-表示"在……之后"，如：post-mortem divorce（分葬离婚书），postnup（婚后协议），post-synch（影片后期配音）等。

b. fore-表示"先、预"，如：foreverness（永恒），foreperson（领班），foreclosure（止赎权）等。

c. ex-表示"从前的"，如：ex-wife, ex-husband, ex-boyfriend 等。

d. re-表示"再次"，如：reanchor, rewild, regift, regreen 等。

e. step-表示"过继、后"，如：step wife（丈夫前妻），step family（再婚家庭），step aerobics（上下踏步有氧运动）等。

（4）表示方位的旧前缀及新词语

a. in-表示"在……中间"，如：in-state（州内），in-thing（流行的事物），in-group（集团内），in-crowd（圈内人），in-house（内部的），in-band（同频带信号传输）等。

b. trans-表示"横跨、变化"，如：transumer（旅游购物狂），trans-fat（反式脂肪），transsexual（异性转化欲者），transplantate（移植器官）等。

c. retro-表示"在后"，如：retrophilia（怀旧），retro-tech（过时的技术），retrospective（个人作品回顾展），retromercial（重播早期广告）等。

（5）表示使动和否定旧前缀及构成的新词语

a. en-或 em-表示"使"，加上名词或形容词构成动词，如：empower（使能做事），embitter（使……更加痛苦），embourgeoisement（资产阶级化）等。

b. be-表示"使、看作"，加名词或形容词构成动词，如：befriend（亲近），befog（把笼罩在雾里）。

c. de-表示"除掉"，加上名词构成动词，如：deoil（去油），demall（把室内购物中心变为室外露天购物中心），de-alert（自核武发射系统拆除核子弹头），decapitation（斩首），de-conflict（化解冲突），decarbonize（无碳），deleb（已故名人），dejunk（打扫），dejab（不戴头盖），de-café（去咖啡因）等。

d. dis-表示"除掉、剥夺"，加上名词构成动词，如：disintoxicate（使戒毒），disposable（一次性物品），disforest（把树林砍掉）等。

e. out-表示"出、向外"，加上动词构成名词，如：outlet（出口，直销），outbound（开往外地的）等。

f. un-表示"由……取出、由……解脱"，加上名词构成动词，如：unwedding（解除婚姻），undecorating（卖房前简单装修），unaverage（杰出的），uncool（不从容的）等。

（6）贬低性或褒扬性旧前缀及新词语

a. mal-表示"不良、坏"，如：malodorant（恶臭物），malignant（恶性），maladjusted（调节差的）。

b. bene-表示"好、有益"，如：beneficiary（受益人），benefactive（施益体）等。

（7）表示数量的旧前缀和新词语

a. uni-表示"单、一"，如：unisex（不分男女），unitonal（单声调的），unibrow（连心眉），uni-grad（大学毕业生）。

b. poly-表示"多"，如：polyfidelity（多婚化忠诚），polysemic（多义词描述），polyglot（通晓多种语言的人），polyester（粗俗的）等。

c. multi-表示"多"，如：multi-channel（多渠道），multimillionaire（大富翁），multitasking（多重任务处理），multi-occupation（多户共用），multigym（多功能健身器材）等。

d. semi-表示"半"，如：semi-finished（半成品的），semi-vegetarian

（半素食者）, semi-somnia（半睡眠）, semi-skimmed（半脱脂的）, semi-literate（初等文化的）等。

（8）术语性前缀与新词语

a. bio-表示"生命、生物"，如：biophillia（生物自卫本能）, biopics（真实人物的电影）, biorhythm（生物周期）, biosphere（生物环境）, biodisel（有机油）, biopiracy（生物剽窃）, biofraud（生态欺诈）, bionomics（生态经济学）, biohacker（分子生物学黑客）, biomom（生物意义上的母亲）, biomimicry（生物仿生）, biopharming（生物制药）, biodiversity（生物多样性）, biodegradable（生物可降解的）等。

b. geo-表示"地球"，例如：geocaching（地理藏宝）, geofence（地理围栏）, geotagging（相片定位）, geotextile（土工纺织物）。

2. 旧后缀构成的新词语

后缀的语义不如前缀明显，但后缀有很强的语法意义，能决定词的语法属性，用来构成名词、动词、形容词和副词等各种词类。旧缀使后缀被赋予新的含义成为新后缀。下面是由旧后缀构成的新词语。

（1）构成名词的后缀及新词语

a. -er 表示"……行为者、器具"，如：diner（餐车；进餐的人）, downshifter（追求生活事业简单化）, bed blocker（害怕孤独赖在医院不出院的人）, trainer（训练鞋）, boomeranger（青年回潮族）, domainer（注册销售域名的人）, downager（装嫩的人）, dumpster driver（大垃圾装卸卡车）, fiver（5美元）, deather（相信美国健康医疗保险导致更多人死亡的人）。

b. -st 表示"……行为者"，如：sewist（裁缝）, rawist（食鲜者）, architourist（建筑旅游者）, politainer（艺人身份的政治家）, andrologist（听力学家）, exemtionalist（免责主义）, foliologist（树叶变色专家）等。

c. -rian 表示"与……有关的人"，如：flexitarian（偶尔吃素食的人）, breatharian（吸食空气者）, cybrarian（网络数据应用专家）, pescetarian（鱼素食者）, pollotarian（只吃白肉不吃红肉的素食主义者）。

d. -eer 表示"从事……的人"，如：pumpkineer（西瓜王）, fisioneer（冷核聚变研究员）。

e. -ity 表示"性质、状态、程度"，如：visibility（预见度）, visitability（残疾人友好的建筑）等。

f. -ism 表示"具有……性质或……主义、学术理论",如:green urbanism(绿色城市主义),declinism(衰退论),endism(终结论),presenteeism(强迫出席症),sageism(歧视老年妇女),ageism(老年歧视)。

g. -ing 表示"状态",如:songlifting(盗版歌曲),voicelifting(嗓音整形),wardrobing(穿后退货),streaking(裸奔)。

h. -ion 表示"动作的过程、状态或结果",如:glocalization(全球本土化),inequity aversion(不平等回避),white pollution(白色污染),hyper-evolution(超进化)等。

i. -ship 表示"职业、行业"或"的性质和状况",如:one-uppermanship(胜人一筹),one-upwomanship(女人胜另外女人一筹),earthship(地球船,指生态循环住宅)。

j. -cide 表示"杀",如:bullycide(校园欺辱而自杀),adulticide(杀成虫药)。

k. -ness 表示"……的性质或状态"。如:worklessness(无业)。

l. -ure 表示"的行为或事实、被……状况",如:biotecture(生态建筑),foreclosure(止赎权)。

(2)构成动词的后缀及新词语

a. -ify 表示"化",如:gentrify(美化房间和环境),nullify(抵消、无效)等。

b. -ize 表示"使",如:posterize(多色调分色印),dollarize(美元化),hybridize(使杂交)等。

(3)构成形容词的后缀及新词语

a. -able 表示"能、可",如:T-shirt-able(可印图像的 T 恤),grubbifiable(劳动后可能弄脏的),offshorable(离岸外包)等。

b. -ful 表示"充满的",如:viewtiful(时髦的、漂亮的)等。

c. -ed 表示"有……的、有……特点的",如:mentally challenged(智障的),vertically challenged(超重的),follicularly challenged(无发的),hymenally challenged(不是处女的)。

d. -cious 表示"具有……的、充满的",例如:babilicious(女性美丽姣好的,迷人的),bootylicious(曲线优美的,性感的),beaulicious(漂亮美味的)等。

（4）构成副词的后缀及新词语

-wise 表示"在……方面、朝……方向"或"以某种特别的方式"，如：moneywise（在钱的方面），street-wise（适应都市环境的），weather-wise（在天气方面），educationwise（就教育而言），taxwise（在税收方面）；housingwise（就住房问题来看），curriculumwise（在课程方面），manpowerwise（根据人力），等等。

（三）新前缀和新后缀构成的新词语

1. 新前缀构成的新词语

20 世纪末期，信息科学和电子技术迅猛发展，人们生活的各个方面有了质的变化。电子网络词汇大量出现。如 electronic 本义是"电子的"，但是为了方便起见，人们使用 e-取代 electronic，e-成为新的词缀。大量以 e-为词缀的新词语产生。例如 e-wallet, e-business, e-commerce, e-signiture, e-tailer, e-cycling, e-book, e-mail, e-shopping, e-tailing, e-card, e-zine, e-fence, e-thrombosis 等。同样，以 web 为前缀的新词层出不穷。如 webrarian（网络数据管理员），web cramming（网络堵塞），web master（网络管理员）。Podcast 是 Ipod 和 broadcasting 的缩写。是一种数字广播技术，是借助"iPodder"的软件与一些便携播放器相结合而使得网友将网上的广播节目下载到自己的 iPod、MP3 播放器或其他便携式数码声讯播放器中便于随身收听。根据这一构词法，人们创出以 pod 为前缀的新词，如 podcatching（播客），podjacking（把他人电脑音乐下载到自己的 Ipod 上）。cyber-本来是一个词素，形容词，表示"计算机的、网络的"。20 世纪 90 年代它频繁出现于媒体和大众生活后，就以词缀形式进入英语语言中，并构成大量新词语。例如：cyber-alert（网络警觉），cyber-bully（网络凌辱），cybercafé（网吧），cybercrime（网络诈骗），cyber-dating（网络约会），cyberdepot（网上商店），cyber-fraud（网络诈骗），cyberlink（网络连接），cyberhate（网络仇恨），cy-berspace（网络空间），cybertech（网络技术），cyber world（网络世界），cybertron（赛博坦），cyber nationalism（网络民族主义），cyber Monday（周一网购高潮），cyber law（网络法），cybernetics（控制论），cyberpunk（电脑高手），cyber racism（网络种族主义），cyber-safety 或 cybersecurity（网络安全），cybespeak（网络语言），cyberterrorism（网络恐怖主义），

cyberwarfare（网络军事战争），cybercasting（网络直播），cybervigilantit-ism（网络联防）。I-是苹果公司为电脑 IMac 的命名。根据公司的解释，i-代表 internet。后来公司相继推出其他产品，分别以 i-为前缀进行命名：iPod, iTunes, iPhone, iLife, iPodder, iPad, iPhone 等。在它的影响下，其他公司以 i-前缀分别命名自己的产品、网址或搜索引擎等。例如：iGoogle, BBC 的播放器 iPlayer, icoke（网址），电视节目 iCarly 等。Blog全称是 Web Log, 是"网络日志"的意思。最早一个博客（blog）就是一个网页，它通常是由简短且经常更新张贴的文章构成，展现出博客本人的世界。新的思想及现象不断出现，人们用 blog 作为前缀，创出大量新词。例如：blogosphere, blogger, blogcritics 等。nerd 是指"那些每天只懂读书、考试，但生活、社交能力都很弱的年轻人"。然而，最近人们对于 nerd 的看法有了很大的改变，赋予它更多的褒义。由于电脑是由 nerd 发明的，the macintosh/apple and windows 也是由 nerds 发明创造的，Bill Gates 也是一位 nerd, 他的成名及暴富使得 nerd 这一词汇的消极含义几乎消失殆尽。nerd 作为词缀随之被大众广泛使用。例如：nerdistan（科技园区），nerdom（IT 精英）。

近些年来，绿色生活受到人们的推崇，环保事业受到越来越多的关注。在英语中出现许多表示环境生态、以 eco 为前缀的新词汇。例如：eco-friendly（环境友好），ecodevelopment（经济—生态均衡），ecocrisis（生态危机），ecocide（物种灭绝），eco-atmosphere（生态气层），eco-cli-mate（生态气候），eco-catastrophe（生态灾难）。ecoradical（激进的环保分子），eco-efficiency（生态效率），ecotecure（生态建筑），eco-anxiety（生态焦虑），eco-bling（生态技术与设施），eco-driving（生态驾驶），eco-tourism（生态旅游），eco-freak（生态反常），economics（生态经济），eco-scam（生态垃圾），eco-labelling（环保标签），ecobabble（环保术语）。美国购房者对于新房和旧房改造的要求越来越高，热衷于使用可持续性材料。eco-house（生态屋）和 eco-perch（生态环保树屋）也受到大众的追捧。

纳米技术是人类发展史上的重大突破，是人类对于世界的贡献。鉴于此，出现了许多与纳米有关的新词，如 nanocomputer（纳米微电脑），nanotube（纳米管），nanochemistry（纳米化学），nanoelectronics（纳米电子学），nanobiology（纳米生物学），nanoarchitecture（纳米建筑），nanolithography（纳米刻蚀技术），nanobioelectronics（纳米生物电子学），nanoethics（纳米道德），nanoneedle（纳米针），nanofilm（纳米膜），nanoplankton（纳米浮生物），nanocarbon（纳米碳），nanosilver（纳米银），nanoproduct（纳米产品），nanopyramid（纳米陈列），nanosatellite（纳米卫星），nanosurgery（纳米手术），nanosyringe（纳米注射），nanodisc（纳米盘），nanotechnology（纳米技术），nanoweapons（纳米武器），nanorobotics（纳米机器人），nanomaterials（纳米材料），nanoparticle（纳米分子），nanopublishing（纳米出版）。

人们利用克隆、转基因技术攻克一些不治之症，生产出更加健康、美味、持久的粮食。Frankenfish（发光转基因鱼）能够满足人们对于美味鱼肉的需求。富含维生素 A 的 golden rice 有助于防止发展中国家儿童失明。然而消费者依然对这种 Franken food 怀有恐惧反感的心理，并未获得批准进行生产。20 世纪克隆羊获得成功后，克隆技术飞速发展，派生出许多以 clone 为词根的新词。例如：Clonality, clonable, cloners, clonee, cloned 等。

美语中许多新词都以总统名字命名，而且影响巨大。1993—2001 年 Clinton（克林顿）执政。在执政过程中走了一条"中间道路"。克林顿本人属于民主党的温和派，但是他淡化民主党的自由主义立场，把共和党受人欢迎的一些思想接过来，作为自己的政策目标，成为民主党温和派。在此期间多数选民从国家经济发展中得到实惠，他们认可 Clintonomics（克林顿的经济政策或主张）。此外还有 Clintonian（与克林顿政策有关的或克林顿政策的支持者），Clintonspeak（闪烁其词、犹抱琵琶半遮面的说话方式），Clintonize（使克林顿化，使适合或适应克林顿的政策），Clintonmania（克林顿热），Clintonite（克林顿派的），Clintonlingo（克林顿官话），Clintonism（克林顿主义，指克林顿在竞选中和执政之初提出对国内经济进行改革的主张）等。

美国总统奥巴马作为争议颇多的第一个黑人总统，也是颇受欢迎的一个美国总统，给语言带来了一系列新鲜词汇。2008 年 9 月位于美国加州圣地亚哥的全球语言监测机构 Global Language Monitor 的一项研究显示，在过去一年中，ObamaSpeak（奥巴马派生词）成为美国电视媒体中的第二大高频词。奥巴马派生词有 Obamacize（像奥巴马那样去做事），Obamania（奥巴马狂），Obamanomics（奥巴马经济政策），Obamafy

（具有奥巴马特征、色彩）。另外还有 Obamanation（奥巴马王国、奥巴马集团），Barackstar（奥巴马的气质）Barackstar Shirts（奥巴马 T 恤），Obama berry（奥巴马用黑莓手机），Obama beer（奥巴马啤酒，指奥巴马式举杯释嫌），Obama agenda（奥巴马议事日程），Obama administration（奥巴马政府），Obama black（奥巴马式黑色），Obama Biden administration（奥巴马拜登政府），Obama mess（奥巴马一团糟），Obamabot（对奥巴马盲目崇拜的选民），Obamamentum（奥巴马的竞选），Obamican（奥巴马的拥护者），Obama care（奥巴马医改）。

2. 新后缀构成的新词语

新后缀构成的新词语通过在词素后加新后缀形成。这些后缀不是从古延续到今，而是最近几十年出现，并且有些是从词素中分解出来的。受 sit-in 这一词汇影响，美语出现了许多以后缀 -in 构成的新词，例如 lie-in（躺地示威），swim-in（游泳抗议），be-in（自由活动聚会），love-in（爱情聚会），teach-in（大学师生发表意见的宣讲会）。从 dotcom 到 zitcom，sitcom，telecom，zit com，bitcom，slackcom 都是以 com 为后缀构成的新词。

前苏联成功地发射第一颗人造卫星（sputnik）后，一连串以俄语后缀 "nik" 结尾的新词汇纷至沓来。例如：beatnik（垮了的一代），no-goodnik（无用的人），citynik（都市迷），jazznik（爵士迷），computernik（电脑迷），peacenik（和平分子），protestnik（凡事抗议者），moonik（月球卫星），earthnik（居住在地球上的人），boatnik（水上人家），等等。

后缀 -zzi 来自意大利语 paparazzi，以此为词根的词汇还有 snaparazzi（业余狗仔队），hackerazzi（黑客狗仔），rumorazzi（绯闻作家）。

Watergate scandal（水门丑闻）揭露出尼克松说谎丑闻，使得他成为美国历史上第一位辞职的总统。自此以后，政治丑闻甚至其他领域的丑闻都被冠以 -gate 词根。Filegate（档案丑闻）指的是 "克林顿秘密建立潜在共和党政敌档案的丑闻"。Nannygate（保姆门）指克林顿上任后在任命女性司法部长时爆出的丑闻。Pardongate（特赦丑闻）则指 "克林顿卸任前的特赦丑闻"。Monicagate（莫妮卡丑闻）则是克林顿与前白宫实习生 MonicaLewinsky 的桃色事件。尤其是 Monicagate（莫尼卡丑闻）使克林顿处于极为尴尬的境地。英国王子查尔斯与卡米拉的桃色新闻被曝光后，媒体与大众称其为 Camilla-gate。佩林的妹妹与担任州警的丈夫伍腾离婚后，佩林向这位前妹夫的上司莫尼根施压，要求开除伍腾。由于不从，结果莫尼根被佩林开除，被称为 troopergate（警门丑闻）。此外还有 Concussiongate（希拉里脑震荡门），Dianagate（戴安娜丑闻），Whitewatergate（白水门丑闻）。

又如-speak 并不是英语中原有的构词成分，美国作家 George Orwell 在他的著名政治讽刺小说 Nineteen Eighty-Four 中把束缚人们思想，内容空洞的政治新闻称作 newspeak（新语言）。自此以后，-speak 便被用来表示某些专门术语，变成了一个构词能力极强的成分。例如：businessspeak（商业界说法），educationspeak（教育界的说法），econspeak（经济学说法），techspeak（科学家说法）。后来-speak 又被用于某些专有名词之后，表示某个时期，某一机构，甚至某一个人的有特色的语言风格。例如 Vietspeak（美军在越南战争期间所创造使用的词汇），NASAspeak（美国航空航天局发言人拐弯抹角的语言风格），Bushspeak（美国总统布什演说发言风格），Obamaspeak（奥巴马演讲风格）。

（四）加连字符的派生词

除了复合词使用连字符构成新词语现象较多外，派生词使用连字符构成新词语的现象也比较常见。与复合词一样，这种构词法数量呈大幅度增加的趋势，巧妙地体现了现代社会追求简洁、明了的特点。一般情况下连字符只出现在单词词根和派生词缀之间。主要有以下几种情况：

1. 元音字母开头的单词前出现以元音字母结尾的派生前缀，可以使用连字符，避免元音字母双写所引起的重复读音或读音的失误。例如：co-opetition，fake-ation。

2. 在某些外形类似单词的词缀上，以避免误解。例如：ultra-reactionary，construction-wise。

3. 用在专有名词前，用来隔开小写和大写字母。例如：Anti-Yankeeism，Pro-British。

4. 用于在临时缀合或尚未获得公认的派生词中。例如：post-liberation，neo-creo，de-alert，de-conflict，de-proliferate。

（五）词缀的文体意义

英语中有的词具有字面意义（denotative meaning）或隐含意义（connotative meaning）或兼而有之。词缀也有类似意义。有些词缀带有褒义或贬义色彩，有些常用于书面体，还有些用于口语体，有些用于正式场合，有些用于非正式场合等。因此词缀的学习也要涉及语体问题。只有这样，才能正确使用它们。词缀的文体意义是指词缀本身具有的褒、贬、亲、疏的色彩，例如：

1. 前缀 mega-表示"超大、巨大"，有明显的贬义，如：megahouse，megastore。

2. 前缀 un 表示"不、非、解除"等贬义，例如：undecorating（不进行大装修，简单装修），unwedding（解除婚姻）等。

3. 后缀-ling 表示"小"，常含有轻视、藐视的味道，如：professorling（小教授），weakling（体弱的人），underling（下属）等。

4. 后缀-ster 既可以表示"干某个不好行业的人"，如：smockster（爱搞女人的人），gangster（歹徒），thugster（刺客），也可以表示"蹩脚、低级"，含贬义，如：rhymester（蹩脚诗人），daubster（拙劣的画家），wordster（花言巧语的人）等。

5. 后缀-ard 表示"某种行为不良的人"，含贬义，如：drunkard（醉鬼），sluggard（懒汉），dullard（笨蛋）等。

6. 后缀-ie 表示"亲昵、关系的密切"，常用于非正式场合。例如：knewbie（大侠），newbie（菜鸟），freebie（免费白送的物品），pokie（老虎机），halfie（混血）等。

7. 前缀 dys-的意思和 dis-相类似，但是它出现在含有"不正常"、"患病"、"令人不快"等意义的词里，如 dysfunction（功能丧失），dyslexia（读写困难），dysbasia（步行困难），dysarthria（构音困难）等，这样构成的新词用于正式文体，而且一般是医用词。

8. 后缀-aholic 或-oholic，来自 alcoholic 一词，与名词、动词结合，构成新名词，表示对某物需要，喜好程度达到似乎上瘾的人。然而这样构成的名词用于非正式场合，并且往往为了达到诙谐的效果。例如：chocoholics，milkhaulic，workaholic，creamholic，nutaholic，shopaholic 等。

9. 以-y 为后缀的形容词常常含有"不满意的"贬义含义。例如：

touchy（棘手的，需要小心处理），nosy（爱打听消息的），bossy（爱发号施令的），tricky（微妙的），trendy（打扮入时的）等。

四　拼缀法

著名语言学家汪榕培在《英语词汇学教程》一书中写道："……如果加上无数学科的专门术语和俚语、方言、新词，英语的词汇远远超过200 万个，并以每年至少 850 个新词的速度增加，……"实践证明，英语中的新拼缀词也是如此。20 世纪以前，拼缀词的数量并不大，但是自从 20 世纪之后，尤其是从中期开始，特别受到人们的青睐，并涌现出了大量的新拼缀词，与日俱增。缩合词（blending）即拼缀词或混成词，是指将两个或两个以上的词进行裁剪，取舍其中的首部或尾部的一种新词语构成的方法。也可以是在一个词前或后附上另外一个词的某个部分而构成的新词语。

这种构词法在英语流行新词语中日渐增多，富有生命力。这类词具有表现力强、结构巧妙的特点，符合现代人快节奏的生活方式。

（一）构成形式

1. 将一个单词的首部与另一个单词的尾部拼接起来组成新词。如：crunk = crazy + drunk（狂醉；尽兴），hoffice = home + office（家庭办公），permalancer = permanent + freelancer（永久性自由职业者），infonasia = information + amnesia（记忆健忘症），spork = spoon + fork（叉勺），skort = skirt + short（裙裤），stragmatics = strategic + pragmatic（战略应用学），Eurasia = Euro + Asia（欧洲亚洲），liger = lion + tiger（狮虎），adflation = advertisement + inflation（广告费用上涨），edutainment = education + entertainment（寓教于乐），genetaceutial = genetic + pharmaceutical（基因药），knowbot = knowledge + robot（知识型机器人），vlog = video + blog（视频博客），infortainment = information + entertainment（新闻娱乐化），broadloid = broadsheet + tablid（小型大报），glocalization = globalization + localization（全球化下的本土化/球土化），smirting = smoking + flirting（边吸烟边跟异性搭讪），Chimerica = China + America（中美国），Oxbridge = Oxford + Cambridge（剑桥牛津），milence = smile + silence（笑

而不语），vegeteal ＝ vegetable ＋ steal（偷菜，指开心网上的摘菜），dykon ＝ dyke ＋ icon（女同性恋喜欢的偶像），Japlish ＝ Japanese ＋ English（日式英语），Chinsumer ＝ Chinese ＋ consumer（国外旅行疯狂购物的中国人，出国旅游时挥金如土的中国购物者），cowfeteria ＝ cow ＋ cafeteria（自动奶品小吃店），ballretto ＝ ballet ＋ liberetto（芭蕾舞剧），bionics ＝ biology ＋ electronics（仿生学），catelo ＝ cattle ＋ buffalo（黄牛与水牛的杂交牛），framily ＝ friend ＋ family（朋友家人），frienemy ＝ friend ＋ enemy（友敌），jumbrella ＝ jumbo ＋ umbrella（巨型伞），newsgram ＝ news ＋ program（新闻节目），stagflation ＝ stagnation ＋ inflation（经济滞胀），multiversity ＝ multiple ＋ university（多校联合大学），telescript ＝ telecision ＋ script（电视广播稿），telecast ＝ television ＋ broascast（电视广播），private ＋ utopia（管理严格有隔墙的私人住宅小区），promzilla ＝ prom ＋ Godzilla（自私的毕业舞会高中女生），yestersol ＝ yesterday sol（火星的前一天）。

2. 由一个单词的首部与另一个单词的全部构成新词。如：agrigenetic ＝ agriculture ＋ genetic（农业基因学），narcomillionaire ＝ narcotic ＋ millionaire（因贩毒而暴富的百万富翁），navaid ＝ navy ＋ aid（助航设备），radwaste ＝ radioactive ＋ waste（放射性废物），feminazi ＝ feminism ＋ Nazi（女权纳粹或极端女权主义），broccoflower ＝ broccoli ＋ flower（球花甘蓝），architourist ＝ architecture ＋ tourist（建筑观光），portafuel ＝ portable ＋ fuel（营养式快餐），geomythology ＝ geology ＋ mythology（地质神话学），narcotoursist ＝ narcotic ＋ tourist（买卖毒品的旅游），biosphere ＝ biological ＋ sphere（生物圈），ecocatastrophe ＝ ecology ＋ catastrop（生态灾难），econobox ＝ economic ＋ box（经济型汽车），e-government ＝ electronic ＋ government（电子政府），e-reader ＝ electronic ＋ reader（电子阅读器），e-marketing ＝ electronic ＋ marketing（网络营销），e-textbook ＝ electronic ＋ textbook（电子教科书），e-card ＝ electronic ＋ card（电子贺卡），camgirl ＝ camera ＋ girl（视频女），emotionormal ＝ emotion ＋ normal（情绪稳定），suihide ＝ suicide ＋ hide（躲猫猫），disemvowel ＝ dismiss ＋ vowel（发送短信或电子邮件时为省事，只写辅音不写元音的输入方式），diabulimia ＝ diabetes ＋ bulimia（抑郁症与饮食障碍）。

3. 由一个单词的全部与另一个单词的尾部构成新词，如：

bridezilla = bride + godzilla（新娘狂躁症），brideorexia = bride + anorexia（新娘婚前厌食症），chillax = chill + relax（冷静放松），beerios = beer + cheerios（啤酒麦圈），deskfast = desk + breakfast（办公室早餐），warmedy = warm + comedy（温情喜剧），eatertainment = eat + entertainment（娱乐餐），beercycle = beer + bicycle（自行车肋骨开瓶），bustaurant = bus + restaurant（巴士餐厅），dellionaire = Dell + millionaire（靠戴尔股票发迹的人），homepreneur = home + entrepreneur（家族企业），zillionaire = zillion + millionaire（亿万富翁），boatel = boat + hotel（汽艇旅馆），warphan = war + orphan（战争孤儿），netizen = net + citizen（网民），kideo = kid + video（适合儿童口味的电视节目或录像带），glitterati = glitter + literati（文学界上层人士和知名人士），penputer = pen + computer（笔触式计算机），travelogue = travel + catalogue（旅游纪录片），breathalyser = breath + analyzer（呼吸测醉器），newsgram = news + program（新闻节目），Obamamentum = Obama + momentum（奥巴马的竞选行动，奥巴马的动力，奥巴马的竞选态势或势头），Obamaican = Obama + republican（奥巴马的拥护者），Obamabot = Obama + robot（奥巴马信徒），Obamanomics = Obama + economics（奥巴马经济，奥巴马经济政策），sexting = sex + texting（性短信），funemployed = fun + unemployed（乐失业一族），scxtary = scx + secretary（老板与女秘书的暧昧关系），manny = man + nanny（男保姆），chiconomics = chic + economic（时尚经济），netiquette = net + etiquette（网规），webucation = web + education（网络教育）。

4. 前词原词加上后词的词首部分。例如：cyberorg = cyber + organism（半机械人），listserv = list + service（邮件分类系统的专题通信服务），webcam = web + camera（网络摄像机）。

5. 将两个单词的首部拼凑起来构成新词，如 digicame = digital + camera（数码相机），advid = advertising + videotap（广告性录像带），cermet = ceramic + metal（金属陶瓷），forex = foreign + exchange（外汇），juco = junior + collge（大专），sanpro = sanitation + protection（月经用品），Britpop = British + popular（英国流行文化），telecinetele = television + cinema（电视电影），Sysop = system + operator（系统管理员），comsat = communication + satellite（通信卫星），WiFi = Wireless + Fidelity（无线上网）等。

6. 把一个单词插入另一个单词构成新词，如 togayther = together + gay（同性恋同居），intexticated = intoxicated + text（开车时发短信）等。

7. 由一个单词的首部与另一个单词的中间部分构成新词，如：deleb = dead + celebrity（死名，已死的名人），props = proper + respect（尊重）。

8. 由三个或三个以上的单词缩合而成的新词。如 podcasting = Personal Optional Digital Casting（个人自选数字广播），turducken = turkey + duck + chichen（鸡鸭火鸡），gynobibliophobia = gyno + biblio + phobia（讨厌女性作家）。

（二）拼缀词的用途

为使得拼缀词新奇有趣或语言简洁凝练，撰稿人常常在新闻报道或广告中使用拼缀词。例如 newscast（新闻广播），slanguage（俗语），agflation（食品价格通胀），edvertorial（社论广告，即看似社论实际是广告）等。

进行商业谈判或交易中，为引人注目或便于记忆人们常常使用拼缀词。例如：Eurodollar, Eurocurrency 等。

新生科技事物层出不穷，人们创造出与之相应的新拼缀词。因特网的突飞猛进的发展使得计算机和网络英语词汇激增，例如：infonomics（信息经济），infowar（信息战），womenomics（女性经济学），e-mail（电子邮件 electronic + mail），e-English（网络英语），e-business（电子商务），e-library（自动化图书馆），e-money（电子货币），emoticom（情感符），cybrarian（交互式检索软件，数据专家），cyberrealm（网络世界），netizen（网民），cyberpunk（电脑朋克派，一种科幻小说形式），cyberphobia（电脑恐惧症），cybersight（计算机视域），fortran（公式翻译）等。

为了取得某种形式上的效果，如出于幽默、搞笑或讽刺目的，人们使用拼缀词。人们截取政客搭档或夫妻的一部分名字，构成一个新词，形成一个概念，含有讽刺意味。例如：Billary = Bill Clinton + Hilary。而在影视界，如果使用明星夫妻的部分名字构成一个新词则表示大众对他们的喜爱。例如：Bennifer = Ben Affleck + Jennifer Lopez, Brangelina =

Brad Pitt + Angelina Jolie，Tomkat = Tom Cruise + Katie Holmes。而 Beslin Productions 则是 Desi Arnaz 和 Lucille Ball 所拥有的公司。

随着科技、网络、商业广告、报业的飞速发展，具有简练、新奇、幽默和非正式的拼缀词在英语构词中大量涌现，它们的出现丰富了英语语言，使得它们更加富有简洁性、创意性和多样性。

第四篇
当代美国委婉语和习语

第七章　当代美国委婉语

根据牛津字典定义，委婉语是用温和或模糊的或迂回的表达来替代刺耳的或直接的表达。委婉语的交际功能主要体现在以下三方面：避讳功能、礼貌功能和掩饰功能。委婉语在社会生活中起着双重作用。一方面它避免了某些尴尬和不雅的场面，能够体现人们的文化素养。在当今高速发展的社会，人与人之间的交流越发密切，而语言交际又是人类赖以维持社会关系和人际关系的重要手段，因此使用委婉语能避免双方不快从而协调人际关系。可以说，委婉语是社会前进所必需的润滑剂；另一方面，委婉语用得过滥会混淆视听，掩盖本质。例如政治化妆词和疾病委婉语。在现代英语中，委婉语几乎涉及个人和社会生活的方方面面，从政治到生老病死和婚丧嫁娶。委婉语从不同程度上反映出人们普遍接受的说话和行为准则、思维方式和共有的价值观和品行。委婉语亦被称为 gilded words 或 cosmetic words。在当代美国社会，委婉语的产生与美国社会息息相关。委婉语为数众多，运用范围涉及美国社会生活的各个方面。

一　委婉语特性

（一）民族性

不同国家、不同民族所处的自然环境与社会环境不同，他们的生活方式、风俗习惯、价值观念也各有差异，因而语言中的委婉语必然也存在相当大的差异，常常带有较强的民族色彩。棒球是美国人喜爱的运动，棒球大赛是全民关注的赛事，以棒球指代性的委婉语不计其数。如 hitting a home run 指代"第一次约会的性关系"，batting both ways，switch-hitting 或 batting for the other team 指代"双性恋或同性恋"。

（二）地域性

不同的地域有着不同的历史文化，风俗习惯有着很大差异，这种差异体现在语言当中就表现为语言的地域性差异。如 turkey 是美国特有的动物，火鸡肉也是美国人喜食的肉食。肉食店销售的肉类少不了火鸡肉。圣诞大餐和感恩节大餐中火鸡和火鸡食品更是每家餐桌上必不可少的食品。因而美语出现了许多与火鸡有关的委婉语。例如，turkey farm 指代政府或私营机构中那些工作无能，又不能开除的人所待的地方，cold turkey 表示突然戒毒，而 talk turkey 则表示"直率地说或谈正事"，say turkey to one and buzzard to another 表示"厚此薄彼"。

（三）语域性

无论是在不同的语境中，还是在同一语境中，人们由于年龄、身份、地位或受教育程度不同，委婉表达方式也有所不同。例如：上厕所，女士可能说 powder my nose 或 to fresh up；男士可能是说 go to the toilet, to relieve myself, answer nature's calls 或 nature is urgent；而儿童可能说 go to the pot。总体来说，女子使用委婉语的频率高于男子，因为女子比男子更受社会规则约束，说话谨慎小心。

上层人士使用率高于平民，他们为了标榜其高贵，大量使用委婉语。

（四）时代性

社会的需要和发展决定着语言的变化。语言处在不断地变化中，新词不断出现，旧词逐渐消失。作为语言变体的委婉语更是如此。例如：表示"失业、被解雇"的委婉语在英语中曾先后出现如下这些表达方式：从 dismissed, fired, early retired, 到 laid off, furloughed, given the pink slip, downsized, rightsized, capsized, brightsized, smartsized。

（五）模糊性

委婉语是用较不准确的词语去替代那些更加准确的词语。还有很多委婉语利用语言的模糊性，使某些词义扩大得以形成。委婉语的模糊性可以掩饰残酷战争、不幸的疾病和灾难。如伊拉克战争中，美国政府把这场由自己一手发动的不符合国际法的战争命名为 Iraqi Freedom（伊拉克自由之战），标榜此次战争是 for justice and peace（为了正义与和平）。用 shock and wave（震慑行动）和 asymmetric capacity（非对称力量）掩盖军队对于伊拉克进行 48 小时大规模的轰炸，乔治·布什政府创出 Regime change 婉指美国对于伊拉克的政权更迭所进行的军事打击。更是使用 decapitation strike（斩首行动）一词婉指处决伊拉克首脑萨达姆行动。

二　委婉语构成方法

委婉语的构成方法多种多样，丰富多彩，可分为下面几种类型：

（一）传统构词法

1. 合成法（compounding）。两个或两个以上的词合成一个意思的委婉语。如：full figured，extra large 委婉表达 fat。

2. 反成法（backformation）。反成法是通过删除假想中的词缀来构成委婉词。由于这种构词法产词量不大，所以造出的词大多新颖别致，用来代替常见的敏感词，也能收到委婉的效果。如：burgle 由 burglar 删去词尾而成。

3. 首字母组合法（acronym），首字母组合法是用委婉语的第一个字母拼合在一起借以掩饰。如：BM（bowel movement，大便），the Big C（癌症）。

4. 截短法（clipping）。截短法是将一些词语斩头去尾。如：gents（Gentlemen's Room，男厕所），lav（lavatory，厕所）。

5. 替代法（synonyms）。使用同义词或替代词将不愿意启齿的词语隐去。如：用 to the big house 替代 to the jail。

6. 外来借词法（borrowing）。一般认为，英语中的本族词多为平民百姓的口语词，不登大雅之堂。所以很多人，尤其是知识分子和学生都喜欢借用法语词或拉丁词来婉指那些令人尴尬的事物。如：法语中的 toilette 替代英语中的 bathroom。

（二）修辞法

1. 模糊词语法（fuzzy words）。通过泛化原则，把特定的语义给予

149

模糊处理，使之一般化、泛化，以此冲淡人们的厌恶和恐惧之感。如：使用 developing country 和 emerging country 替代 underdeveloped country，senior citizen 替代 old people。

2. 反面着笔法（negation）。从相反的角度去表达那些令人不快的事物，效果有时会比正面直说婉转些。如：使用 unwedding 婉转表达离婚事实（解除婚姻）。用 misspoke 来掩饰发言中所犯下的错误言论。

3. 比喻法（metaphorical transfer）。根据禁忌事物的特点，将其描绘成具有相同特点的可以接受的事物。如：pay nature's debt, left the building, join the majority 等来表示 die。

4. 迂回说法（periphrasis）。迂回说法是将不便直言的事物用拐弯抹角的方式表达出来。结果是"短词长写""短话长说"。如：用 adjustment downward 表示 drop（下跌），cash flow problem 表示 short of cash（资金不足），用 vertically challenged 表示 short，chronologically-challenged 表示 late，用 economical with the truth 替代 liar。

三 委婉语的隐喻及语用

美语委婉语为数众多，其运用范围涉及美国社会生活的各个方面，大致分为以下几个方面：

（一）避讳老病死等消极词汇

老年是人类生存过程中的一个必经阶段。在西方，人们认为衰老意味着思想僵化、知识老化、迟钝，是爱唠叨、固执、怪癖的代名词，他们忌讳变老，因此创造了许多委婉语来替代"老"这个词。例如 senior citizen, getting on years, second childhood, third age, sunset year, elderly people, past one's prime, the longer living, golden ager, distinguished gentleman, the seasoned。养老院就有许多委婉语，如：nursing home, retirement home, elder hostel, private hospital, rest home, golden age club, adult day care center, loneliness industry。虽然疾病是生活中常见的现象，但是一些致命疾病，如癌症、艾滋病都是死亡的代名词。英美人不愿意谈及，即使谈及到，也必须用一些委婉语来替代。如：用缩写 AIDS 替代艾滋病，用 accident 来替代 stroke，flu 代替 influenza（流行感冒），big C 替

代 cancer。死亡委婉语更是如此。死亡是人类不可避免的事实。人们对于它的恐惧永远存在，也是一种普遍的感觉。但是人们不敢直言，也不愿直言。如此一来，死亡的委婉语层出不穷：cross over the Divide，join the majority，last sleep，asleep in Jesus，release，happy release，to go to the heaven，to go to better world，to go to another world，to pay one's debt to nature，to be gone，left the building 等。

（二）生育婚恋委婉语

自 20 世纪 60 年代以来，社会发生巨大变化，妇女地位得到提升，人们的价值观念发生巨大变更，婚姻法随之发生变革。离婚变得易如反掌，美国家庭婚姻发生了裂变。美国的离婚率达到 50%。离婚容易，再婚也不难，产生许多婚姻裂变的衍生物。许多人对婚姻没有信心，不相信白头到老，他们在婚前签署 prenuptial agreement，以免离婚时财产分割不清。婚姻形式多种多样，分别被婉曰 serial marriage（系列婚姻），blended family（混合家庭），marriage of convenience（形式婚姻），starter marriage（起步婚姻），companionate marriage（友爱婚姻），cove-nant marriage（契约婚姻）。离婚被冠以 renovate，unwedding，matchcrupt-cy。非婚同居者美其名曰 cohabitee，companion，paramour，partner。婚外情、婚外恋被粉饰为 affair 或 extramarital affair，夫妻互相容忍对方的外遇或通奸的婚姻被婉称为 open marriage。同居爱人被称为 live-in lover，私生子被婉称为 a love child，outside child，natural child，baby of love，non-wedlock child，irregular child。

同性恋婚姻被称为 same sex marriage 和 broke back marriage。同性恋者出柜被称为 come out of closet。同性恋被称为 queer，homo，same sex person，dyke。男同性恋者被称为 gayboy，queen，closet queen。女同性恋者叫做 lesbian，leslie，fair lady，dyke。lipstick lesbian 为"漂亮优雅的女同性恋"，luppie 表示"女同性恋雅皮士"。当然，同性恋中不乏名人，他们中有很多人是很有名的艺术家、影视明星、体育明星和政治家，他们被称为 celesbian（名人同性恋），他们的曝光率高，承载巨大压力，有时不得不 lanced（被迫承认是同性恋）。

为了避免尴尬，表示文雅，人们创出许多生育的委婉语。例如 in the club，in a family way，eating for two，swallow a watermelon seed，wear the apron high；未婚先孕而结婚被称为 shotgun marriage（奉子成婚）；生孩子被冠以 visit from the stork。

（三）尊重他人，表示礼貌的需要

委婉语在社会语言交际中的恰当使用能增强交谈者的自尊、增强信心，同时还能协调人与人之间的关系，缓解矛盾与冲突，达成和平与谅解。人们用 adult entertainment, adultmaterial, gentlemen's special interest literature 替代 pornography；adult beverages 替代 beer 或 liquor；au natural 替代 naked；chronologically-challenged 表示 late；break wind 表示 pass gas；economical with the truth 替代 liar；用 mentally challenged 替代 with an intellectual disability。金钱社会使得人们嫌贫嫉富，在谈及贫穷或者相关的情况时，为表示尊重，不使对方不快或恼怒，人们使用许多委婉语表达"贫穷"。如 the underprivileged, down and out, to be down on one's luck, low income。教育界人士常常使用积极词汇评价学生，缩小教育者与学生间的距离，维护学生尊严，同时又能起到良好的教育作用。例如：愚钝的学生被婉称为 slow learner, underachiever 等，差生被委婉地称为 below the average。learning difficulties 和 special needs 替代 idiot 和 imbecile。

人们对相貌、体态的说法也十分委婉，体现出对人的尊严的维护，现实生活中的一些实际称呼伤害他人的感情和尊严，造成交际障碍。出于这种原因，美语中出现许多委婉语。例如人们使用 plain, homely 替代 ugly（丑陋的）；用 slim（苗条）或 slender 替代 skinny（皮包骨头）。肥胖的委婉语更是不计其数，如 big, curvy, fluffy, zaftig, plus-sized, thick-boned, full-figured, heavy-set, Rubenesque, extra large, plump, heavy。人们用 vertically-challenged 指代 short, lame 和 disabled 等词被 physically challenged, differently abled, people with disabilities 所替代。

同性恋被委婉地称为 serial bachelor, light in the loafers, confirmed bachelor, rides the bus, friend of Dorothy, lesbian, gay, queer, male-oriented, female oriented 等。the poor 被委婉语 economically depressed, underprivileged 和 culturally deprived 所替代。人们用 I misspoke, bend the truth, white lie, fudge, colour the truth, be economical with the truth, dissemble, political spin, unreliable 替代 tell a lie。用 a little thin on top 表示

bald。打小抄时学生不说 cheat 而是说 peer homework help, comparing answers, collaborating, harvesting answers。一个人如果很怪则被称为 special, unique, 而不是 quirky 或 odd。当别人欠自己的钱时，人们不说 you own me money 而是以 looking forward to settlement of the account 来婉求还钱。仅被解雇、炒鱿鱼就有多种委婉的表达方式：

语气婉转委婉语

laid off

discharged

dismissed

made redundant

furloughed

separated

given the pink slip

outplaced

rifed

bought out

released

unassigned

cut ties

uninstalled

separated

语气强硬，表示"你不在此工作了"

services no longer required

early retired

eased out

forced resignation

stepped down

assignment ended

position eliminated

given the package

released from the talent pool

declined to extend

assignment expired

helped her with exit

going in different directions

one-person layoff

managed out

career transition

career change opportunity

contract not renewed

end of trial period

involuntary separation

freed up for the future

relieved of duties

taking it for the team

promoted to customer (retail workers)

大面积裁员委婉语

downsized

rightsized

capsized

brightsized

dumbsized

smartsized

layoffs and massive layoffs

re-engineered

reorganized

outsourced

headcount reduction / adjustment

heads rolling

decruitment

regime change

make internal efficiencies

contracted out

off shoring / best shoring

streamlining operations

operational simplification

personnel realignment

personnel surplus reduction

reduced headcount

rationalize the workforce

reduction in force

skill mix adjustment

streamlining operations

cutting the fat

workforce adjustment

re-prioritizing labor expenses

slashing, cutting or chopping jobs or positions

trimming the workforce

taking a hard look at expenses

（四）职业委婉语

社会分工的不同，会使得一些人群往往产生低人一等的感觉。他们需要一些委婉语来称呼自己所从事的职业，以期获得人们的尊敬或是避免称呼上的尴尬。反之，其他阶层人士为尊重他人也需要使用委婉语来避免称呼上的尴尬。如将专门的技术工人冠以工程师之类的头衔。如：garbage collector（垃圾清运工）被称为 sanitation engineer（公共卫生工程师）；automobile mechanic（汽车修理工）被称为 automobile engineer（汽车工程师）；secretary（秘书）被称为 administrative assistant（行政助理）；servant（仆人）被呼为 gentleman's gentleman（绅士家的先生）；domestic engineer 被用来指代 maid 等。人们用 correctional facility 指代 prison custodian；caretaker 替代 janitor；transparent-wall maintenance officer 指代 window cleaner；rodent officer 替代 rat-catcher；cemetery operative 替代 gravedigger。为避免尴尬，性工作者被冠以 comfort woman，service provider 被用来指代 sex worker 和 callgirl，exotic dancer 替代 stripper。

155

（五）人体器官与生理现象委婉语

英语中部分表示人体器官、生理现象等方面的词语，传统上一般被人认为是粗俗、猥亵或者是肮脏的，直接说出来不雅，因此往往由另外一些被认为是含蓄或高雅的词语来替代。例如身体排泄物的词汇都被认为是禁忌语，被委婉语所替代。Men's lavatory 被称作 Gent's，the John，the washroom；Women's lavatory 被称作 Lady's，the powder room，Mrs Jones；to urinate 被 take a piss，take a leak，to empty，take a slash，relieve myself，take a whiz，Number one 来替代；shit 被称作 number two；WC 被 restroom 替代。与性有关的词汇也都有替代的委婉说法。有关两性交欢的词语，采用委婉的比喻手法使之含蓄化，如 do it，make love，go to bed with someone，sleep with somebody，intimacy，fraternalize，get laid，screw，score，go all the way，the birds and the bees，hide the sausage，making whoopee。Condoms 被人们冠为 rubbers，sheaths，love gloves。Thomas 被用来婉指"控告性骚扰者"，hit on sb 婉指性骚扰。所有这些词经过委婉语的修饰，就可以堂而皇之地使用了。

（六）粉饰美化事实真相的战争政治委婉语

委婉语也常被政客们和媒体利用，用来美化或粉饰事实真相。美国在军事上常常使用委婉语掩盖侵略战争的本质。involvement（介入）被用来替代 aggression（侵略）。明明是进攻，却美其名曰 preventive war（防御性战争），active defense（主动防御），似乎是为了制止战争不得已而为之，以此掩饰侵略的本质。air strike 是战争的委婉表达，给人的印象是自己的行为是为了遏制他人的行为而发生的，从而企图掩盖其发动战争的不道德性和非正义性。美国政客和媒体还创出 panda hugger（熊猫拥抱者）一词，表示美国亲中国派，hawk 婉指美国鹰派。bamboo curtain（竹帘）被用来指共产主义国家。从越南战争到海湾战争，再到最近的伊拉克战争，美国政府在四处出兵的同时从来不忘为自己的军事行动作一番"辞令包装"。

美国在"越战"时期，为了掩盖其暴行，创造过大批委婉语。他们把空中的狂轰滥炸说成是 logistical strikes（后勤行动）和 close air support（近距离空中支援），用 wasting the enemy（消耗敌人）表示杀戮，本来是 civilian casualties（平民伤亡）却粉饰为 collateral damage（附带损伤）；明明是进攻却换成 pacify the area（绥靖）；本来是 destroying crop（毁灭庄稼），却掩饰为 defoliation（落叶行动）；明明是 aggression（入侵）却被掩饰成 police action（警察行动）；等等。

委婉语的使用，不仅对外缓和战争的影响，对内也满足了美国民众在道德、个人利益之间的平衡感，使美国政府更加冠冕堂皇地博得美国民众的支持。在以美国为首的北约对南联盟的这场"战争游戏"中，美国国防部宣布有一些美国大兵"have joined the immortals"（加入了不朽者的行列），替代阵亡，借此来淡化战争的残酷，昭示士兵的伟大。1983年，美国把入侵格林纳达标榜为 a rescue mission（援救任务），空袭利比亚掩饰为 surgical attack（外科手术式的打击），用 Operation Restore Hope（重拾希望行动），表示其入侵行动为索马里人道主义和维和行动。美国政府和媒体把入侵伊拉克行动粉饰为 Operation Iraqi Freedom（自由伊拉克行动）。把大量杀伤性武器（WMD——Weapons of Mass Destruction）称为 Cruise, Scud, Tiny Tim, Honest John, Blood Hound, Hound-dog, Davy Crocket, Exocet, ICBM-intercontinental ballistic missile。海湾战争时空中轰炸和地面进攻偷袭分别被婉称为 air operation（空中行动），air support（空中支援），air interdiction（空中封锁），ground operation（地面行动），preemptive defense（先发制人的进攻）。

阿富汗战争也不乏委婉语。美国把自己侵入他国称为 presence，对塔利班的控制称为 pacification action 和 crisis humanitarian intervention（危机人道主义干预）。与他们的交火称为（armed）conflict 或 tension。刺杀行动婉称为 targeted killing（定点清除）。对于俘虏的刑讯逼供美化为 enhanced interrogation technique（强化审讯技术）。美国还把阿拉伯一些国家政变美其名曰 Arab Spring（阿拉伯之春）。

核武器杀伤力无敌，为了掩盖其攻击力和杀伤力，美国社会给予它体面的名称。如 counterforce weapon（打击敌对部队导弹），counter value weapons（攻击城市的导弹），nukespeake（核语言）。核事故被轻描淡写地冠以 incident 或 event（事件）。虽然核反应堆几近爆炸并可能失控，但还是被谨慎地称为 superprompt critical（超瞬发临界事故）。

美国新闻中出现的战争委婉语美化政府形象，颠倒是非，为他们不得人心的政策和无能以及战争罪行辩解、开脱。例如，在2003年伊拉

克战争爆发后，我们可以在 VOA 中听到出现频率最高的词语 disarm Iraq
（解除伊拉克武装）和 take military action against Iraq（对伊拉克采取军
事行动）。这两个委婉语躲开了 at war，attack，invasion，aggression 等敏
感的字眼，达到了委婉的效果。

美国政客还惯于使用委婉语，隐藏自己的政治目的，对于一些过错
欲盖弥彰。在语言上倾向于使用委婉语达到这些目的。例如，间谍被冠
以 source，undercover，operator。水门事件中盗窃情报的人员被美化成
plumber。motivation（动机）被用来替代 bribe（贿赂）。take legal action
（采取法律行动）被用来替代 sue（控告）。委婉语 glass ceiling 被用来表
示女性在职场提升上的困难，glass wall 婉指其他种族在职位上难以提升
的尴尬境地。反政府人士被称作 dissident（持不同政见者），riot（骚
动）被称为 disturbance（扰乱）。罢工被说成 walk-out 和 down tools，而
不是 strike。

里根入主白宫后，便开始增税，违背了竞选时向美国大众所做减税
的许诺，在为他的增税政策辩护时，里根大谈 revenue enhancement（增
收财源），避谈 tax increase（增税），粉饰他违背诺言的行为。2008 年美
国经受了前所未有的经济危机，政客们将经济危机委婉说成 economic
downturn，economic slow down 或 cashflow problem。

美国虽然是一个高度法制的民主国家，但是其犯罪率居高不下，持
枪杀人的暴力事件时有发生。为了避免这些不雅说法，人们使用大量的
委婉语：偷窃被称为 to hook，to palm，to work the hole，to walk away with。
抢劫被婉称为 to put arm on，to break a jug。进监狱被委婉地说成 drop into the bucket，do time，to walk the last mile。毒品分别被婉称为 lady snow，
joy powder。吸毒后产生幻觉被称为 trip out。吸毒者的聚会被称作 big
party 或 smoke-in。

英语委婉语不仅能淡化禁忌语及粗俗语，还起着净化语言的作用，
它起着推动社会前进的重要作用。委婉语的使用已经成为对所涉及敏感
话题进行交际的最佳方式之一。作为一种语言变体的委婉语，它的社会
语言学研究具有捕获人类思维和目的的作用。外语学习者若掌握委婉语
并在交际中恰到好处地应用委婉语，将会在社交语境中立于不败之地。
随着人类文明程度和品德修养的提高，委婉语的使用将会无处不在，使
用委婉语的人也将越来越多。

第八章　当代美国习语

一　习语的概念

对于什么是习语，词典和学者所下的定义并不尽相同。原因是他们对于习语理解的视角不同。牛津英语字典的定义：a group of words established by usage as having a meaning not deducible from those of the individual words. (*New Oxford Dictionary of English*, 1998)

美国韦伯斯特大字典是这样下的定义：Idiom is an expression established in the usage of a language that is peculiar to itself either in grammatical construction or in having a meaning that can't be derived as a whole from the conjoined meanings of its elements. (*Webster's Third New World International Dictionary*, 1976)

学者对于习语的定义多种多样，下面看看两个具有代表性的观点：

An idiom is a set phrase of two or more words that means something different from the literal meaning of the individual words. (Ammer, 1997) (习语是两个或多个词组成的固定词组，它的意义与各组成词的字面意义不同)

An idiom is a combination of two or more words which functions as a unit of meaning. (Cowie, 1975) (习语是两个或多个词的结合，它们起到一个语义单位的作用)

另外还有 McCarthy, Cooper, Carter, Moon, Wray and Perkins 等。这些专家对于习语的界定各有侧重，有的界定范围宽，有的范围窄，有的强调语义，有的强调语用，有的强调结构。各有所长，各有利弊。综合以上定义，可把习语归纳为语音、词法和句法形式相对固定的表达方式，表达完整意义，其意义不能从各个部分的意义推断出来。

习语是在英语的长期发展过程中提炼出来的相对固定的语言形式，是英语的民族形式和各种修辞手段的集中表现，包括比喻性词组（metaphorical phrases）、俚语（slang）、俗语（colloquialism）、谚语（proverb）等等，是英语词汇中不可或缺的重要组成部分。

二 美语习语的特征

美语习语在英语中广泛应用于会话、讲座、电影、电视节目口语体和报纸、杂志等各种书面材料中。英语习语有广义和狭义之分。广义的美语习语包括口语体、谚语、格言等。它具有三个较为重要的特点。

（一）语义的整体性

内容的整体性是指组成的各个词表示一个整体意义而不是表示单个词的意义。例如，Glass ceiling 是由惠普公司的管理人员 Katherine Lawrence 和 Marianne Schreiber 于 1976 年在发表的文章中提出的。它主要描述的是无形的种族或性别歧视阻碍女性和有色人种在事业上获得提升，虽然表面上看来提升之路一片平坦。它不是 glass 加上 ceiling 单个词汇的字面意义组合。

其他例子还有 quit cold turkey 在美语中表示"戒毒"或"戒酒"，get laid 是"发生性关系"，get with it 表示"开门见山直截了当说"，power lunch 和 power breakfast 表示"一起吃早饭或午饭，并商谈事务"。The glass is half empty 表示"悲观的人"。shoot for the stars 表示"某人目标高远、追求卓越"。又如名词性的俗语俚语：Target A 表示"美国白宫"，New York's Finest 代表"纽约市的警察"，bottle neck 表示"交通路口的瓶颈"。eye candy 是"养眼物品或尤物"，arm candy 表示"蜜糖伴侣"，nose candy 是"可卡因"的别称。steal one's thunder 表示"抢了某人的风头"，spill the beans 指"泄露秘密"等。这些习语无法通过组成它们的单词来推断整个习语的意思，整个习语表示一个完整的意义。

有的习语也可能有其字面意思，但它作为习语的意义（比喻意义）必须是其修辞意义。例如，over the hill 的字面意义是"在山那边"，而作为固定习语的意义是"古老的"。更多的例子还有 A sight for sore eyes（极受欢迎的人），a close shave（侥幸脱险），to get the ball rolling（使某种活动开始起来）等。

还有一些习语通过普通词汇创造出来的新词进行搭配，使这两个结构相似的词素进行重叠，以构成一个叠音词，许多是不能从字面猜测出字义的。如 tiptop（非常杰出的），super-duper（特别大而引人注目的，显著的），lovey-dovey（挚爱的，多情的），chitchat（亲切而闲适的谈话），ding-dong（精神饱满的，坚强的），dilly-dally（游手好闲），hugger-mugger（邋遢的），fuddy-duddy（老古板），whishy-washy（优柔寡断的），hocus-pocus（诡计），razzle-dazzle（欺诈行为），wiggle-waggle（摇摆，聊天，嚼）。

（二）结构的固定性

习语形势比较固定，常常被认为是固定词组。它的固定性表现在三个方面。一是词语的词序比较固定，不能随意更改。例如，head over heel 的意思是"完全"，不能改成 heel over head。二是不能任意增减单词，一字之差会导致误义。例如 been there done that 表示"经历过"，不能改成 have been there，did that。三是不能随便更改单词。如 Top-notch（最出众的人或其他东西）不能改成 high-notch，这些词的更改会让人疑惑不解或造成歧义。

需要说明的是，在实际生活中，由于语言使用者出于需要，对于习语进行处理，其表现效果比原来的习语形式更加生动形象，言简意赅。这种对于语言的灵活运用被称为语言的变体，也是新习语产生的根源。例如，birds of a feather meeting（电脑技术贸易展），The dead lion is in preference to the live dog（宁要死狮不要活狗）等。

（三）字面理解困难性

绝大多数习语不是独立单词意义构成的总和，从字面上很难猜到它们的含义，这就造成理解上的困难。它们带有浓厚的民族、地理、文化和历史色彩，造成理解上的难度。例如，white bread 在美国不但超市有卖，就连廉价药店 Walgreen 的柜台上通常都会摆满名为 Wonder 牌的白面包。这种面包是典型的美式面包，平淡无味，比较细腻，容易消化。所以一直是美国人餐桌上必不可少的食物。鉴于白面包的特性，美国人常常用 white bread 指那些中规中矩、平凡无味、非常直白的美国人。他们的特点是：盲目消费、具有从众心理。他们住在中产阶级所独有的那种方方正正的房子里，信奉基督教，持保守的政治观点，并且大多从事白领职业。

美国人对糖和甜食喜爱有加，因而创造出 eye candy，表示"某些人和东西只能用来养眼，但拿不来或不属于自己"。例如，女伴们在一起逛街，看到一件很漂亮又性感的上衣，但价格不菲又不适合平时穿，考虑再三，女伴会劝说道：

You can look if you want, but we both know that's just not for you, it's only eye candy. （你如果想看看可以，但是你知道那不适合你，好看但不实用。）

而 He wanted to put some eye candy on their web site 则表示"网站上的图片或广告看起来美丽，但实际上很肤浅，华而不实"。

eye candy 另外一个含义是"非常性感、吸引人的女性"，例如：

When I was walking the mall I scoped out some nice eye candy. （我在购物中心闲逛时发现了一个美女。）

三　美语习语分类

专家学者为了便于学生掌握习语，从不同方面对习语进行分类，如按构成习语的主词分类、按主题分类、按英语和汉语习语的异同分类等。

（一）按构成习语的主词分类

有些单词可以与不同的介词、副词等搭配形成习语，如：to come a-bout（发生，产生），to come across（偶然遇见），to come up（出现），to come round（苏醒，恢复健康）。eat a humble pie, as American as apple pie, to have a finger in the pie（多管闲事；干涉）。to lift a finger（尽举手之劳），with a wet finger（毫不费力地），to let... slip through one's fingers（让机会溜走）。

（二）按习语内在的暗喻主题分类

我们的世界观反映在我们用以描述世界的习语中。例如，下列句子中的习语都反映了"Time is money."这一主题。You're wasting my time.（你在浪费我的时间）。This device will save you hours.（这种装置可以节省时间）。How do you spend your time?（你是如何支配时间的）？You need to budget your time.（你需要对时间进行预算）。He's living on borrowed time.（他侥幸地活了下来）。

（三）按来源分类

习语的来源非常丰富。它们来源于历史事件、寓言、故事等。如，来源于《圣经》的习语有：to cast one's bread upon the waters（做好事不图报答），cast pearls before swine（对牛弹琴），Job's news（噩耗，坏消息）等；来源于历史的习语有：to send sb. to Coventry（拒绝和某人来往），to do a Dunkirk（仓促撤退）等。

（四）按功能分类

为了便于掌握习语的用法，也便于记忆，学习者可以按功能来分类习语，这样可以提高记忆效率。例如，可以将电话中用来表示祝贺、致谢、赞美或对赞美作答的习语分别进行归类。电话中经常使用的习语有to make a phone call（打电话），answer the phone（回电话），on the phone（在打电话），over the phone（用电话），hold the line（别挂断），hang up（挂断）等。

（五）按语法和结构分类

按语法和结构可以将习语分成动词性习语、名词性习语、形容词性习语和副词性习语。

动词性习语。如 black out（封锁，涂掉），zero in on（向……集中火力），face the music（勇于承担后果），fall flat（完全失败），bad mouth（说某人坏话），go nuts（发疯）等。

名词性习语。如 narrow escape（九死一生），a friend at court（有势力的朋友），little green man（小绿人，外星人）等。

形容词习语。fair and square（正大光明的），up in the air（悬而未决的），as cool as a cucumber（泰然自若的）等。

副词性习语。heart and soul（全心全意地），behind the scenes（在幕

后），with flying colors（成功地）等。

（六）按修辞方法分类

按习语的修辞方法进行分类不但能够便于掌握习语，而且还可以提高使用修辞的意识。习语中常涉及的修辞方法有比喻、拟人、夸张等。

比喻：like a cat on hot bricks（像热锅上的蚂蚁），a wolf in sheep's clothing（衣冠禽兽）。

拟人：a walking dictionary（活字典），firendly gestures（友好的姿态）。

夸张：split hairs（鸡蛋里挑骨头），blow one's top（勃然大怒）。

（七）按语体色彩分类

英语习语按语体色彩可以分为属于口语、俚语以及书面语和口语共核部分。这种分类便于培养学生使用语言的得体性。例如，带有口语色彩的习语有 take it easy（别太在意），under the weather（不舒服，有病），run the show（掌管一切）等。俚语习语如 to carry the can（代人受过），be in Dutch（处于困境），to chance the duck（不管三七二十一，冒险）。共核部分的习语数量最大，如 hold up（阻塞），in short（简而言之），to let loose（放手，松手）等。

（八）按与母语的异同分类

英语习语和汉语习语有三种类型的关系：对应关系、半对应关系和不对应关系。对应关系指两种语言的习语在语义和形象上都是一致的。例如，to burn one's boats（破釜沉舟），lose（one's）face（丢脸），like fish out of water（如鱼离水）。这些习语对中国学生非常容易，因为在两种语言中这些习语是相似的。但是，具有这种对应关系的只是少数习语。大量的习语在两种语言中只是部分对应或完全不同的。

最难理解和掌握的是在两种语言中无任何对应关系的习语，如 Dutchman's courage（酒后之勇），black and blue（鼻青脸肿），Hobson's choice（无选择余地），a Jack in office（自命不凡的小官吏）等。hands of sb/sth. 是"断绝关系，推卸责任"不是"洗手（不干）"；pull one's leg 是"开玩笑"；handwriting on the wall 是"不祥之兆"；an apple of love

是"西红柿"。

（九）按语义分类

学术界把表示不同语义，如不同情绪、不同动作、不同态度等的习语进行分类比较。还有的习语按不同领域来进行分类，便于学习者学习。这在新习语学习中占了很大一部分，下面进行逐一介绍。

1. 医学整形：美国是世界整形美容超级大国，各种整形手术都有可能被完美地实现。为了 perma-youth（驻颜）和美丽，人们进行 plastic surgery 或 cougar lift（整形），breast augumentation，lip enhancement，eyelide surgery，tummy tuck 等美容整形手术。

2. 经济：这类词有：nailing jelly to a tree（处理烂摊子），open the kimono（揭露），put skin in the game（巨大投资），put the pants on it（补充），starve the beast（饥饿疗法），bucket list（一生计划），cockcroach problem（棘手问题），drop your pants（清仓降价），eat what you kill（应得的财富），juggle eggs（完成难度大的任务），low hanging fruit（容易的任务）等。

3. 社会生活：这类习语有：prenuptial agreement，dirty old man，office park dad，waitress mom，soccer mom，speed date，tom boy，honey trap，low profile，power nap，eye candy，window shop，trophy wife，brokeback marriage，wedding moon，destination marriage。此外还有 parellel parenting，leather spinster，toxic bachelor，cradle robber，gold digger，sugar daddy，sugar mom，shotgun marriage，unwedding ceremony，migratory divorce、bling-bling，shopgrifting，flip flop，alpha girl，alpha mom，bright collar，open collar，distance work，silver collar，couch potato，mouse potato，rat race，veg out，go nuts，go green，peaches and cream，slow food，spinach cinema，top banana，white bread，cold turkey，social butterfly，house sit，petsit，lame duck，white elephant。dinner table test（晚饭桌测试，是否礼貌），dog that caught the car（获得一个目标没有下一个目标），drink the kool aid（坚定信奉者），face palm（掩面失望）等更是最近较新的习语。

4. 汽车：car schooling（在车中教育孩子），windshield time（车上工作时间），car cloning（汽车克隆），cut and shut（别车），phantom accident（碰瓷），bait car（诱饵汽车），speed bump（减速坡），mobile

speedbump（流动减速坡），road rage（路怒族），walking bus（健走人形校车）。有些人宠爱 cuddle tech（大众车新车技术），成为 beetlemania（甲壳虫车迷）。有些人吃住在 motor homes 里，露营者们开着 tent trailers（篷式拖车），sport utility vehicle（运动型多功能汽车）成为大众推崇的车型。

5. 政治：punch out computer cards（打卡投票），rolling-pin vote（家庭妇女的选票），secret ballot（无记名投票），blood diamonds（血色钻石），chicken hawk（逃兵），dark biology（生化武器研究），White watergate（白水事件）。mission from god（上帝使命，不容失败），moon the giant（挑战巨人，蔑视），more cold bell（更上一层楼），throw it over the wall（部门互踢球），torch-and-pitchfork（暴民），wave a dead chicken（无益但必要的步骤）。共和党支持率较高的州在大选地图上用红色标示，被称为 red state，而 blue state 则代表支持民主党的州等。

6. 体育与休闲：zen house（瑜伽屋），forest bathing（森林浴），apple tourism（采摘苹果），extreme tourism（极限旅游），black-water rafting（黑水漂流），glacier walk（冰川健走），chick lit（女性文学），lad lit（青少年文学），misery lit（悲惨题材文学），issue literature（问题文学），Kmart realism（描写工人阶级奋斗的现实主义文学），lad mag（青少年杂志）。

7. 语言：Murphy willing（不出错的话），this close（如此接近），bad hair day（坏发型日），get a life（获得新生活），break a leg（祝好运），blow off（放鸽子），head over heels（完全，彻底），could care less（一点也不在乎），knock off（停止），have no beef with（没有关系），hear from grapevine（小道消息），rain check（改日），full of beans（精力充沛）等。

8. 科学技术：social swarming（社交聚会），social networking（社交网络交流），social notworking（工作时间浏览社交网络），social networking fatigue（社交网络疲劳），socially produced（合作创建的网络），social book marking（网址收藏夹），tweet up（网友见面），tweet seats（剧院推特专位，专供观众上网发微博的座位），zombie computer（僵尸电脑），mousetrapping（捕鼠陷阱）。guru site（权威网站），multiple-channel shopping（多渠道购物），birds of a feather meeting（电脑技术贸易

展），pajama hadeen（揭错博客），rain dance（雨中舞，查找电脑故障），sucking mud（网络电脑瘫痪），electric can opener question（电动起罐器问题）等。

四 习语的变体

虽然英语具有固定不变和语义整体的特征，在实际生活中，由于语言使用者出于需要，对于习语进行处理，其表现效果比原来的习语形式更加生动形象，言简意赅。这种对于语言的灵活运用被称为语言的变体，由于长期的习用性，原来精辟、寓意深刻的习语逐渐失去它们的光泽，最终被淘汰。人们在使用习语时，不断丰富它们的内涵与外延，不仅赋予习语以新的活力，而且通过对已有习语的创新增加了语言的表现力，丰富了习语的宝库。

英语变体语言具有创造出无数个句子的潜在可能性，它本身具有创造性。社会文化不断地发展，出于语言经济原则，加上交际过程中语境的约束和人们求新求异的心理，导致美语习语具有临时变体的特性。

美语习语的临时变体较为多样，人们对习语组成部分进行增扩、减缩、替换、拆分、移位等，赋予习语新意，使其成为新习语，增加了习语的表现力。

1. 增扩：就是在原有习语中加上修饰性成分，以限制其内容，赋予其新意。如：carpeted ivory towers（舒适的象牙塔）来自 ivory tower（象牙塔），live a hand to mouth life（勉强糊口的生活）来自 from hand to mouth。

2. 减缩：通过减字或使用连字符等手法把原有习语改造，使其短小精悍，便于灵活使用，压缩而成的新词基本保持原有习语的意义，但往往也会引起词性转换。如：birds of a feather meeting（电脑技术贸易展）是 birds of a feather get together 的减缩，截取前半部分省略后半部分。

3. 替换式：主要是改换原有习语中的个别单词，如一些名词、动词、介词、冠词、代词等。也就是说，原有习语的框架和比喻关系基本不变，但习语的基本意义有所变化，能达到特定的修辞效果。如：like mother like daughter（有其母必有其女）来自 like father like son（有其父必有其子）。down and out（贫困潦倒）来自 down but not out（潦而不倒）。Wine was thicker than blood（酒浓于血）来自 Blood is thicker than water（血浓于水）。keep up with the Wangs 是 keep up with the Joneses（与邻居攀比物质方面的享受）的变体。go with the stream 来自 flow with the tide（随波逐流）。whine and dine（吃饭和抱怨）是 wine and dine（盛宴款待）的变体。

4. 重新排列式，即灵活安排习语中对应的两个成分，颠倒其次序。例如：the canary had swallowed the cat 是习语 The cat had swallowed the canary（自鸣得意，踌躇满志）的重新组合。from riches to rages（由富变贫）来自 from rags to riches（由贫变富）。

美语习语的临时变体在习语精练简洁的特点上增添了新奇生动的文体效果，既避免了陈词滥调，又做到了通俗易懂，进一步增强了语言的表达力和艺术感染力；同时，习语变体弥补了原习语在表达新事物、新现象或新的经验领域的不足，增强了语言表达的精确性和形象性；此外，习语变体是在"说话人对受话者共有知识和语言文化背景的假设"基础上对原有习语所做的合乎当前交际情境的恰当改变，它容易在说话人与受话者之间产生认同感，从而缩短了交际双方的距离，是交际双方互动关系的直接体现。

第五篇
美语新词语研究与新词语翻译
原则和方法

第九章　美语新词语研究

abroadness　n.

English definition：state of being outside of one's country of residence for the purpose of higher education

Chinese equivalent：出国深造

type of word formation：derivation from abroad（overseas，usually for the purpose of studying）and-ness（a noun-forming suffix）

context：I'm going to be really burned out after four years of Rice，so I'm looking forward to a little abroadness.

www. rice. ruf. edu

active aging　n.

English definition：an aging process in which people remain active physically and mentally

Chinese equivalent：积极变老

word formation：compounding from active and aging

context：EIWH is anxious to stress that disease and disability，depression and dependency are not inevitable accompaniments to growing old，that good policies can and do make a difference. The buzzword in gerontology circles at the moment is "active" ageing.

——Aine McCarthy，"Research bias against women"，The Irish Times，July 22，1996

affluenza　n.

English definition：an extreme form of materialism in which consumers overwork and accumulate high levels of debt to purchase more goods

Chinese equivalent：富裕病

type of word formation：blending affluence and influenza

context：Our society is more troubled by problems of overabundance. We are three times richer than in the 1950s, and diseases particular to "affluenza" clog our social and individual arteries. We are more overworked, more stressed, more depressed and much fatter....

—Anne Manne, "Sell Your Soul And Spend, Spend, Spend," Syndey Morning Herald, April 14, 2003

agritourism　n.

English definition：a tourist who watches and participates in agricultural activities

Chinese equivalent：农业观光

type of word formation：blend of agriculture and tourism

context：Agricultural tourism is a commercial enterprise at a working farm, ranch or agricultural plant conducted for the enjoyment or education of visitors, and that generates supplemental income for the owner.

sfp. ucdavis. edu/agritourism/30 Nov 2012

airrage　n.

English definition：an airline passenger's physical or verbal assault of crew members or other passengers

Chinese equivalent：飞行愤怒族

type of of word formation：analogy from road rage

context：Three (passengers) helped to pin down and handcuff (another passenger) after he threatened to kill the pilot and headbutt a passenger, smashed a seat and indecently assaulted a stewardess in an hour of mid-air mayhem.

http：//wordspy. com

alpha earner　n.

English definition：a wife who earns all or most of her household's income

Chinese equivalent：养家太太

type of word formation：compounding from alpha and earner

context：They call them the new alpha earners. They are women, they bring home America's bacon and they are set to take over.

—Joanna Walters, "America's alpha career women leave men at the kitchen sink," The Observer, May 18, 2003

alpha geek n.

English definition：The person with the most technological prowess in an office or department

Chinese equivalent：技术达人

type of word formation：compounding from alpha and geek

context：Those who study apes call the dominant member of the group the "alpha male". In the office or workplace, the most technically knowledgeable person often is called the alpha geek, reports Wired magazine.

— "Handbook for Retirees Answers Big Questions," The Orlando Sentinel, October 26, 1n. The dominant woman in a group of mothers, 1995

anchor store n.

English definition：a major retailer in a shopping mall, particularly one that attracts many customers to the mall

Chinese equivalent：锚店

type of word formation：compounding from anchor and store

context：Many malls will have two to five anchor stores strategically placed around the cluster of smaller stores that are found at the core of the layout of the mall.

wisegeek. com

ape diet n.

English definition：a vegetarian diet that emphasizes soy protein, soluble fiber, nuts, and leafy green vegetables

Chinese equivalent：类猿餐，素食

Type of word formation：compounding from ape and diet

context：The ape diet, heavy in whole grains, nuts, soy and fruits and vegetables, is also cheaper than medicine, has fewer side effects and, if properly prepared, tastes a heck of a lot better.

— "WWKD?" Salt LakeTribune, July 26, 2003

apple picking n.

English definition：snatching a person's iPhone, iPad, or iPod

Chinese equivalent：偷抢苹果系列通信设备，行为

type of word formation：compounding from apple and present participle of picking

context：Nabbing electronic devices isn't new. But lately it is growing "exponentially" according to a 2011 report from the New York Police Department. The lucrative secondhand market for today's niftiest handsets has produced an explosion in "Apple picking" by thieves. A used iPad or iPhone can fetch more than $400.

—Rolfe Winkler, "Fighting the iCrime Wave," The Wall Street Journal, July 27, 2012

apple tourism n.

English definition：a person whose vacation consists of visiting apple orchards and purchasing apples and apple-related products

Chinese equivalent：苹果采摘

type of word formation：compounding from apple and tourism

context：At harvest time, it is not uncommon to see enormous buses—the kind you see taking gamblers to casinos on the East Coast—pull up in front of roadside stands around the state and disgorge scores of apple tourists.

—John Seabrook, "Crunch" (subscription required), The New Yorker, November 21, 2011

arm candy n.

English definition: an extremely beautiful person who accompanies a member of the opposite sex to a party or event, but is not romantically involved with that person

Chinese equivalent: 蜜糖伴侣

type of word formation: analogy from eye candy

context: Now that gossip and society columnists are popularizing the phrase "arm candy" to refer to an attractive young thing who is escorted by an older, more powerful person for others to eye appreciatively, how long will it be before they begin using a companion term, 'room candy,' for a similarly attractive young thing who is invited to receptions or parties for decorative purposes?

—Stuart Elliot, "Twenty, count 'em, 20 questions on media and marketing to astound and amaze your friends," The New York Times, November 30, 1998

—Marcia Froelke Coburn, "Marilyn's enduring appeal," Chicago Tribune, August 21, 1992

arrival city n.

English definition: a slum, shantytown, neighborhood, or other urban area that serves as an initial destination for a large population of rural migrants or foreign immigrants

Chinese equivalent: （移民）首到城市

type of word formation: compounding from arrival and city

context: The capital became, as it remains, an "arrival city", crammed with new communities: first from rural England, then Wales and Ireland, then continental Europe, then the former Empire, then the whole world.

—Boyd Tonkin, "Brenton Brown, By Alex Wheatle," The Independent, August 12, 2011

auto-eating n.

English definition: eating without thinking or without being hungry

175

Chinese equivalent：机械地吃东西

type of word formation：derivation from auto and eating

context：Women can munch their way into a bigger dress size in weeks by "auto-eating" the calorie equivalent of a Big Mac a day. . . . Boredom is the main reason for auto-eating.

—Jo Willey, "Boredom makes women put on weight," Daily Express, May 24, 2010

bait car　n.

English definition：A vehicle, monitored by the police, that is used to tempt a car thief into stealing it

Chinese equivalent：诱饵车，钓鱼执法车

type or word formation：compounding from bait and car

context："Sometimes we have a bait car, put a device in it and see whether it is disturbed," McCormick said. "But this is such a quick act. You need a law enforcement officer right there."

—Terry Richard, "Prevention can stop car clouts on the prowl at forest parking lots," Portland Oregonian, October 18, 1989

baller　n.

English definition：any ballplayer that has significant talent and some sort of reputation with women

Chinese equivalent：受女球迷喜欢的天才球员

type of word formation：clipping (ballplayer)

context：Did you see that convertible? He is such a baller!

www. rice. ruf. edu

beat　n.

English definition：ugly

Chinese equivalent：丑陋；难看

type ofword formation：zero derivation/semantic change

context：I wouldn't want to go out with her; she's beat.

176

www. rice. ruf. edu

big hair houses n.

English definition: a house that has a garish style and that is overly large compared to its lot size and to the surrounding houses

　　Chinese equivalent: 豪宅

　　type of word formation: analogy from big hair

　　context: Yet the newest residential rage in Dallas is the antithesis of the traditional neighborhood: the gated community. Depending on your income and level of anxiety, these private enclaves may contain golf courses, health clubs and equestrian centers, surrounded by big hair houses of indecipherable pedigree and protected round the clock by cameras and private police.

　　—David Dillon, "Where we live: Dallas' neighborhoods," The Dallas Morning News, May 2, 1999

biodiesel n.

English definition: a truck and bus fuel made from discarded restaurant grease

　　Chinese equivalent: 地沟油，生态油

　　type of word formation: affixation of bio-to diesel

　　context: One industry source suggests that a biodiesel fuel made from a less expensive product, like grease, could be more viable.

　　—Caroline Humer, "Vegetable oils play role in alternative fuels industry," Chemical Marketing Reporter, April 6, 1992

birther n.

English definition: a person who believes that U. S. president Barack Obama was not born in the United States, and is therefore ineligible to be president

　　Chinese equivalent: 奥巴马非美国生的坚信者

　　type of word formation: affixation of -er to birth

　　context: Last December, in dismissing the birth-certificate argument as a "canard," Gilbert wrote, "The 'birthers' are the new 'truthers.'" Soon, birther met its counterpart, deather — that is, someone who insists that health care reform will lead to "death panels" eager to pull the plug on "granny."

——Leslie Savan, "On Language: From Simple Noun to Handy Partisan Put-Down," The New York Times, November 18, 2009

bling-bling n.

English definition: shiny metal trinkets, necklaces; objects of luxury

Chinese equivalent: 亮晶晶的首饰、饰品

type of word formation: sound symbolism

context: Many of today's popular TV shows, from "Entertainment To-night" and "Access Hollywood" to practically anything on the E Channel, suggest we've become a bling-bling society. TV specials showcase the opulence of our favorite entertainers — Ben Affleck, Jennifer Lopez, Will Smith, etc. Newscasts report the price of diamonds and other jewelry worn by stars at popular award shows.

——Davey D, "Fixation on bling-bling isn't limited to hip-hop," San Jose Mercury News, August 8, 2003

blogbrity n.

English definition: a famous or popular blogger

Chinese equivalent: 名人博客

type of word formation: blend of blog and celebrity

context: It's been quite a turnaround for Hilton, who said that before becoming a blogebrity he had been in a deep depression and last year filed for bankruptcy and was fired from a job at a celebrity weekly magazine.

——Erin Carlson, "Love him or loathe him, celebrity blogger Perez Hilton says he'll 'always be an outsider'," The Associated Press, November 6, 2006

bridezilla n.

English definition: a woman (about to be married) who is exceptionally spoiled, meticulous and domineering especially about details of her wedding.

Chinese equivalent：新娘狂躁症

type of ord formation：blend from bride and Godzilla

context：bridezilla "They are perfectly normal women — until they get a ring," says Ms Spaemme. "They run around screaming：'It is my day! Bow down and kiss my feet!' They demand attention, gifts and money and treat family and friends like servants.

—Steffi Kammerer, "Drama, chaos, greed and a white dress," The Dallas Morning News, August 27, 2002

bridorexia n.

English definition：the regimen of restricted diet or exercise, undertaken in order to lose weight during the time period leading to her wedding day, especially to fit into her wedding dress

Chinese equivalent：新娘养生，新娘节食

type of word formation：blend of bride and anorexian

context：But some brides might be taking it too far. A new term has been creeping around magazine articles lately called "bridorexia." It's where women starve themselves weeks even months before the wedding so they can "get skinny" by the big day.

www. abslocal. com

bowling-alone adj.

English definition：not participating in the social life of a community

Chinese equivalent：自己玩，自己打保龄球

type of word formation：metaphor

context：Individuals now lead more atomised and anonymous lives in which they are more likely to be watching television and "bowling alone" than participating in collective activities alongside politicians.

—Robert Buddan, "MPs, careers, and salary controversies," The Gleaner, February 16, 2003

brick-and-mortar adj.

English definition: describes a site that has a physical presence in the real world (as opposed to a virtual presence in the online world)

Chinese definition: 实体店的

type of word formation: compounding from brick and mortar

context: No single company has been able to succeed thus far as an online threat to brick-and-mortar shopping malls anchored by giants such as Wal-Mart, Target or Sears. If Amazon does—and analysts say the chances are good—it could be a booster rocket for electronic commerce in the consumer market.

—Steve Rosenbush, "Amazon will be a Net mall," USA Today, September 30, 1999

brokeback marriage n.

English definition: a current or former marriage in which one partner is gay or has had a gay affair

Chinese equivalent: 断背婚姻

type of word formation: compounding from broke back and marriage

context: We are ecstatically happy together. This is no Brokeback Marriage!

—photo caption, "An Army of Davids Attacks Barry C. Lynn," Wonkette, March 7, 2006

carbon neutral adj.

English definition: emitting no net carbon dioxide into the atmosphere

Chinese equivalent: 碳中和

type of word formation: compounding from carbon and neutral

context: Burning wood for fuel also generates carbon dioxide emissions, but as long as new trees are planted to replace those used as fuel, the level of emissions doesn't change as the new trees are soaking up carbon to offset the emissions from the wood fuel. So wood fuel is "carbon neutral."

— "Better management of forests across Europe would tie up much more carbon," Irish Independent, March 9, 2004

carbon offset　n.

English definition：a donation or other act that aims to remove a certain amount of carbon dioxide from the atmosphere to compensate for the same amount of carbon dioxide that someone or something has added to the atmosphere

Chinese equivalent：碳抵消

type of word formation：compounding from carbon and offset

context："Whether you're a secretary, a bookkeeper or a senior executive, you can take actions to make your institution greener," says Doyle. Ideas include buying ecofriendly office supplies (see thegreenoffice. com), asking your company to buy carbon offsets for corporate travel and pushing for more opportunities to work from home so fewer employees have to commute on a daily basis (for more ideas, see treehugger. com).

—Anna Kuchment, " Going Green at Work," Newsweek, June 11, 2007

carcooning　n.

English definition：using one's car for working, playing, eating, grooming and other tasks normally performed at home or at the office

Chinese equivalent：以车为家；车茧

type of word formation：blending of car and cocooning

context：Academics have coined the word "carcooning" to describe how people increasingly outfit their cars for comfort, entertainment and productivity. Phone systems are built in. New stereos pull in satellite radio broadcasts and play MP3 files downloaded from the Internet.

—Jim Wasserman, "Inattention at the wheel: It's so much more than cell phones," TheAssociated Press, August 22, 2002

car-schooling　n.

English definition：educating or instructing a child while driving in a car

181

Chinese equivalent：车内教育

type of word formation：compounding from car and schooling

context：Grant and others who educate their children at home offer the following tips on turning the summer break into an educational opportunity. . . . In the car：As Grant has found, an extended education often involves travel. "We basically do car-schooling," she said.

——Jill Smith, "Keep kids learning on summer break," The Oregonian, June 15, 2000

casualization   n.

English definition：1. the trend toward a more casual atmosphere in the workplace, particularly regarding the clothes worn by office workers. 2. the trend toward using casual workers (workers who are called in as they are needed) instead of permanent full-time or part-time workers

Chinese equivalent：轻松工作气氛；休闲装

type of word formation：affixation from casual and-zation

context："While dress-down Fridays have contributed to the casualizationof the American workplace, they have also led to upgrading of casual clothes."

—— "Teen Boys Have Slob Appeal," The Boston Herald

celetoid   n.

English definition：a person, particularly one with little or no talent, who is briefly famous

Chinese equivalent：一夜成名转瞬即逝

type of word formation：blending from celebrity and tabloid

context：propose celetoid as the term for any form of compressed, concentrated, attributed celebrity. I distinguish celetoids from celebrities because, generally, the latter enjoy a more durable career with the public. . . .

——Chris Rojek, Celebrity, Reaktion Books, September 21, 2001

chairobics　n.

English definition：aerobic exercises performed while sitting in a chair or wheelchair

Chinese equivalent：椅子有氧运动

type of word formation：blending from chair and aerobics

context：Abilities Rehabilitation Center programs include "chairobic" exercises and the Gamefield Wheelchair Sports Course.

——Pat Fenner, "Paraplegic seeks access to Gulf," St. Petersburg Times, July 24, 1987

cheapuccino　n.

English definition：an inexpensive, low-quality cappuccino, particularly one from a vending machine; a cappuccino made from brewed or instant coffee

Chinese equivalent：质低价廉卡布奇诺

type of word formation：blend of cheap and cappuccino

context：Wondering what a Blended Cheapuccino is? Well, it's a blended coffee drink that you make at home. Since most of us are trying to cut costs, a great way to save a whole lot of money is to give up the Starbuck's habit.

—— "Blended Cheapuccino," That Girl Can Cook! June 8, 2010

Chermany　n.

English definition：China and Germany taken together, particularly as an economic entity or market

Chinese equivalent：中德

type of word formation：blending from China and Germany

context：The U. S. perpetually runs large trade deficits with the rest of the world (especially "Chermany") because other countries are far more focused on export-led growth.

——Steven Capozzola, "Chermany," Manufacture This, March 18, 2010

chick flick　n.

English definition：a movie with themes, characters, or events that appeal more to women than to men

Chinese equivalent：女性喜欢的电影

type of word formation：compounding from chick and fllick

context：So what is a chick flick exactly? A movie where everyone talks a lot, preferably at the hairdresser? A movie that makes women and certain sensitive men cry faster than frying onions?

—Charlotte Bauer, "Chick schtick," Sunday Times, October 20, 2002

Chimerica　n.

English definition：the interrelated elements of the economies of China and America, particularly the Chinese supply of credit to America and the American purchase of cheap Chinese goods

Chinese equivalent：中美国

type of word formation：blend of China and America

context：Chinese savings were a key reason U. S. long-term interest rates stayed low and the borrowing binge kept going. Now that the age of leverage is over, "Chimerica" — the partnership between the big saver and the big spender — is key.

—Niall Ferguson, Monday, November 17, 2008, Washington Post

chip　v.

English definition：to implant a microchip, particularly a radio frequency identification (RFID) transponder, into an animal or person

Chinese equivalent：植入芯片

type of word formation：conversion

context：In the face of raging immigration debates across the nation, Applied Digital Corp. 's Chairman and Chief Executive Officer Scott Silverman suggests "chipping" immigrants to help gain control of the situation.

—Joni Morse, "RFID tagging debated for immigration control," RCR Wireless News, May 22, 2006

clubbing　v.

English definition：to go out to a dance club or a nightclub to dance or simply hang out

　　Chinese equivalent：泡吧

　　type of word formation：affixation of club and-ing

　　context：Are you a club kid, or a club kid in the making? Is the rave scene or going club hopping your idea of fun? If this sounds like you then you can't afford to skip this list of eight essential things every club kid must know.
www. teenadvice. about. com

　　comfort TV　n.

　　English definition：television programs with unsophisticated or home-spun themes that comfort or provide solace

　　Chinese equivalent：安慰性电视节目

　　type of word formation：compounding from comfort and TV

　　context：But by mid-September, the Condit story was a faint memory. "Comfort TV," fed by nostalgia for more innocent times, came on strong, typified by huge viewership for a Carol Burnett special.

　　—James Hebert, "The big-budget blowout 'Pearl Harbor' fed into post-Sept. 11 patriotism," Copley News Service, December 28, 2001

　　completist　n.

　　English definition：a person who obsessively gathers the complete collection of a particular set of items

　　Chinese equivalent：集全（物品）者

　　type of word formation：affixation of ist to complete

　　context：Hendrix completists, and they are legion, already will have these volumes cataloged with previous versions on quadraphonic vinyl, 8-track and Betamax.

　　—**Bill Lammers**, "Latest CD Offers More of Hendrix," The Plain Dealer, July 25, 1999

　　concrete collar　n.

　　English definition：an extensive system of roads or highways that sur-

185

rounds a city

Chinese equivalent：水泥领

type of word formation：compounding from concrete and collar

context：Ashford's controversial ring-road has gone two-way —a move town officials hope will aid the town's regeneration.

The road has been coined a "concrete collar" by its critics who point to it restricting the growth and development of the town centre.

— "Ashford ring-road goes two-way," Kent News, July 2, 2007

condop n.

English definition：A cooperative incorporated within a condominium building

Chinese equivalent：合作式共管公寓

type of word formation：blend of condo and co-op

context：This three-bedroom, three-bath apartment is on the 28th floor of the 37-story Grand Sutton tower at 59th Street and First Avenue.

The building, a so-called condop (a co-op that operates like a condominium), has only two apartments on each floor. Windows in every room of this apartment offer panoramic views of the city and East River, with multiple exposures.

—Meredith Daniels, "Home of the Week," Newsday, May 13, 2005

cookprint n.

English definition：the energy and other resources used while preparing meals

Chinese equivalent：碳足迹

type of word formation：blend of cooking and footprint

context：What do you call the impact you make on the planet when you cook?

It's your "cookprint" — the entire chain of resources used to prepare meals, and the waste produced in the process.

—Kate Heyhoe, "Cookprint: A New Green Buzzword," New Green Basics, February 26, 2008

cord blood bank n.

English definition: a repository for umbilical cord blood, which is rich in stem cells that can be used for research or to help the donor in future medical procedures—cord blood banking pp

Chinese equivalent: 干细胞库

type of word formation: compounding from cord blood and bank

context: "In France, scientists are considering establishing a cord blood bank to use for children who don't have a compatible donor relative," Dr Vowels said.

—Jane Southward, "Medical breakthrouh to save Andrew," The Sun-Herald, October 13, 1991

cosplay n.

English definition: a play or skit in which fans dress up as their favorite Japanese cartoon characters

Chinese equivalent: 真人模仿秀

type of word formation: blend from costume and play

context: The cult of cosplay sprang to life more than 15 years ago, when Japanese anime otaku (fans) began dressing up as their favourite cartoon characters at annual anime meets, where fans attended talks, meet-the-artist sessions and caught up with each other.

—Clara Chow, "Spider can eat my shorts," The New Straits Times, March 8, 2002

cot potato n.

English definition: an infant or toddler who spens a great deal of time watching TV

Chinese equivalent: 幼儿土豆；小电视迷

type of word formation: analogy from couch potato

context: Cot potato, USA Today has said television, video games and fear of the world outside the front door is creating a world where today's children are under "house arrest." And White Dot, the International Campaign Against Television (http://www.whitedot.org) is trying to turn back something called "Baby First TV" which, White Dot says, is out to turn infants into "cot potatoes."

—Roy MacGregor, "Little could television's inventor imagine how low the medium could go," The Globe and Mail, September 18, 2006

cougar　n.

English definition: middle-aged woman who seeks sexual or romantic relationships with younger men

Chinese definition: （专门勾引年轻男士的）熟女

type of word formation: conversion

context: Now the cougars have more than 20 members, including two males who have been dubbed Manthers (aka male panthers), but they'd like more, to expand their fundraising strength.

—Steve Newman, "Cougars Conquering Cancer campaign underway," Your Ottawa Region, February 10, 2011

cube farm　n.

English definition: a collection of cubicles in an office

Chinese equivalent: 办公室隔段

type of word formation: blending of cubicle and farm

context: The beloved Cube Farm began to crop up on our office landscape in the 1970s with what Haworth design manager Jeff Reuschel calls a "noble purpose": replacing the "bullpens full of desks" that were the norm back then with "a more flexible, fluid solution."

—Dale Fuchs, "The OK Work Corral; New Breeds of Cubicles Keep Coming," The Commercial Appeal

cuddletech:　n.

English definition: technology, such as the new Volkswagen or the iMac computer that is marketed as cute, friendly, or just plain cuddly

Chinese equivalent：让人爱不释手的科技产品

type of word formation：blend of cuddle and technology

context：Signs of cuddletech have been popping up for the past several years — a rounded corner here, an unexpectedly bright color there. Perhaps it was a rounded bumper on your new car. Or a beeper or cell phone made of plastic that resembles raspberry sorbet.

—Alisa Gordaneer, "Cuddletech: New products so cute you just wanna pinch their cheeks," Metro Times (Detroit), October 14, 1998

cup-holder cuisine　n.

English definition：food meant to be consumed while driving in a car or truck and that comes in a package designed to fit inside a cup-holder

Chinese equivalent：置杯座食物

type of word formation：compounding from cup-holder and cuisine

context：Cup-holder cuisine is the latest salvo in the commuter food (1987) wars. In fact, drive-time dining (1997) has become so popular that the food industry now has a separate food-in-the-car (1998) category to keep an eye on the latest trends.

www. wordspy. com

dashboard dining　n.

English definition：eating a meal while driving

Chinese equivalent：仪表盘快餐

type of word formation：compounding from dashboard and dining

context：Dashboard dining seems to be a phenomenon of our times. More and more busy people find their car takes the place of the breakfast table.

—Fran Berkoff, "Time to Go Back to Breakfast," The Toronto Sun, August 23, 2000

daycation　n.

English definition：a day trip or other short vacation that does not re-

189

quire an overnight stay

Chinese equivalent：一日游

type of word formation：blend from day and vacation

context：Seniors are invited to take a "daycation," a day traveling with a group of people using the bus and/or light rail system to entertainment and shopping destinations throughout the area.

— "Campbell shorts," San Jose Mercury News, April 15, 2010

decarbonise v.

English definition：to make an area or process environmentally cleaner by removing existing carbon or by reducing the amount of carbon produced

Chinese equivalent：去碳；脱碳

type of word formation：affixation from de-and carbon and-ise

context：Our commitment is also influenced by the CO2 we have already released, the positive feedback loops that amplify climate change, global dimming and the speed at which human economies can decarbonise themselves.

—Tim Flannery, "The Weather Makers," Atlantic Monthly Press, February 28, 2006

dejab v.

English definition：to stop wearing a hijab

Chinese equivalent：不戴头盖

type of word formation：affixation of de-to hijab

context：I say this based on my own dejabbing experience：yes, there were some base, practical reasons, but also many complex, illogical feelings which explained why it took me almost six months to fully dejab.

—Nicole Zaghia. "NPR's Dejabbing Sideshow," Muslim Media Watch, April 25, 2011

dejunk n.

English definition：to simplify；to tidy up a room, closet, office or other area by removing unneeded or unwanted items

190

Chinese equivalent：打扫；清除

type of word formation：affixation of de-and junk

context：First of all, "dejunk" the bedroom. Get rid of extra furniture. Move out some of the sentimental accumulation. Either give it to a charity or pack it into labeled boxes and put it in long-term storage areas. Move out clothing that you don't wear anymore.

　　—Bonnie McCullough, "Home Rule: How to 'Dejunk' Your Bedroom," Los Angeles Times

Denglish　n.

English definition：speech or text that uses a mixture of German and English words

Chinese equivalent：德式英语

type of word formation：blending from Deutch and English

context：speech or text that uses a mixture of German and English words

In Germany, there is an ongoing debate about language, specifically what they call "Denglish" — the increasing use of English.

http://wordsp. com

diabulimia　n.

English definition：an eating disorder in which a diabetic personattempts to lose weight by regularly omitting insulin injections

Chinese equivalent：抑郁饮食障碍；放弃胰岛素引起的饮食紊乱

type of word formation：blending from diabetes and bulimia

context："Diabulimia" Mercer explains, "is characterized by a person with diabetes who is intentionally skipping insulin therapy to keep blood glucose levels elevated, which in turn causes dangerous weight loss. "

　　—Julia McKinnell, "When to reveal your insulin pump," Maclean's October 27, 2011

digital native　n.

English definition：a person who grew up in a world with computers,

191

mobile phones, and other digital devices

Chinese equivalent: 数码熟练一代

type of word formation: compounding from diabetes and bulimia

context: Almost half the working population of the United States has not known a world without video games, Prensky said. These are people who grew up with what once was considered "gee-whiz" technology such as personal computers, wireless phones and pagers. Prensky called this younger group the "digital natives."

—Mark Watson, "Games people play put to work," The Commercial Appeal, January 27, 2001

distance work n.

English definition: office work performed at a remote location

Chinese equivalent: 在家工作

type of word formation: compounding from distance and work

context: telecommuters must be able to direct and discipline their own performance and manage their time well.

—Victor Y. Haines III et al. , "Environmental and person antecedents of telecommuting outcomes," Journal of End User Computer, July 2002

dollarization n.

English definition: abandoning a country's national currency in favor of the U. S. dollar

Chinese equivalent: 美元化

type of word formation: affixation from -zation to dollar

context: The main reason for dollarization is because of greater stability in the value of the foreign currency over domestic currency. The downside of dollarizationis that the country gives up its right to influence its own monetary policy by adjusting the money supply.

www. investopedia. com

doughnut pattern n.

English definition: an urban development pattern in which businesses and affluent residents migrate to surrounding suburbs and edge cities, resulting in a "hollowed out" downtown core consisting of mostly poorer residents

Chinese equivalent：多纳圈发展模式（富裕居民移居到郊区，形成穷人留存在市中心的发展模式）

type of word formation：metaphor

context：The numbers are new, but the story remains the same. Growth in income, population and jobs in the Chicago area continues to follow a doughnut pattern, with the central city coming up empty.

—Tom Andreoli, "Chicago continues to lag suburbs on income growth," Crain's Chicago Business, July 6, 1992

downsize n.

English definition：1. an employee who quits to take another job and later returns to the company 2. an employee who is laid off and then rehired as a consultant or contract worker

Chinese equivalent：裁员，被裁员后再次受雇

word formation：compounding from down and size

context：One interesting phenomenon of workers in the last two categories is the boomerang-style contract worker. Many organizations are hiring the very highly skilled people they just downsized out of a job. These people then come back on a much more tenuous basis as contract workers in their areas of expertise.

—Donna G. Albrecht, "Reaching new heights," Workforce

drunk dialing n.

English definition：a phone call made while drunk

Chinese equivalent：酒后打电话

type of word formation：compounding from drunk and dialing

context：Have you ever committed a "drunk dial?" (Called someone up when you were drunk and said things you wouldn't say when you were sober?)

—Cheryl Lavin, "Gentlemen, start your engines," Chicago Tribune, August 24, 1997

duppeies n.

English definition: a depressed urban professional; a person who once had a high-status or high-paying job and must now work in a menial or lower paying job

Chinese equivalent: 郁闷的雅皮士

type of word formation: acroym of depressed urban professional

context: In the dry argot of government statisticians, they're the "under-employed" — people who aren't working as much as they'd like to. But a better name for them might be "Duppies" — depressed urban professionals.

Leslie Haggin Geary, "Here come the 'duppies'," CNN/Money, June 17, 2003

earworm n.

English definition: a song that repeats over and over inside a person's head, usually refers to the time when the song has stopped playing

Chinese equivalent: 余音缭绕；耳熟能详

type of word formation: compounding of ear and worm

context: An earworm is a piece of music that sticks in one's mind so that one seems to hear it, even when it is not being played.

www. wikipedia. org

eatertainment n.

English definition: a restaurant that also offers entertainment such as wall-mounted memorabilia, video displays, or live music

Chinese equivalent: 娱乐饭店

word formation: blending from eat and entertainment

context: Eater-tainment has become the industry buzzword for restaurants such as Hard Rock CaféDave & Buster's and Jillian's, which bring together dining and play under the same roof.

—Lornet Turnbull, "Theme Restaurants Looking for a Hook," The Columbus Dispatch, August 21, 1999

eco-friendly　n.

English definition：the ability to manufacture goods efficiently and with as little effect on the environment as possible

Chinese equivalent：生态友好

word formation：affixation from eco-to friendly

context：McDonough and Alston contend it is not enough for the corporate world to embrace "eco-efficiency" — a business buzzword coined in the early 1990s.

—William Grady, "Environmental care encouraged," Chicago Tribune, November 4, 2001

edutainment　n.

English definition：software that entertains while teaching sth to the user

Chinese equivalent：寓教于乐电脑软件

type of word formation：blending from education and entertainment

context：ManyEdutainment Showsappear on PBS, the most famous example being Sesame Street.

www. tvtropes. org

egosurf　n.

English definition：to look oneself up on the internet using an internet search engine, especially to improve one's self-esteem

Chinese equivalent：网上搜索本人信息以提振自信

type of word formation：compounding from ego and surf

context：You know how to ego-surfwith Google but Addict-o-matic can help you find occurrences of your name across a much larger web and that too, very quickly.

www. labnol. org

eldering　n.

English definition：sharing wisdom and knowledge with people who are younger than oneself

Chinese equivalent：与比自己年轻的人分享智慧和知识

type of word formation：affixation of -ing to elder

context：Thus, we affirm the success of eldering or "saging," not aging. Although we admire and love our young, significant wisdom lies with our elders. Those who can recognize this wisdom and incorporate it in their lives, can feel proud of themselves and enjoy life to its fullest.

　　—Rabbi Chaim Richter, " 'Eldering' provides positive connotation," Sun-Sentinel, April 7, 1995

elderweds　　n.

English definition：people who get married later in life

Chinese equivalent：晚年新婚

word formation：analogy from newlyweds

context：Orville Abbott, 76, and his wife, Arlene, 65, have been married seven years... What do experts say about marriages like theirs? How about children of such brides and grooms? And what do "elderweds," as they are called, think about such relationships themselves?

　　—Robert A. Masullo, "Once and Again," Sacramento Bee, September 26, 1999

eternity leave　　n.

English definition：paid leave given to a person who needs to provide full-time care for a dying spouse or family member

Chinese equivalent：带薪留职（照顾将去世的家人）

word formation：compounding from eternity and leave

context：They say just as the parent of a newborn child receives maternity leave, the care provider for a terminally ill person — often a child taking care of a dying parent — should get "eternity" leave.

　　—Mark Quinn, "A plea for 'eternity care'," The Medical Post, April 27, 2000

ethical eater n.

English definition：a person who only or mostly eats food that meets certain ethical guidelines, particularly organically grown food and humanely raised meat, poultry, and fish

Chinese equivalent：伦理食者

type of word formation：compounding from ethical and eater

context：choosing to become a more ethical eater doesn't mean you have to become a vegetarian, or shop only at farmers' markets or buy only fair-trade, free-range, shade-grown coffee sold by nonprofit groups that donate all their money to literacy programs in developing countries. Rather, it means being clear on what your values are, and in deciding how far to go to practice them.

—Jeremy Iggers, "Ethical eating," Star Tribune, July 13, 2006

Eurogeddon n.

English definition：an extreme European economic, political, or military crisis

Chinese equivalent：欧洲危机

type of word formation：blend from Europeand Armageddon

context：As the debt-ridden, fractious European family gathered in Brussels for what was billed as crunch time, analysts coined a term for the chaos predicted to ensue if the euro fails: "Eurogeddon."

—Karen Kissane, "Eurogeddon threatens the postwar dream of unit" The Age, December 10, 2011

exercise bulimia n.

English definition：compulsive behaviour in which people count the calories ingested during a meal, and then tailor a workout to burn off the same number of calories

Chinese equivalent：运动强迫症

type of word formation：compounding from exercise and bulimia

context：Less studied, but perhaps more common today, is a phenome-

197

non that some therapists have dubbed "exercise bulimia" .... Instead of vom-
iting or taking laxatives, however, some bulimics purge by burning off calories
with huge amounts of exercise.

—Leonard Bernstein, "Perils of exercise, diet addicts," Los Angeles
Times, April 16, 1987

exercise widow n.

English definition: a woman who spends little time with her husband because of his frequent and extended exercise sessions

Chinese equivalent: 运动寡妇

type of word formation: compounding from exercise and widow

context: The exercise widow often wakes to an empty bed—a sure sign of
a morning workout—and may find dinner plans spoiled by a sudden avoidance
of anything heavy before a night run.

—Kevin Helliker, "A Workout Ate My Marriage," The Wall Street Journal, February 1, 2011

extreme ironing n.

English definition: a pastime in which participants iron a few items of
laundry while engaged in an extreme sport or some other dangerous activity

Chinese equivalent: 极限熨烫

type of word formation: compounding from extreme and ironing

context: Extreme ironing is described on its website as "the latest danger
sport that combines the thrills of an extreme outdoor activity with the satisfac-
tion of a well-pressed shirt".

— "Strike while ironing's hot," MX (Melbourne, Australia), April
18, 2001

facation n.

English definition: a vacation where a significant amount of time is spent
reading email and performing other work-related tasks

Chinese equivalent: 伪度假

type of word formation：blend from fake and vacation

context：Instead of taking a vacation, I take a facation. You know what I mean, don't you? It's a fake vacation. You stay connected and though you're not in the office, you still do all the things you'd normally do if you were at your desk and in your office.

—Phil Gerbyshak, "Don't Take a Facation!," EveryJoe, February 16, 2009

fakeaway　n.

English definition：a homemade meal that is similar to a takeaway meal purchased from a restaurant

Chinese equivalent：类外卖食物

type of word formation：blending from fake and takeaway

context：Alison Austin, head of sustainability at Sainsbury's, said："Fakeaways are here to stay. They're created for a fraction of the cost of traditional takeaways, you know what's going into them and they use up food that would otherwise be chucked out and sent to landfill. "

— "Sainsbury's reports the emergence of the 'fakeaway'" Twelve Thirty Eight, July 17, 2008

familymoon　n.

English definition：a honeymoon in which the bride and groom also bring their children from previous marriages

Chinese equivalent：全家度蜜月

type of word formation：blending from family and honeymoon

context：With three birthdays, a wedding and a "familymoon," we've had a lot of celebrations in our family lately.

—Jennifer Hansen, "End of this school year true cause for celebration," The Arkansas Democrat-Gazette, June 2, 1999

fast-casual　adj.

English definition：of or relating to a restaurant that offers a slightly higher quality of food, service, and atmosphere than a fast-food restaurant

Chinese equivalent：休闲快餐

type of word formation：compounding from fast and casual

context：Besides bumping up a notch from fast food, the fast-casual res-taurants, including chains such as Chipotle, Panera Bread Co. , Qdoba and Noodles & Co. , offer up more atmosphere.

——Kelly Pate, "Einstein buyout fills hole in owner's plans," The Denver Post, July 2, 2001

filmanthropy n.

English definition：moviemaking that aims to shed light on and raise money for a cause or charity

Chinese equivalent：慈善电影

type of word formation：blend from film and philanthropy

context ：Leonsis, for now, has curtailed his work in feature films. Pro-ducing documentaries on such serious subjects as the Japanese destruction of Nanking and a national soccer program for the homeless, he coined the word, "filmanthropy," which he described as "shedding light on a big issue" while raising money for charity.

——Bob Cohn, "Capitals owner eyes own ' compelling event ' ," Pitts-burgh Tribune Review, December 26, 2010

flash mob n.

English definition：a large group of people who gather in a usually prede-termined location, perform some brief action, and then quickly disperse

Chinese equivalent：暴闪族

type of word formation：compounding from flash and mob

context：Organizing a "flash mob" basically involves e-mailing a bunch of people with instructions to show up at a certain place for a few moments, then disappear.

——Kim Lamb Gregory, "Briefs," Ventura County Star, July 1, 2003

flexitarian　n.

English definition：a person who eats a mostly vegetarian diet, but who is also willing to eat meat or fish occasionally

Chinese definition：弹性素食者（偶尔可吃一些肉食或鱼肉的素食者）

type of word formation：blend from flexible and vegetarian

context：She has a passion for the occasional pork rind and describes herself as a "flexitarian," meaning that she is flexible about what she eats.

—Anne Schamberg, "Nell Newman brings dad's philosophy, her taste to Kohler," Milwaukee Journal Sentinel, May 5, 1999

flirtationship　n.

English definition：a relationship that consists mostly of flirting

Chinese equivalent：调情关系

type of word formation：blend from flirt and relationship

context：I think the average high school relationship probably lasts two weeks. Raging hormones and a desire to be the center of attention keep most teenagers moving on quickly, having mostly "flirtationships" and never really settling down.

—Courtney Phelan, "Phelan：High school relationships not always easy," Kane County Chronicle, August 2, 2012

food mile　n.

English definition：the distance that a food item travels from its source to the consumer

Chinese equivalent：食物里程

type of word formation：compounding from food and mile

context：Food miles are the distance food has travelled from its point of origin to you. In America, retail experts calculate that the average distance for any one item of food is around 1, 100 miles. The contents of the average European shopping trolley travel 2, 200 miles.

—Joanna Blythman, "Eat local and sever the food chains," The Independent, October 23, 1993

Frankenfish   n.

English definition: genetically engineered fish that glow

Chinese equivalent: 发光转基因鱼

type of word formation: blend from Frankenstein and fish

context: Genetically modified Atlantic salmon — known by critics as "Frankenfish" — may soon be available in your local grocer's seafood aisle. www. livescience. com

Freegan   n.

English definition: a person, usually a vegan, who consumes only food that is obtained by foraging, most often in the garbages of restaurants, grocery stores, and other retailers

Chinese equivalent: 免费一族

type of word formation: blend of free and vegan

context: It's about 7 : 30 on a mild Tuesday evening in one of Melbourne's northern suburbs. I'm in a small Toyota station wagon with Tim, Shane, G (Gareth) and Danya. They are "freegans": people who minimise their impact on animals and the environment by living on what supermarkets throw out.

—Peter Singer and Jim Mason, "Food for nought," The Age, May 20, 2006

freshmore   n.

English definition: 1. a second-year high school student who must repeat some or all of his or her first-year classes; 2. Freshmen and sophomores as a group

Chinese equivalent: 大一大二课程生；大一大二学生组

type of word formation: blending of freshman and sophomore

context: "I've been going along with it," said Smith's friend Chris York, a self-described "freshmore" at Patrick Henry. (He takes freshman and sophomore classes）

—Betty Hayden Snider, "Colorado hits home for teens," Roanoke Times & World News, April 25, 1999

friend v.

English definition: on a social networking website, to add a person to one's list of acquaintances, and vice versa

Chinese equivalent: 加为好友

type of word formation: conversion from noun to verb

context: students post profiles of themselves, go on a frenzy looking for friends on the system, and friending them on the site. If their friend does the same friending process, they're listed on each other's profiles.

— "Putting on your Face and find a Friend," Connecticut Post, November 4, 2004

functional food n.

English definition: a food product that has been enhanced with vitamins or pharmaceuticals to provide specific health benefits

Chinese equivalent: 功能性食品

type of word formation: compounding from functional and food

context: Other functional food products include higher-calcium yogurt, calcium-added ice cream, anti-oxidant enriched eggs, soy products and nutritionally enhanced sweets.

—Megan Davis, "Convenience, conviviality mark mealtime trends for future," Milwaukee Journal Sentinel, January 2, 2000

fuzzword n.

English definition: a word or phrase that is deliberately confusing or euphemistic

Chinese equivalent: 委婉语；迷惑之词

type of word formation: blending from fuzzy and word

context: These days, the buzzword — actually it's more like a fuzzword—

in urban policy is "empowerment," a concept endorsed by both President Bill
Clinton and the new Republican majority in Congress.

—Tim Poor, "'Empowerment' proposals don't sway everybody," St.
Louis Post-Dispatch, September 30, 1995

garage mahal   n.

English definition: a large or opulent garage or parking structure

Chinese equivalent: 巨型车库或停车场

type of word formation: analogy from Taj Mahal

context: Baylor's $ 15 million parking garage, with steeples and towers,
has been called "Garage Mahal" and will house a Starbucks.

—photo caption, The Dallas Morning News, July 13, 2003

garden to fork   adj.

English definition: describing or relating to food grown in a person's own
garden

Chinese equivalent: 自家花园种植的食物

type of word formation: compounding from garden, to and fork

context: Last week I ate the first head of lettuce it was amazing, all that
garden to fork crap is true.

— "Lettuce Give Thanks," The Big Fat Food Manifesto, August 8,
2009

Generation XL   n.

English definition: children or young adults who are overweight

Chinese equivalent: 肥胖一代

type of word formation: analogy from lost generation and generation
millenium

context: If researchers are correct that people in their 20s today — the
so-called Generation X — are heavier and less physically active than people in
that age group five to 10 years ago, that would make them Generation XL,
wouldn't it?

—Bob Molinaro, "Speeding up baseball," The Virginian-Pilot (Norfolk), July 14, 1995

ginormous　n.

English definition：massive, huge, or large, in either a physical or metaphorical sense

　　Chinese equivalent：大量的，巨大的

　　type of word formation：blending from gigantic and enormous

　　context：This is Jazz, a ginormous weird looking planet just showed up in the suburbs of Denver.

www. rice. ruf. edu

graffiti　n.

English definition：a drawing or inscription made on a wall or other surface located in a high location or altitude

　　Chinese equivalent：高处涂鸦

　　type of word formation：blending from giraffe and graffiti

　　context：It's presumably a combination of the words graffiti and graffe because Hughes said it involves spray painting a picture or graffiti signature, called a tag, as high as possible off the ground.

　　—Richard Watts, "Make spray paint a controlled substance to stop graffiti: Victoria councillor," The Canadian Press, January 4, 2001

glass cliff　n.

English definition：a senior job or important project, particularly one given to a woman, with a high risk of failure

　　Chinese equivalent：玻璃悬崖；给予女性重要但很可能失败的工作

　　type of word formation：analogy from glass ceiling

　　context：The barriers to women's progress in leadership and management are well known-from the "glass ceiling" or "glass cliff" to the "Mommy track".

　　—Sharon Mavin, "Venus envy: sisters are ruining it for themselves,"

Personnel Today, August 8, 2006

glass wall n.

English definition: a social prejudice that prevents an individual from moving laterally within an organization

Chinese equivalent: 玻璃墙；阻止一个人提升的偏见

type of word formation: analogy from glass ceiling

context: "Folks of color don't leave because of title and money," Poriotis said. "They want to expand their portfolio and they can't in the company. The glass walls are more impenetrable than the glass ceiling."

—Christopher Mele and Andrea Rubin, "Plenty of room at the top," Journal News (Westchester County, NY), March 24, 2002

Google v.

English definition: use an internet resource to look up or find out information, especially Google itself

Chinese equivalent: 用谷歌搜索信息

type of word formation: zero derivation from noun "Google" to verb "google"

context: So if you're Googling your prospective dates, a word of warning: Don't jump to conclusions about someone just because Google says she murdered 50 people. Chances are, that's an overstatement.

—Amy Gilligan, "Googling is newest date thing," Telegraph-Herald, January 14, 2001

GOOMBY n.

English definition: a person who hopes for or seeks the removal of some dangerous or unpleasant feature from his or her neighborhood

Chinese equivalent: 主张离开我的后院之人

type of word formation: acronym from Get out of My Backyard

context: NIMBY has been joined by other acrimonious acronyms of the waste wars: GOOMBY (Get Out of My Backyard), LULU (Locally Undesirable Land Use）and NIMEY（Not in My Election Year）.

　　—Melinda Beck，"Buried Alive," Newsweek，November 27，1989

grab and goer　n.

English definition：a person who dislikes shopping，or does not have much time for shopping，and so tends to select items quickly and without much thought

Chinese equivalent：（在商店）拿着买到的东西就走的人

type of word formation：compounding from grab and goer

context：There are thousands of workers out there in desperate need of some serious morning nourishment that they can literally just "grab and go"... Unfortunately，convenience and healthy eating don't always go hand in hand，but for the health-conscious grab-and-goer you could always put together some kind of bag meal：a yogurt，some fruit juice，a single-use cereal and milk container，or even a filled bagel.

　　—Stuart Ferguson，"Breakfast on target," Caterer & Hotelkeeper，January 10，2008

granny bank　n.

English definition：savings held by grandparents and used to pay for their grandchildren's education，first home，and other expenses

Chinese equivalent：祖母银行

type of word formation：compounding from granny and bank

context：God bless the granny bank. It's helping to fund tens of thousands of college educations.

　　—Jane Bryant Quinn，"Praising the Granny Banks," Newsweek，April 29，1996

graze　v.

English definition：eating a number of small meals throughout the day；eating a selection of appetizers as your main meal

Chinese equivalent：少吃多餐；只吃零食

type of word formation：new meaning in old word

context："Grazing was the way our body was designed to eat," says nutritionist Antony Haynes. "Large meals burden the digestive system, often causing bloating and lowered energy while the body struggles to digest them."

——Helen Foster, "Good grazing guide," Daily Mail, June 12, 2001

green roof n.

English definition：a roof that is covered with plants, particularly one in which special membranes and other layers serve to protect the roof top and hold the plants and soil in place

Chinese equivalent：绿色屋顶

type of word formation：compounding from green and roof

context：Although considered a new concept in Canada, green roofs have been used extensively in Europe for more than a decade. More than 10 percent of flat roofs in Germany containgreen-roof infrastructure.

— "Green roofs Qualify for Government of Canada Energy Efficiency Funding," Canada Newswire, May 12, 2004

groceraunt n.

English definition：a business that combines a grocery store and a restaurant

Chinese equivalent：副食饭店（既卖副食又经营饭店的企业）

type of word formation：blend from grocery and restaurant

context：Allegedly, the new groceraunt features wide-screen televisions, a chef performing in-store cooking lessons, a wine-tasting bar and a brick-oven pizza counter. Yum!

——Heather Strang, "Spend Date Night at Whole Foods." Retail Design Diva, April 18, 2008

group coupon n.

English definition：a consumer discount that only applies if a minimum number of people sign up for the deal

Chinese equivalent：团购

type of word formation：compounding from coupon and group

context：The recession has bred a new type of coupon：the group coupon. In recent months, several Web sites have launched in the District and nationwide giving customers discounts on restaurant meals, sporting events, spa treatments, golf outings.

——Nancy Trejos, "The Humble Coupon Joins Social-Media Web," The Washington Post, September 1, 2009

gurgitator n.

English definition：a person who competes in eating contests

Chinese equivalent：大胃王

type of word formation：affixation from -or to gurgitate

context：Maybe you've heard of Thomas, who is 38, manages a Burger King at Andrews Air Force Base and is the darling — and No. 1-ranked American "gurgitator" — of something called the International Federation of Competitive Eating (IFOCE) tour.

——Kevin Cowherd, "It's no gag when the Black Widow sits down to eat," Baltimore Sun, May 2, 2006

guru site n.

English definition：a web site, put together by an expert on a particular subject, that contains a large amount of useful, accurate information on that subject

Chinese equivalent：专题网址

type of word formation：compounding from guru and site

context："Finding a guru site in the area you're researching is like stumbling across a consultant or research librarian and tapping into their expertise, for free."

——Reva Basch, quoted in Jargon Watch

halfie n.

English definition: an individual who is half one ethnicity or race and half another

Chinese equivalent: 混种人

type of word formation: affitation from-ie to half

context: How to Date a Brown Girl (Black Girl, White Girl, or Halfie) is a satirical short story by Junot Díaz. The story takes the guise of an instructional manual, purporting to offer advice as to how to act or behave depending upon the ethnicity and social class of the reader's date.

www. wikipedia. org

hand-me-ups n.

English definition: a used object, especially an article of clothing, passed from a younger person to an older person

Chinese equivalent: (过时不穿) 传给父母的衣物、服饰

type of word formation: conversion

context: But some families put a twist on the trend. Instead of hand-me-downs, they share hand-me-ups. Older offspring who tire of wearing the same old threads pass garments to their parents, who might not be as picky about fit or fashion.

—Michele M. Melendez, "Frugal families 'hand-me-up' when size is right," The Star-Ledger (Newark, NJ), September 15, 2002

heirloom pork n.

English definition: pork that comes from a relatively rare breed of pig that has been raised in humane and environmentally friendly conditions for a number of generations

Chinese equivalent: 生态有机猪肉

type of word formation: compounding from heirloom and pork

context: The first time I had heirloom pork was at Cabbage Hill Farm in Westchester County, which is dedicated to saving historic breeds.

The pork I had last week, at Gramercy Tavern, is available by mail and will eventually be in some New York City grocery stores. Sold under the brand

Niman Ranch, which is known for its fine beef, the pork had first been described to me several months ago in terms of its environmental soundness rather than its taste.

　　—Marian Burros, "Pork With a Pedigree," The New York Times, September 22, 1999

helicopter parent　n.

English definition：a parent who hovers over his or her children

Chinese equivalent：直升机家长

type of word formation：compounding from helicopter and parent

context：Kids aren't the only ones who use slang in school. Here's some vocabulary that teachers aren't teaching: Helicopter parent: A nosy grown-up who's always hovering around. Quick to offer a teacher unwanted help.

　　—Ned Zeman, "Buzzwords," Newsweek, September 9, 1991

himbo　n.

English definition：man who is good-looking, but unintelligent or superficial

Chinese equivalent：肤浅无脑的靓男

type of word formation：analogy from bimbo

context：After three Garbage albums, Manson hasn't yet become a tedious pop princess. Undeniably charismatic, she can be distinguished from most of the pop world's thrusting teens and vainglorious himbos by one easy test: she has opinions.

　　—Sacha Molitorisz, "Talking Trash," Sydney Morning Herald, January 25, 2002

hiving　n.

English definition：making one's home the focus for social activities and work

Chinese equivalent：以家为社交和工作中心

type of word formation：new meaning in old words

context: Hiving is the response to this craving for comfort and connection. Hiving is the embrace of others in a safe setting a buzz with activity and engagement. Home is an integral part of hiving, yet hiving is not just about home. A hive is command central for a more fully engaged and more broadly connected lifestyle.

—J. Walker Smith, Craig Wood, "The Buzz About Hiving," Direct, February 1, 200

hotelling n.

English definition: an office setup in which mobile workers do not have permanent desks or cubicles and so must reserve a workspace when they come into the office

Chinese definition: 多人用临时办公设施

type of word formation: new meaning in old words

context: Welcome to the concept of "hotelling," where employees make reservations for work space, check in for an afternoon, a day or a week, and then move along to make room for someone else.

—Michael Kinsman, "Checking into a desk du jour," The San Diego U-nion-Tribune, April 17, 2002

hockey mom n.

English definition: a woman with hockey-playing children, particularly one who spends lots of time driving her children to the rink and watching their games and practices

Chinese equivalent: 冰球妈妈

type of word formation: analogy from soccer mom

context: Alaska neighbors love their hockey mom VP Candidate. http://edition. cnn. com/2008/politics/palin. alaska

huppies n.

English definition: a Hispanic urban professional

Chinese equivalent: 西班牙裔城市专业工作者

type of word formation：acronym from Hispanic urban professional

context：Mr. Munoz stresses that the crime rate has been dropping in Little Village and that he backs a tax-increment financing district in his ward — a controversial stance in other Hispanic areas. Because the neighborhood is improving, "folks like me — yuppies, luppies, huppies, whatever you want to call them — will be able to find homes here," he says, referring to the Latino and Hispanic variations of young urban professionals.

—Greg Hinz, "Vying for Hot Hispanic Votes," Crain's Chicago Business, February 15, 1999

hurried child syndrome　n.

English definition：a condition in which parents overschedule their children's lives, push them hard for academic success, and expect them to behave and react as miniature adults

Chinese equivalent：催熟儿童现象

type of word formation：compounding from hurried, child and syndrome

context：No parent wants to yell at children all the time, so my husband and I go to work and let the sitter do it. To avoid the dreaded hurried child syndrome, we avoid scheduling activities every day, so the children have some time to read, play, do homework and torture one another. Each has no more than two extracurricular activities a week.

—Roberta Zeff, "When the Clock Strikes Summer," The New York Times, June 2, 2002

hyper-dating　n.

English definition：dating many different people over a short period of time

Chinese equivalent：短时间内频繁约会多人；超级相亲

type of word formation：affixation of hyper to dating

context：Statistics suggest that in just three years' time more than 50 per cent of single people will meet a partner online (in New York, internet dating

213

has taken off to such an extent it is now sometimes referred to as "hyperdating"; people set up 10 online dates every week, sometimes several a night).

—Rachel Cooke, "Couples: The Search," The Observer, April 20, 2003

hypermiler n.

English definition: a person who attempts to maximize gas mileage by using driving techniques that conserve fuel

Chinese equivalent: 超级省油者

type of word formation: affixation from hyper- to miler

context: She is part of a small and extremely dedicated group of drivers around the country who call themselves "hypermilers." They almost exclusively drive hybrid vehicles, and their goal is simple: squeeze every mile they can out of each drop of gas.

—Chris Williams, " 'Hypermiler' drivers try to squeeze every mile they can out of a gallon of gas," The Associated Press, May 29, 2007

hyperparenting n.

English definition: child-rearing style in which parents are intensely involved in managing, scheduling, and enriching all aspects of their children's lives

Chinese equivalent: 超级家长

type of word formation: affixation from hyper to parenting

context: While older teens were making America miserable, the infants checking out of maternity wards were the "Millennial" babies born in 1982 and after. These babies, the flip side to the 13th Generation, would experience hyper-parenting — academic preschools, school uniforms, strict curfews.

—Richard Whitmire, "Social turnaround baffling," The Salt Lake Tribune, December 24, 1996

hyperpower n.

English definition: a nation that has vastly greater economic, political, or military power than any other nation

Chinese equivalent：超级大国

type of word formation：affixation of hyper- to power

context：Long the principal superpower and now the single superpower — or a "hyper-power," in the favoured phrase of the French — the U. S. is the contemporary Rome. Its power, much of it invisible because it's based on culture or technology rather than just upon smart bombs and cruise missiles, reduces the power of all others, whether the European Union or China or Russia, let alone Canada, to the third rank, sort of like Gaul's status at the height of the Roman Empire.

—Richard Gwyn, "U. S. and Them," The Toronto Star, December 29, 2001

hyperwhite　adj.

English definition：relating to speech and dress patterns devoid of non-white influences, particularly among nerds

Chinese equivalent：超级白人

type of word formation：affixation from hyper- to white

context：Many different types of nerds have surfaced in the past few decades：the Bill Gates nerd, Screech nerd, Millhouse nerd, Dwight Schrewt nerd and Michael Scott nerd.

They all have their own little quirks, but they share one similarity：they're all "hyperwhite."

—Justin Fritscher, "Nerds lack street credibility, cool kicks," The Daily Reveille, November 7, 2007

informavore　n.

English definition：a person who consumes information

Chinese equivalent：信息消费者

type of word formation：affixation from -vore to information

context：Which of these activities occupies more of your time：foraging for food or surfing the Web? Probably the latter. We're all informavores now, hunting down and consuming data as our ancestors once sought woolly mammoths and witchetty grubs. You may even buy your groceries online.

—Rachel Chalmers, "Surf like a Bushman," New Scientist, November 11, 2000

intexticated adj.

English definition: preoccupied by reading or sending text messages, particularly while driving a car

Chinese equivalent: 开车时忙于查看、发信息

type of word formation: analogy from intoxicated

context: A British study has found that "intexticated" drivers are worse than intoxicated ones, and even as dangerous as those who do drugs and drive.

Nearly 50 percent of the drivers ages 18 to 24 surveyed said that they sent text messages while driving, according to the study by Britain's Royal Automobile Club.

—Ginny MacDonald, "Texting while driving worse than drunken driving, British study finds," Birmingham News, March 30, 2009

intellidating n.

English definition: dating that emphasizes intelligence, particularly by attending lectures, readings, or other cultural events

Chinese equivalent: 智慧约会

type of word formation: blend from intelligent and dating

context: Intellidating is also a boon for the shy. In contrast to speed-dating, which demands rigidly timed discussions about pretty much whatever pops to mind, events such as lectures and viewings offer built-in conversational pegs.

http://wordspy.com

Iraqification n.

English definition: the process of controlled supervision of government reconstruction based on the formula used in Iqaq

Chinese equivalent：战争伊拉克化

type of word formation：derivation from Iraq and -fication

context：While Iraqification will not solve our immediate security problems, we must move more quickly to transfer meaningful political authority to Iraqi leaders.

——Washington Post, 9 Nov. , 2003

Jihadist　n.

English definition：a person engaged in or supporting a jihad

Chinese equivalent：圣战者；圣战支持者

type of word formation：regularization composed of jihad and -ist

context：Hillary Clinton has called for increased US military and political intervention in north Africa, and warned of a long, difficult but necessary struggle against a "spreading jihadist threat" in the region.

www. guardian. co. uk

jamais vu　n.

English definition：the illusion or impression of never having experienced something that has actually been experienced many times before

Chinese equivalent：旧事如新

type of word formation：loan from French

context：There's a condition in epilepsy called jamais vu which means, literally, "never seen. " It's the opposite of déjà vu; what happens here is that, when the sufferer comes round after a seizure, the whole world is new. He or she has, or so it seems, never seen any of it before.

—Lucretia Stewart, " The Reunion," The Independent, October 30, 1999

Japanimation　n.

English definition：an Anime and other Japan-based cartoons and animation

Chinese equivalent：日本动漫

type of word formation：blend from Japan and animation

context："Ghost in the Shell" (Manga Entertainment/Pioneer LDMA-529-3, two discs, CAV, wide screen, $49.95) is a high-tech sci-fi futuristic tale made in the process that has come to be known by its devoted followers as Japanimation.

——Richard Christiansen, "Blurred Colors Clear Up on New 'King and I' Release," Chicago Tribune, January 30, 1997

jumbrella n.

English definition：a large umbrella or canopy, particularly one used to cover the outdoor patio of a restaurant or bar

Chinese equivalent：巨型大伞

type of word formation：blend from jumbo and umbrella

context：With council permission, the side entrance has been "fenced off" with attractive period railings and behind it a "jumbrella", a state of the art canopy complete with powerful tiny heaters in its roof, set up.

——Mike Chapple, "Pub Refurbishment," Daily Post, June 10, 2006

junk sleep n.

English definition：low-quality sleep caused by disruptions from nearby electronic devices such as cell phones, computers, and TVs

Chinese equivalent：垃圾睡眠

type of word formation：analogy from junk and sleep

context：Researchers fear an entire generation is suffering from the effects of this "junk sleep," disrupted sleep blamed on electronic devices, whether it be a computer game played into the wee hours or a cell phone tucked under a pillow.

——Sue Gleiter, "Ever-present electronic devices disrupting teens' sleep", The Star-Ledger, February 26, 2008

just in time learning n.

English definition：the acquisition of knowledge or skills as they are needed

Chinese equivalent：现用现学的知识

type of word formation：compounding from just, in time and learning

context：The new flexible space created in the curriculum by the 20% rollback in technical requirements would be used in very different ways by different engineering schools. Following their tradition of diversity, some might focus on advanced specialized technical training; ... some might experiment with radical departures from conventional curricula such as "just in time learning."

—M. Granger Morgan, "Accreditation and diversity in engineering education," Science, August 31, 1990

kidfluence n.

English definition：the direct and indirect influence that kids have on their parents' purchasing decisions

Chinese equivalent：孩子（对于父母购买决定）影响

type of word formation：blend from kid and influence

context：Because of Disney's particular position in the marketplace, it has become an analyzer and advocate of "Kidfluence," Disney's term for the power kids hold over purchasing patterns.

http://wordspy.com

kidnapping v.

English definition：to redraw electoral boundaries so that most or all of an incumbent's district becomes part of another district that has a popular incumbent from the same party, meaning the two must run against each other

Chinese equivalent：赎回选票；重划选区同党竞争

type of word formation：new meaning in old word

context：The oddly shaped Twelfth District in Pennsylvania is a good example of "kidnapping" — in effect, moving an incumbent's established constituency out from under him or her.

—Don Peck and Casey Caitlin, "Packing, cracking, and kidnapping:

219

the science of gerrymandering," The Atlantic Monthly, January, 2004

kipper   n.

English definition：an adult son or daughter, particularly one aged 30 or more, who still lives with his or her parents

Chinese equivalent：啃老族

type of word formation：acronym from kids in parents' pockets eroding retirement savings

context：Have you got akipper in your nest? The first withering acronym of the year has been coined by the British building society Prudential to describe adult children reluctant to fly the nest. "Kippers" — Kids In Parents' Pockets Eroding Retirement Savings — are a million strong in Britain.

—Louise Holden, "Have you got a kipper in your nest?," The Irish Times, January 13, 2004

knowbie   n.

English definition：a knowledgeable and experienced Internet user

Chinese equivalent：网络大虾

type of word formation：zero derivation from knew and -bie

context：The best method for learning your way around the Internet is to read as much as you can (especially the Frequently Asked Questions lists associated with some Web sites, mailing lists, and newsgroups), learn the ins and outs of Netiquette, and to ask questions. Thus does the "newbie" turn into a "knowbie".

http：//wordspy. com

lance-ing   v.

English definition：to force a celebrity to reveal that he or she is gay

Chinese equivalent：迫使名人宣布出柜

type of word formation：conversion

context : There's a new way to describe celebrities who are coming out of the closet. Lance-ing is the new it term, referring to ＊NSYNC member Lance

Bass, who announced months ago he was gay and in a relationship with Reichen Lehmkuhl of The Amazing Race fame.

—Chad Martin, "Celebrities get lanced," Calgary Sun, October 24, 2006

laptop zombie　n.

English definition：at a coffee shop or similar establishment that offers free wireless Internet, a person who is oblivious to everyone and everything except the screen in front of them

Chinese equivalent：电脑僵尸

type of word formation：compounding from laptop and zombie

context：The dude sitting next to you in his comfy Starbucks chair might as well be a thousand miles away—his mind probably is... We have become a Nation Of Laptop Zombies.

—Tom Wright, "Are We Becoming A Nation Of Laptop Zombies?," Open Salon, February 17, 2010

LATs　n.

English definition：a situation in which an unmarried couple live in separate residences while maintaining an intimate relationship; a person in such a relationship

Chinese equivalent：分开同居

type of word formation：acronym from living apart together

context：In most cases, a living apart together couple would happily choose to get married or live common law except that circumstances prevent shacking up.

http：//wordspy. com

latte factor　n.

English definition：seemingly insignificant daily purchases that add up to a significant amount of money over time

Chinese equivalent：拿铁因素；每天看似较少的购买但随着时间推

221

移加起来非常多

type of word formation：new meaning in old word

context："You get a mocha at Starbucks and it costs $3. You buy a biscuit for $1. 50. At work, you get a diet Coke and Snickers. Before you know it, you've spent $10 a day," Holt said. "It's the latte factor."

—Deborah Adamson, "Money makeover," The Honolulu Advertiser, October 19, 2003

leather spinster　n.

English definition：a heterosexual or asexual woman who is happily unmarried and has no desire to seek a mate

Chinese equivalent：坚硬的独身女

type of word formation：compounding from leather and spinster

context：To call oneself a leather spinster is a powerful way of saying, I'm a happily unmarried straight (or asexual) woman and proud of it. The difference between leather spinsters and single women (most) is a purposeful personal choice not a accident or "I don't have a choice in the matter singlehood just happened", it's a lifestyle choice.

— "Leather Spinster Origins," Leather Spinsters. com, 1998

left Coast　n.

English definition：Joshing reference to the west coast, particularly the west coast of the United States or Canada

Chinese equivalent：左海岸（西海岸）

type of word formation：compounding from left and coast

context：If you're standing in Texas looking north, as Texans frequently do, the left coast is where Hollywood is. And to the folks from Warner Brothers in Hollywood, Willie Nelson's Eighth Annual Fourth of July Picnic was the perfect vehicle for promoting the release of the singer's new motion picture.

—John M. Crewdson, "The last of the best little picnics in Texas," The New York Times, July 6, 1980

Lexus lane　n.

English definition：a highway lane that is normally restricted during rush hour to vehicles carrying multiple passengers, but that can also be used for a fee by single-occupant vehicles

Chinese equivalent：凌志专用车道；特权车道

type of word formation：compounding from Lexus and lane

context：In San Diego County, officials will soon open a "Lexus lane" so called because solo drivers — mostly luxury car owners, critics say — can buy their way into less-congested car-pool lanes.

—Richard Simon, "Street Smart," Los Angeles Times, September 15, 1995

Lexus liberal　n.

English definition：a person who is liberal in words but not in deeds

Chinese equivalent：凌志自由党（口头上是自由党但行动上不是）

type of word formation：compounding from Lexus and liberal

context：Vello's big campaign promises were to get youth gangs off the street and clean up public transit. The plan turned out to be a model of efficiency. He would do both at once: Put the youth gangs on buses as security guards, and let them clean the floor with those who don't stand behind the yellow line. This is San Francisco, so the plan is applauded by Lexus liberals as a model for rehabilitating troubled youth.

—Rob Morse, "Anon., and on and on," The San Francisco Examiner, January 28, 1996

lifecasting　n.

English definition：using a portable camera to broadcast one's activities over the Internet 24 hours a day

Chinese equivalent：（24 小时）网络生活播报

type of word formation：blend from life and broadcasting

context：For over a week, Kan has been video blogging nonstop, 24/7. Everything he does（including going to the bathroom）streams live on http: //www. Justin. tv, where his phone number is posted for fans to call him and a chat room facilitates discussion. He calls it "lifecasting."

—Jake Coyle, "Justin Kan vlogs (with sponsorship) all day and all night on Justin. tv," The Associated Press, March 27, 2007

lightscape n.

English definition: the total illumination or the pattern and distribution of lights in a picture or vista

Chinese equivalent: 灯景

type of word formation: analogy from landscape

context: Christmas decorations, including dozens of lightscapes on downtown streets, will add to the festivities.

—Jan Galletta, "Holiday homes tour," Chattanooga Times/Chattanooga Free Press, November 30, 2001

lipstick effect n.

English definition: during a recession, the tendency for consumers to purchase small, comforting items such as lipstick rather than large luxury items

Chinese equivalent: 口红效应

type of word formation: compounding from lipstick and effect

context: If you've been following domestic news in recent weeks, you've probably heard about the "lipstick effect." As described in such outlets as NBC, The New York Times, and The Wall Street Journal, the idea is that, during a recession, women substitute small, feel-good items like lipstick for more expensive items like clothing and jewelry. And indeed, between August and October, lipstick sales were up 11 percent over the same period last year.

—Norm Scheiber, "Replacement Killers," The New Republic, January 7, 2002

locavore n.

English definition: a person who eats only locally grown food

Chinese equivalent: 土食族

type of word formation：affixation from -vore to local

context：In California, a group of "concerned culinary adventurers" called **Locavores** committed to eat only foods grown or harvested within a 100 radius of San Francisco for one month, August, 2005.

—Christopher B. Bedford, "Meeting the challenge of local food," In Business, January 1, 2006

low-hanging fruit　n.

English definition：the easiest task or the most readily achievable goal

Chinese equivalent：容易的工作；易获的目标

type of word formation：metaphorical use

context：Other examples of "low-hanging fruit" that agents are encouraged to ignore, according to a department memo explaining the decline in tickets, are illegally parked cars in residential areas during early-morning hours on Sundays, expired inspection stickers, cars faced the wrong way on dead-end streets and wheels aligned more than 12 inches from the curb.

—Lisa W. Foderaro, "Fewer Tickets As Goal Shifts From Revenue," The New York Times, September 12, 1993

luppies　n.

English definition：a latino urban professional

Chinese　equivalent：拉丁雅皮士

type of word formation：acronym from latino urban frofessional

context：There's nothing surprising about Hayek occupying Latina's cover—every issue is devoted to the Latin community. But, then again, there's nothing surprising in any part of their July issue. They're going after the "luppies," but apparently these ladies don't want to read anything risque.

— "On the Newsstand," New York Post, June 21, 1999

makeunder　n.

English definition：a change of appearance in which a person is given a simpler look, especially one with little or no makeup and a basic hairstyle

Chinese equivalent：素颜

type of word formation：analogy from make up

context：The makeover section, where a tatty subject is given a physical reconstruction as a pleasant way of saying "you are a total barker, get your life in order", is good viewing. It's been mooted that a refreshing change would be to see the reverse operation; a sort of makeunder.

http://wordspy.com

mancation　n.

English definition：a vacation in which the participants are all men

Chinese equivalent：清一色男性度假

type of word formation：blend of man and vacation

context：Buddies on vacation don't go to spas. And, unless they're ancient Druids getting in touch with their inner shaman, they don't group-bathe, either.

——Alfred Lubrano, "These are no trips for manly men,' The Philadelphia Inquirer, January 13, 2007

manny　n.

English definition：a male nanny

Chinese equivalent：男奶妈

type of word formation：blending from male and nanny

context：Although it is still rare to find guys on traditional nannying-courses, attitudes are fast changing. In Manhattan, for instance, mannies are as hip as Hermes scarves and every yummy mummy wants one — even Ally McBeal and Rachel from the TV show Friends.

——Penny Fray, "Manny splendid role model," Daily Post (Liverpool, England), August 18, 2003

marmalade dropper　n.

English definition：something that is extremely shocking or upsetting, particularly a newspaper headline or article

Chinese equivalent：震惊事件

type of word formation：new meaning in old word

context：You could argue, too, that the novel sometimes seems to be enjoying the horrors a little too much. But Burn has written a memorable, upsetting and clever book which is indeed to borrow Norman Miller's ultimate praise-phrase "a real marmalade dropper", although it might be sensible not to read Fullalove over breakfast.

　　—Mark Lawson, "Sleazy does it" (book review), The Sunday Times of London, August 27, 1995

marriage lite　n.

English definition：mildly derogatory term for an unmarried couple who live together or a couple who have formed a civil union or similar partnership

Chinese equivalent：同居

type of word formation：compounding from marriage and lite

context：But the other side of the coin is that is that a civil partnership is, face it, marriage lite. Terms and conditions apply, if you're gay your results will definitely vary from the bride and groom down the road. Because civil partnerships simply do not come with all of the legal rights of marriage.

　　—Cahir O'Doherty, "Irish Government introduces gay marriage (lite)," Irish Central, June 26, 2009

Mcjob　n.

English definition：a job that is low-paying, temporary and offers no incentives or benefits

Chinese equivalent：低薪临时工作

type of word formation：an analogy blend from McDonald and job

context：As McDonald's seeks to beef up its workforce, it's also trying to upgrade its image as the poster child for low-wage jobs by redefining the term "McJob."

　　John W. Schoen from msnbc. com

McMansion　n.

English definition：a large, opulent house, especially a new house that has a size and style that doesn't fit in with the surrounding houses

Chinese equivalent：雷同的豪宅

type of word formation：analogy from Mcjob

context：In a world of bloated S. U. V. 's and rambling McMansions, there are times when smaller is better.

—Steven E. Brier, "Nikon's New Digital Camera Fits Easily in a Pocket," The New York Times, August 16, 2001

meat tooth　n.

English definition：a craving or fondness for meat

Chinese equivalent：肉食者

type of word formation：compounding from meat tooth

context：In a couple of months, I rediscovered my love for meat. Sausages, steak, buffalo wings, crab legs, brisket, pork dumplings, those chicken legs served at Dim Sum. Others craved chocolate or cheesecake; I had a "meat tooth. "

—Kevin Chong, "Vegging out," The Vancouver Courier, September 10, 2003

meatloaf　n.

English definition：forwarded messages, jokes, lists, and other unsolicited noncommercial email messages sent by an individual to a large number of people

Chinese equivalent：群发信息

type of word formation：new meaning in old word

context：In the online world, meatloaf refers to unsolicited mass e-mail sent out by an individual. These people post their personal rants and raves to an extensive mailing list compiled by collecting personal addresses from discussion groups, chat parties and so forth. These are then fired off at any time of the day or night, regardless of whether the receiver cares for what's inside.

— "Lexicon," The Herald, January 24, 2001

megashed n.

English definition: a massive store or distribution warehouse, particularly one with a plain or unattractive exterior

Chinese equivalent: 仓储商店

type of word formation: affixation from mega-to shed

context: Outside the business pages, it will probably be Tesco the bull-dozer that makes headlines, as it is lambasted for supposedly demolishing traditional high streets and replacing small shops with its category-killing-megasheds.

—George MacDonald, "Tesco needs to spread word of its good work," Retail Week, April 21, 2006

mentally challenged adj.

English definition: relating to a person with a mental disability

Chinese equivalent: 智障的

type of word formation: compounding from mentally and challenged

context: Kennedy last year helped found Facing the Challenge, Inc., a nonprofit group that he said tries to raise people's awareness of barriers faced by "the physically and mentally challenged." He said he rejects the terms "handicapped" and "disabled".

—Dan Wascoe Jr., "Ted Kennedy Jr. says sports helped recovery," Minneapolis Star-Tribune, April 28, 1986

menoporsche n.

English definition: angst and anxiety exhibited by some men upon reaching middle age, especially when those feelings manifest in the purchase of a sports car or an affair with a younger woman; a sports car purchased by a man undergoing a mid-life crisis

Chinese equivalent: 男性中年危机焦虑感（购买运动轿车或发展婚外情）

type of word formation：blending of menopause and Porsche

context：Some doctors believe that midlife crises often stem from men's waning testosterone levels. Dr. Harry Fisch, a New York physician and author of the "Male Biological Clock," drolly refers to the phenomenon as "menoporsche," noting that testosterone treatment may prove a better antidote for the condition than the purchase of a new sports car.

—Shari Rudavsky, "Manopause," The Indianapolis Star, March 14, 2005

metrosexual　n.

English definition：an urban male with a strong aesthetic sense who spends a great deal of time and money on his appearance and lifestyle

Chinese equivalent：都市玉面男

type of word formation：affixation from metro- to sexual

context：The typical metrosexual is a young man with money to spend, living in or within easy reach of a metropolis — because that's where all the best shops, clubs, gyms and hairdressers are. He might be officially gay, straight or bisexual, but this is utterly immaterial because he has clearly taken himself as his own love object and pleasure as his sexual preference.

—Mark Simpson, "Meet themetrosexual," Salon. com, July 22, 2002

Millennial Generation　n.

English definition：the generation born in 1978 or later

Chinese equivalent：千禧年一代

type of word formation：compounding from millenial and generation

context：The youngest generation is still taking on members. These Millennial Generationtots, born beginning in 1982, are entering a childhood today's collegians would hardly recognize.

—William Strauss and Neil Howe, "The Cycle of Generations," American Demographics, April, 1991

millionerd　n.

English definition：a wealthy person who made their money in computer software or some other high-tech industry

Chinese equivalent：网络或高科技行业富翁

type of word formation：blend from millionaire and nerd

context：When a millionerd like Steve Forbes can bring excitement to the Republican presidential nomination contest, anything is believable.

—Robert Haught, "Clinton and Dole Might Not Be All That Popular in Libya Either," Daily Oklahoman (Oklahoma City, OK), February 1, 1996

misteress　n.

English definition：a man who has an extramarital affair with a woman

Chinese equivalent：婚外情郎

type of word formation：analogy from mistress

context：DEAR ANNIE You recently printed a letter from "Equal Rights in Michigan." She said a woman who has an affair with a married man is called a "mistress," but what do you call a man who has an affair with a married woman? ... Houston：How about "misteress"?

—Kathy Mitchell and Marcy Sugar, "Annie's Mailbox," South Coast Today, March 30, 2004

moonscape　n.

English definition：a view of or resembling the surface of the moon, characterized by rockiness and barrenness

Chinese equivalent：月景

type of word formation：blending from moon and land scape

context：Moonscape is a free and freely downloadable high-definition documentary about the first manned Moon landing.

moonscapemovie. blogspot. com

morganatic marriage　n.

English definition：a marriage between a person of royal birth and a partner of lower rank, in which the latter has no royal status or title

Chinese equivalent：皇族与平民的婚姻

type of word formation：compounding from morganatic and marriage

context：It may be that many people in Britain would not seriously object to Charles marrying Camilla. . . . That being so, what should Camilla's status be? Our constitutional law, rightly, does not admit morganatic marriage.

　　—Paul Johnson, "Don't they deserve a break now?," The Daily Mail (London)

mouse potato　n.

English definition：a person who spends a great deal of of time in front of a computer

Chinese equivalent：鼠标土豆

type of word formation：analogy from couch potato

context：It's enough to turn a diehard football fan into a mouse potato, planted in front of a PC, beer in lap.

　　—David Einstein, "Super Bowl's tangled Web," The San Francisco Chronicle, January 24, 1996

mouse race　n.

English definition：a lower-stress lifestyle that results from moving to a smaller community or taking a less demanding job

Chinese equivalent：轻松工作

type of word formation：analogy from rat race

context："We wanted to leave the rat race and join the mouse race," said Phyllis, who among other jobs worked at a Jewish day school, a private high school, an affordable housing program and as a cake decorator.

　　—Tom Wharton, "Mouse Race Pace Suits Them Fine," SaltLake Tribune, May 3, 2003, Saturday

mouth feel　n.

English definition：the way that a food product feels inside a person's mouth

Chinese equivalent：口感

232

type of word formation：compounding from mouth feel

context：Mouthfeel is a product's physical and chemical interactionin the mouth, an aspect of food rheology. It is a concept used in many areas related to the testing and evaluating of foodstuffs, such as wine-tasting and rheology.

www. wikipedia. org

mushroom v.

English definition：to multiply, grow, or expand rapidly

Chinese equivalent：急剧扩散、发展

type of word formation：conversion

context：A sleepy capital of a few hundred thousand people has mush-roomed to a crowded city of 2 million.

www. neologisms. us

mother-out-law n.

Engllish definition：the mother of a person's former spouse

Chinese equivalent：前岳母；前婆婆

type of word formation：cf. mother in-law

context：It's equally difficult to describe the peculiar membership of this new lineage. Does your first husband's mother become a mother-out-law?

—Ellen Goodman, "The Very Extended Family," The Washington Post, August 20, 1983

nanny car n.

English definition：a car that uses computer technology to prevent the driver from making unsafe actions or decisions

Chinese equivalent：傻瓜汽车

type of word formation：compounding from nanny and car

context：Down the road, perhaps, the nanny car will have devices that monitor body fat and cholesterol. If they're too high, the car won't start. Instead a flashing display on the dashboard will say："You're too fat. Get out and walk."

— "Coming soon: nagmobile," The Commercial Appeal (Memphis, TN), October 15, 2002

nanobreak n.

English definition: a brief vacation, particularly one that includes just one night away from home

Chinese equivalent: 纳米休假（短假）

type of word formation: affixation of nano-to break

context: Despite the mounds of luggage in the boot of the prime ministerial Land Cruiser plus one very smart guitar case this is not really a holiday at all. It is more of a nanobreak to show support for the British tourist industry.

—Robert Hardman, "Tony's country jaunt," Daily Mail, August 2, 2002

naycation n.

English definition: time off from work spent without travelling and without spending money on leisure activities

Chinese equivalent: 在家度假

type of word formation: blend of no and vacation

context: Pundits have dubbed 2009 the year of the "naycation." Because the recession has slashed vacation budgets, many families are staying home this summer.

—Gail Borelli, "Invitation to Summer: Spiffing up the backyard," The Kansas City Star, May 24, 2009

Neets n.

English definition: a young person who isn't working, in school, or in a training program

Chinese equivalent: 待业在家的青年，三无青年，无工作、无教育、无培训的青年

type of word formation: acronym from not in employment, education, or training context：Here's another thought, lifted from Ridley's inspiring book："The 21st century will be a magnificent time to be alive," he says, a message which deserves to be disseminated far beyond the literary pages, so as to reach everyone from Neets and unemployed graduates to Lib Dems who cannot believe what they have got themselves into.

—Catherine Bennett, "Phew. At last we can ignore the gurus peddling happiness," The Observer, June 27, 2010

nerdistan　n.

English definition：an upscale and largely self-contained suburb or town with a large population of high-tech workers employed in nearby office parks that are dominated by high-tech industries；any large collection of nerds

Chinese equivalent：高科技工业园

type of word formation：affixation of -stan to nerd

context：South Orange County is a classic nerdistan — largely newly built, almost entirely upscale office parks, connected by a network of toll roads and superhighways to planned, often gated communities inhabited almost entirely by college educated professionals and technicians.

—Joel Kotkin, "Avoiding Excesses Has Buoyed L. A. 's Tech Sector," Los Angeles Business Journal, August 20, 2001

newbie　n.

English definition：a new or inexperienced user, especially one who is ignorant of netiquette and other online proprieties

Chinese equivalent：菜鸟

type of word formation：zero derivation from new and -bie

context："There is nothing inherently bad about being an inexperienced user. It's only when the inexperienced ignore those rules that serve to grease the wheels of Net social interaction that they get branded with the 'newbie' label."

www. neologism. us

news grazing　n.

English definition：getting news from a number of different sources

Chinese equivalent：新闻浏览

type of word formation：compounding from news and grazing

context：To its credit, perhaps, The World Today seemed little different from any other CNN news hour, of which there are many generic varieties. There's something to be said for continuity, and thenews grazers who have grown addicted to dipping in and out of the various shows would find nothing in The World Today to be thrown by.

—Matt Roush, "On CNN, a sluggish 'World'." USA Today, October 17, 1989

NINJA loan　n.

English definition：a loan or mortgage given to a person who has no income, no job, and no assets

Chinese equivalent：给予三无人员的贷款（无收入、无工作、无资产）

type of word formation：acronym from the phrase No Income, No Job or Assets

context：It's not as though the absurd excesses of the mortgage market were some big secret. Lenders brazenly advertised "low-doc" and "no-doc" loans that required borrowers to provide little or no documentation of their ability to repay. They pushed "ninja" loans, requiring no income, job or assets. And adjustable rate mortgages that were barely affordable at their teaser rates.

— "Risky-mortgage meltdown was predictable, preventable," USA Today, August 10, 200

novelty degrees　n.

English definition：a fake degree from an existing university or college; a degree from a non-existent university or college

Chinese equivalent：野鸡大学假学位

type of word formation：compounding from novelty and degree

context：On the site, customers can buy, for $ 50 apiece, diplomas from any colleges they want — including the University of Nebraska, whose "diploma" graces the Web site's main page. The Web site's order form requires customers to sign a statement saying that they will not misrepresent their "novelty" degrees as being the real thing.

　　—Lisa Guernsey, "Company Shuts Down On-Line Operation Selling Fake Diplomas and Transcripts," Chronicle of Higher Education, May 22, 1998

NIMBY　n.

English definition：not in my back yard; a person who hopes or seeks to keep some dangerous or unpleasant underground feature out of his or her neighborhood; the attitude of such a person

　　Chinese equivalent：避邻主义；拒绝在自家附近建有危害的建筑

　　type of word formation：acronym from not in my back yard

　　context：It's not a case of NIMBY, William Tardy says. The popular anti-development cry, which stands for Not In My Back Yard, just doesn't fit the facts of the supercollider proposal. For Tardy, opposing the project is a matter of NUMBY—Not UNDER My etc.

　　—Stevenson Swanson, "The Supercollider: Should it be built at Fermilab?," Chicago Tribune, May 29, 1988

Obamacon　n.

English definition：a conservative voter who supports Democratic candidate Barack Obama in the 2008 U. S. presidential election

　　Chinese equivalent：支持奥巴马的保守选民

　　type of word formation：blend from Obama and conservative

　　context：Why could there be an Obama blowout? One reason is the Obamacons, conservatives who support Mr. Obama. Some, such as columnist Andrew Sullivan, are attracted by Mr. Obama's message of hope and his potential ability to reshape America's image before the world.

　　—John Ibbitson, "Four months out, the smart money is on Obama to win," The Globe and Mail, July 2, 2008

office　v.

English definition: to perform office-related tasks, such as photocopying and faxing

Chinese equivalent: 办公

type of word formation: conversion from noun to verb

context: You can office while the rest of the world wastes time sleeping. You can even **office** while you're supposed to be on vacation in Tahiti.

——Marilyn Gardner, "The Plugged-In Vacation: What's a Beach Without a Fax?" The Christian Science Monitor, June 26, 1997

office spouse   n.

English definition: a co-worker with whom one has a very close but non-romantic relationship

Chinese equivalent: 异性办公搭档

type of word formation: compounding from office and spouse

context: A recent study by Vault. com found that 32 percent of office workers have an "office husband" or "office wife" — that is, a nonromantic relationship — and many have more than one.

——Ieva M. Augstums, "Do you take this co-worker..." The Dallas Morning News, March 12, 2006

office park dad   n.

English definition: a married, suburban father who works in a white-collar job

Chinese equivalent: 居住郊区的白领父亲

type of word formation: compounding from office, park and dad

context: If you're an office park dad, "you're not anti-corporate, because you work for a corporation — or you know you'll be working for one again," said Tom Ochs, political director of the New Democratic Network. "So the 'people versus the powerful' is not the world they live in."

——Carla Marinucci. "Move over soccer moms — here come the 'office park dads'," The San Francisco Chronicle, August 13, 2002

one-handed food　n.

English definition：food that is small enough to hold in one hand and is not messy to eat so that it can be consumed while driving or working

Chinese equivalent：手指食品

type of word formation：compounding from one-handed and food

context："Fast-food restaurants have succeeded best with 'one-handed food,' because the majority of fast-food patrons eat in the car."

——Mary E. Corcoran, "Changing a habit isn't an issue of immediate gratification," The Kansas City Star, September 10, 1996

open collar worker　n.

English definition：a person who works at home

Chinese equivalent：敞领工作人员

type of word formation：compounding from open collar and worker

context：Organized labor is worried about the millions of new "open collar" workers who will be able to do jobs at home that once required an office setting — that may be about 10 percent of our work force by the year 2000.

— "The Small Issue, the Big Picture," The Washington Post, December. 31, 1988

Oprahization　n.

English definition：the increased tendency for people to publicly describe their feelings and emotions and confess their past indiscretions

Chinese equivalent：奥普拉倾向

type of word formation：affixation of -zation to Oprah

context：The Oprahization of our culture — the astonishing propensity to tell all, even the most sacred, private things to an audience of strangers — has fueled the Bobbitt case.

——Molly Mayfield, "The Bobbitt tragicomedy," Denver Rocky Mountain News, January 16, 1994

orange collar　adj.

English definition：relating to a worker who wears an orange safety vest while on the job

Chinese equivalent：橙领

type of word formation：compounding from orange and collar

context：Orange collar staff are identified by their highly technical and specialist skills. They are likely to work in remote locations, and are typified by their level of relevant training, adherence to compliance and long-term commitment to a project.

—John McCarthy, "Most employers bracing for busier times, according to new employment survey," Courier Mail, June 11, 2012

orthorexia　n.

English definition：an extreme desire to eat only healthy food

Chinese equivalent：饮食完美症

type of word formation：analogy from anorexia

context：Orthorexia also can be induced by a host of extreme diets：raw foodism, with the mantra "The greatest enemy of man is the cooking stove"; macrobiotics, which mandates that vegetables be sliced in a certain fashion; the self-explanatory fruitarianism; and breatharianism, extreme fasting.

—Leslie Goldman, "When almost no food is right," Chicago Tribune, October 14, 2001

panda-hugger　n.

English definition：an analyst or academic who believes that China poses no military threat, particularly to the United States

Chinese equivalent：拥抱熊猫者；亲中派

type of word formation：compounding from panda and hugger

context：The very name of Bill Gertz's new book "The China Threat" is an affront to the panda-huggers in our nation's capital. They deny the existence of a threat from China, suggesting that this view is a mindless holdover from the reflexive paranoia of the Cold War.

—Steven W. Mosher, "The new cold war," The Washington Times,

January 2, 2001

parachute kids　n.

English definition: children sent to a new country to live alone or with a caregiver while their parents remain in their home country

Chinese equivalent: 空降孩子

type of word formation: compounding from parachute and kid

context: A 1990 UCLA study, using numbers from visa applications, estimated that there are 40, 000 Taiwanese parachute kids ages 8 to 18 in the United States; smaller numbers come from Hong Kong and South Korea.

—Denise Hamilton, "A house, cash — and no parents," Los Angeles Times, June 24, 1993

parahawking　n.

English definition: a sport where paragliders follow birds of prey that have been trained to look for and follow thermal updrafts that enable the pilots to stay aloft

Chinese equivalent: 滑翔驯鹰

type of word formation: blend from paragliding and hawking

context: Parahawking is simply a fusion between Paragliding and Falconry. The idea being that the birds are trained to "hunt" the thermals, which allow the pilots to stay aloft.

—Scott Mason, "The Himalayan Parahawkers," Falconry & Conservation Magazine, January 1, 2003

parkour　n.

English definition: a sport in which participants run, climb, and leap over urban structures

Chinese equivalent: 跑酷

type of word formation: loan word from French

context: Parkour developed 16 years ago in the suburbs of Paris when sneaker-clad teenagers began navigating public spaces as skateboarders might, but without the skateboards. (The name comes from "parcours," French for circuit or course.) From Paris it made its way to England, and then as far as Finland and Singapore.

http: //wordspy. com

passive overeating　n.

English definition: the excessive eating of foods that are high in fat because the human body is slow to recognize the caloric content of rich foods; eating whatever is put in front of you, even to the point of discomfort

Chinese equivalent: 被动吃

type of word formation: compounding from passive and over eating

context: There's term for eating everything you are served at a restaurant — then realizing you are basically too stuffed to move. It's called "passive overeating" and is the subject of a survey commissioned by the American Institute for Cancer Research, an organization devoted to exploring the link between diet and cancer.

—Lisa Muehlbauer, "Eyeing your driver's license," Buffalo News, February 20, 2001

p-book　n.

English definition: a paper book

Chinese equivalent: 纸质书

type of word formation: analogy from e-book

context: E-books range in price from ＄1 for Dean Wesley Smith's Star Trek: S. C. E. #1: The Belly of the Beast to double-digit figures for books such as Susan Sontag's In America (＄26), and they can be downloaded in seconds. E-books, in general, cost the same or are cheaper than their p-book versions.

—Tara McKelvey, "Easy-on-the-eyes typeface clears screen for better content," USA Today, August 30, 2000

pay per listen　n.

English definition：a music feature that requires the user to pay a small fee each time they listen to a song, album, or audio stream

Chinese equivalent：按次付费

type of word formation：compounding from pay and per listen

context：Music is "content" that will flow across that cable—content that AT&T hopes people will pay for, perhaps on a pay-per-listen basis just as many people now pay per view.

—Patricia Horn, "Music Over the Net Hits a High Note with AT&T," The Buffalo News, March 9, 1999

pescetarian　n.

English definition：a person who supplements a vegetarian diet with fish

Chinese equivalent：鱼素食者

type of word formation：blend from pesce and vegetarian

context：In my research, I have come across other interesting and creative categories, such as pescetarians, who permit themselves fish, and semi-vegetarians, who eat less meat than the average person. Whether these groups should really call themselves vegetarians is somewhat suspect. I have never met a fruitarian, but apparently these are people who subsist on a diet limited to fruit and vegetables.

—Susan Biali, "Vegetarianism: perks and pitfalls," Medical Post, June 26, 2001

phishing　n.

English definition：document used to trick people into giving personal information

Chinese equivalent：网络钓鱼

type of word formation：affixation of -ing to fishing

context：**Phishing**is the term coined by hackers who imitate legitimate companies in e-mails to entice people to share passwords or credit-card numbers. Recent victims include Charlotte's Bank of America, Best Buy and eBay, where people were directed to Web pages that looked nearly identical to the companies' sites.

—Andrew Shain, "Phishing to steal your information," Charlotte Observer, July 25, 2003

physically challenged　adj.

English definition：relating to a person with a physical disability or handicap

Chinese equivalent：残疾的

type of word formation：compounding from physically and challenged

context：According to a study released in the spring, 55 per cent of physically challenged people make an average of four trips a year.

—Vivian Macdonald, "The physically challenged are forced to make extra efforts," Toronto Star, November 14, 2002

pie　v.

English definition：to hit a person, particularly a political or business leader, in the face with a pie

Chinese equivalent：以饼击打

type of word formation：conversion from noun to verb

context：Other prominent Quebecers to be pied recently include former premier Jacques Parizeau, Montreal Mayor Pierre Bourque and former police chief Jacques Duchesneau.

— "Pie-Eyed," The Calgary Sun, January 19, 1999

pluots　n.

English definition：a fruit created by cross-pollinating a plum and an apricot in such a way that the resulting hybrid has dominant plum characteristics

Chinese equivalent：杏李

type of word formation：blend from plum and apricot

context：Pluots are a plum-apricot cross that has more of the characteristic of a plum because it has more plum parentage than apricot: smooth, crisp skin, round shape. However, the skin isn't as bitter as that of a true plum.

—Wanda Adams, "Off the Shelf," The Honolulu Advertiser, September 10, 2003

podcast　n.

English definition: publishing audio feeds that people can subscribe to and have transferred to an iPod or other digital audio player

　　Chinese equivalent: 播客

　　type of word formation: analogy from broadcast

　　context: The idea behind a podcast is simple, yet brilliant. Instead of using portable MP3 players such as the iPod only for listening to music, new software called iPodder allows one to download prerecorded radio shows onto the devices.

　　—Stephen Humphries, "'Podcast' your world," Christian Science Monitor, December 10, 2004

post mortem divorce　n.

English definition: a stipulation that one must be buried separately from one's deceased spouse

　　Chinese equivalent: （夫妻）死后分开埋葬协议

　　type of word formation: compounding from post mortem and divorce

　　context: "In Japan, many women stay with their husbands even though their feelings towards him are cold and they sleep in separate rooms. That way they are economically supported by their husbands," said Haruyo Inoue, a writer who has coined the term "post mortem divorce".

　　—Colin Joyce, "Divorce beyond the grave for Japanese wives," The Daily Telegraph, February 22, 2003

Potterhead　n.

English definition: a person who is a big fan of the Harry Potter series of books

　　Chinese equivalent: 哈利波特迷

　　type of word formation: compounding from Potter and head context: A very ordinary British boy grows up under the cruel care of his aunt and uncle. On the edge of his teenage years, he learns a magical secret: he belongs to a clan of wizards who invite him to a parallel world of dark forests, dragon's eggs, merlins and trolls. So begins a string of books featuring Harry Potter, the hottest thing in publishing. The third book in the series just landed at bookstores this week, and Potterheads set up lawn chairs to wait for the doors to open. Not since "Charlotte's Web" in the early 1950s has a children's tale ruled the roost so completely.

— "Harry Potter's Magic," The San Francisco Chronicle, September 11, 1999

quiet car n.

English definition: a train or subway car where riders cannot have cell-phone conversations or use noisy devices

Chinese equivalent: 寂静车厢

type of word formation: compounding from quiet and car

context: Beginning Oct. 3, a passenger car on every weekday Metrolink train will be designated as a "quiet car." Cellphones, smartphones or electronic devices that can be heard by others will not be allowed.

—Alejandra Molina, "No cellphones on Metrolink's quiet car," Orange County Register, September 28, 2011

quiet party n.

English definition: a party in which talking and other loud noises are prohibited, and where guests communicate using handwritten notes

Chinese equivalent: 寂静派对

type of word formation: compounding from quiet and party

context: The Quiet Party is the brainchild of two New York City friends: Paul Rebhan, who calls himself a life-artist, which means he treats his life as a work of art, and classic rock singer-songwriter-producer Tony Noe. Their Web site, www. quietparty. com, explains how it works.

—Linda Laban, "Bar-scene trendsetters keeping quiet on this one," The

246

Boston Herald, November 4, 2003

purple states　n.

English definition: an American state in which Democrats and Republicans have roughly equal support

Chinese equivalent: 紫色州

type of word formation: compounding from purple and state

context: On U. S. election night maps, Republican states are traditionally shown in red and Democratic states are shown in blue, so pundits of both political stripes now routinely talk about red states (2001) and blue states (2001). States that give both parties roughly equal electoral support — also called battleground states or swing states — are a blend of blue and red, hence they're purple states.

www. answers. com

rawist　n.

Eglish definition: a person who eats only unprocessed, unheated, and uncooked food, especially organic fruits, nuts, vegetables, and grains.

Chinese equivalent: 食生鲜者

type of word formation: affixation of -ist to raw

context: The cornerstone of the "rawist" philosophy is simple: Nature is perfect. Proponents say that raw foods are nutritionally complete, and that cooking food is not only unnatural, but detrimental to its nutritional content. They shun baking, boiling, sauteing, steaming, microwaving, frying and pasteurization—in short, any method of food preparation or processing that requires heat. "If you can't eat a food in its fresh, natural state, you shouldn't be eating it at all" is a popular rawist mantra. "Man is the only animal who cooks his food" is another.

—Jack Rosenberger, "Can a raw-foods diet be balanced?," Vegetarian Times, May 1996

recessionista　n.

English definition：a person who dresses stylishly on a tight budget

Chinese equivalent：危机时尚达人

type of word formation：affixation from-ista to recession

context：A recessionista is a modern sort of girl who is trying to survive the credit crunch the best she can. We're all recessionistas now.

——Ann Marie Hourihane, There's money on it being a bad time to get divorced, The Irish Times, July 14, 2008

regift v.

English definition：to give as a gift something that one received as a gift

Chinese equivalent：转赠礼物

type of word formation：affixation from re-to gift

context：Regifting is a brilliant concept, really. Everyone needs to reroute a few ugly, useless gifts this time of year.

——Maile Carpenter, "The gift you keep on giving," Wilmington Star-News (Wilmington, NC), December 3, 1995

returnment n.

English definition：the act of returning to work after having retired

Chinese equivalent：返聘

type of word formation：affixation of-ment to return

context：Research by insurer Zurich Life suggests that the number of people returning to work and starting their own businesses after retirement — a process they have dubbed "returnment" — will continue to increase.

——Helen Loveless, "Retire to become the boss," Mail on Sunday (London), June 22, 2008

ringxiety n.

English definition：1. the confusion experienced by a group of people when a cell phone rings and no one is sure whose phone it is; 2. mistaking a faint sound for the ringing of one's cell phone

Chinese equivalent : 铃声焦虑

type of word formation：blend from ring and anxiety

context：Many of us will be familiar with the basest form of ringxiety —— when one phone rings and everyone in the vicinity suddenly starts checking their pockets or handbags with frantic abandon. But some cases become far more complex: individuals have reported hearing their phone ring at concerts, or while driving.

——Bobbie Johnson, "Do you suffer from Ringxiety?," The Guardian, June 1, 2006

road rage　n.

English definition：extreme anger exhibited by a motorist in response to perceived injustices committed by other drivers

Chinese equivalent：路怒族

type of word formation：compounding from road and rage

context：Fit of "road rage" has landed a man in jail, accused of shooting a woman passenger who's car had "cut him off" on the highway. Robert Edward Muller Jr. , 40, was in the Lake County Jail on Friday, charged with firing the shot that critically wounded Cassandra Stewart, 20, on U. S. 441 on March 19.

—— "Highway driver accused of 'road rage' shooting," St. Petersburg Times, April 2, 1988

rush-minute　n.

English definition：he time of day when people are going to or from work in an area where the commute is short or has little traffic

Chinese equivalent：尖峰时刻

type of word formation：compounding from rush and minute

context："We used to have the rush-minute," said McCarthy, a Helena native who is the city's mayor. "Now we have the rush half-hour. "

——Susan Gallagher, "Montana's struggles with growth," Chicago Sun-Times, July 28, 1996

salad dodger n.

English definition：an overweight person；a person who shuns healthy foods

Chinese equivalent：不吃沙拉者

type of word formation：compounding from salad and dodger

context：Nicknamed the Salad Dodger, it was clear yesterday Ian Sturgess does not favour a diet of fresh fruit and vegetables. But now the 40-stone lorry driver's love of fried food and dislike of exercise is set to be the death of him.

——Flavia Munn, "Love of food will kill me if I can't have op," Western Daily Press, January 16, 2003

salmon v.

English definition：to ride a bicycle against the flow of traffic

Chinese equivalent：骑车逆行

type of word formation：conversion from noun to verb

context：I am not anarchic；I heed most traffic laws. I do not ride on the sidewalk（O. K., except for the final 25 feet between the curb cut and my front door, and then with caution）. I do not salmon, i. e. ride against traffic.

——Randy Cohen, "If Kant Were a New York Cyclist," The New York Times, August 4, 2012

sandwich generation n.

English definition：people who must care for both their children and their parents；people who have finished raising their children and now must take care of their aging parents

Chinese equivalent：夹心层一代

type of word formation：compounding from sandwich and generation

context：They have been called the "sandwich generation." Some are in their 30s or 40s, caught between the needs of their growing children and the needs of their aging parents. Others are in their 50s or 60s-planning for relaxation and travel, their children grown-when they must take on a new guardian-ship, becoming parents to their parents.

　　—The Globe and Mail (from a story in The New York Times), May 18, 1978

self-checkout　n.

English definition: a retail system that enables a customer to enter and pay for purchases without the aid of a cashier

　　Chinese equivalent: 自助结账

　　type of word formation: compounding from self and checkout

　　context: Other manufacturers predict a promising future and customer acceptance of a self-checkout lane in a store equipped with a conveyor belt that continually passes items along a combination scanner and security surveillance system. At stores with several self-checkout lanes, a cashier close to the checkstands would help customers and answer questions.

　　—Joel Elson, "Computers seen transforming supermarket of the future," Supermarket News, April 23, 1984

sexting　n.

English definition: sending a salacious text message

Chinese equivalent: 发送性信息

type of word formation: blend of sex and texting

　　context: There also are concerns about texting while driving, text-bullying and "sexting," or the term for adolescents messaging naked photos of themselves or others. What might have been intended for a friend can be widely distributed, and the texting of lewd photographs of minors can lead to criminal charges.

　　—Donna St. George, "6, 473 Texts a Month, But at What Cost?," The Washington Post, February 22, 2009

shock and Awe　n.

English definition: a military strategy in which massive amounts of firepower are unleashed early in a conflict in an effort to force the enemy's regime to collapse or surrender

Chinese equivalent：震慑打击

type of word formation：compounding from shock and wave

context：The phrase Shock and Awe has been trademarked by the Japanese electronics giant Sony for use in computer games. Sony registered Shock and Awe just one day after the US and British forces started the war in Iraq. The Americans coined the phrase to describe the heavy bombing of Iraq during the first few days of the conflict.

——Paul O'Kane, "Sony banks on war game," Sunday Tribune (Ireland), April 13, 2003

shoefiti n.

English definition：one or more pairs of shoes tied together by the laces and dangling from a powerline or other type of overhead wire

Chinese equivalent：电线挂鞋

type of word formation：blend of shoe and graffiti

context：Shoe-flinging, or shoefiti, has emerged as one of the more inexplicable forms of cultural expression in inner-city Melbourne.

——Lyndal Cairns, "Heels and toes and then a fling," Northcote Leader, January 3, 2007

surrogate boyfriends n.

English definition：a man hired to accompany a woman on a shopping trip

Chinese equivalent：陪购男友

type of word formation：compounding from surrogate and boyfriend

context：Women can hire "surrogate boyfriends" to take them shopping while their real other halves relax in a men-only zone, under a pilot scheme taking place today.

——Graham Hiscott, "Shop-hating boyfriends can hire stand-ins for their partners," Press Association, November 9, 2001

sight jogger　n.

English definition：sightseeing while running

Chinese equivalent：赏景慢跑者

type of word formation：compounding from sight and jogger

context：If you find the panoramas as appealing as the perspiration, consider yourself a "sight jogger."

http：//wordspy. com

slow food　n.

English definition：agricultural and gastronomic movement that emphasizes traditional, organic growing methods and the appreciation of fine food and wine

Chineseequivalent：慢餐

type of word formation：compounding from slow and food

context：Instead of drive-up burgers, tacos and chicken wings, slow food followers carve out a little bit of time in their hectic schedules to appreciate locally grown food, to preserve traditional cooking techniques (which usually require patience, not speed) and to celebrate the bounty with family and friends.

—Kathy Stephenson, "Taste Not Haste," The Salt Lake Tribune, April 24, 2002

slugging　n.

English definition：commuting to work by accepting a ride from a stranger who requires one or more extra passengers to legally qualify to drive in a high occupancy vehicle lane

Chinese equivalent：临时拼车

type of word formation：new meaning in old words

context：The Virginia Department of Transportation does not openly plug slugging; it fears liability for accidents or crime in the lots. But VDOT loves slugs, who number perhaps 10, 000, because each of them represents a car off the road.

　　—Patrick Lackey, "In northern Virginia, rides are free and everyone wins," The Virginian-Pilot, May 9, 2003

soccer mom　n.

English definition: a white, suburban woman who is married and has children

Chinese equivalent: 足球妈妈；家有学龄孩子、住在郊区的白人妇女

type of word formation: compounding from soccer and mom

context: One last word before we file The Year of the Soccer Mom into the political calendar of cliches. Somewhere along the way, the stressed-out, minivan-driving juggler of lives and roles was awarded the title of MVP in the competition for voters. She became the icon of 1996, nearly running over the Angry White Male of 1994 in her new Dodge Caravan.

　　—Ellen Goodman, "Meet the worried woman," The Boston Globe, November 10, 1996

social networking　n.

English definition: using a web site to connect with people who share similar personal or professional interests, particularly where the people in the site's database are connected to each other as friends, friends of friends, and so on

Chinese equivalent: 社交网络

type of word formation: compounding from social and networking

context: In San Francisco, where unemployment is rampant and social networking is nearly an obsession for just about everyone under 35, it seems everybody looking for a job is using sites like Friendster, Linkedin, Tribe. net, or Ryze, all of which allow you to join only if you invite friends to join with you, or if you are yourself an invitee.

　　—David Kirkpatrick, "I Get By With A Little Help From My Friends Of Friends Of Friends," Fortune, October 13, 2003

sock puppetry　n.

English definition：a fake persona used to discuss or comment on oneself or one's work, particularly in an online discussion group or the comments section of a blog

Chinese definition：网上假名

type of word formation：compounding from sock and puppetry

context：Sock puppetry may be rampant online, but journalists writing for their employer's Web site have a greater responsibility to be honest than run-of-the-mill posters.

— "Sock Puppet Bites Man," The New York Times, September 13, 2006

soft power　n.

English definition：power based on intangible or indirect influences such as culture, values, and ideology

Chinese equivalent：软实力

type of word formation：compounding from soft and power

context：What is needed is increased investment in "soft power," the complex machinery of interdependence, rather than in "hard power" — that is, expensive new weapons systems.

—Joseph S. Nye, Jr. , "The misleading metaphor of decline," The Atlantic, March, 1990

speed dating　n.

English definition：taking part in a series of short conversations with potential romantic partners

Chinese equivalent：速配

type of word formation：compounding from speed and dating

context：Speed dating is a growing phenomenon after the system was dreamt up by a New York rabbi：the usual method is that about two dozen men and women have just three minutes to impress each other before being moved on to the next table.

——Helen Rumbelow, "High-speed daters may find their love's labour's lost," The Times (London), January 31, 2003

spinach cinema   n.

English definition: movies that are not very exciting or interesting, but that one feels one must see because they are educational or otherwise uplifting

Chinese equivalent: 菠菜电影；励志电影

type of word formation: compounding from spinach cinema

context: Barmak's film "Osama" got a kind of affirmative-action boost from being the only movie from Afghanistan anybody in the West has ever seen (it's just the 43rd Afghan feature ever), but it's been playing in the United States for six weeks and keeps spreading to more cities. Its now apparent this is one of those little foreign films that won't quit, and if you've seen it you understand why. If you haven't seen it because it sounded too much like spinach cinema, I'm here to tell you not to miss out.

——Andrew O'Hehir, "Beyond the Multiplex," Salon. com. March 25, 2004

step-wife   n.

English definition: the current wife of a woman's ex-husband; the ex-wife of a woman's current husband

Chinese equivalent: 前夫之妻；丈夫前妻

type of word formation: affixation from step- to wife

context: "We never really knew what to call each other," Ms. Oxhorn-Ringwood said. "When Evan was a kid, I would call Louise my ex-husband's new wife, but after 10 years I couldn't do that anymore. We came up with stepwives to describe the relationship between ex-wives and current wives."

——Alex Witchel, "Wives No. 1 and No. 2 Bury the Sandals," The New York Times, May 12, 2002

sunlighting   n.

English definition：doing paid work while taking time away from one's day job

Chinese equivalent：白日兼职

type of word formation：analogy from moonlighting

context：In Spain the title of civil servant has long been a misnomer. They are civil enough. But they rarely serve. Bureaucrats practiced moonlighting to such an extent it turned into sunlighting. It was not unusual for them to hold down two, sometimes three — and in one case, a reliable source swears, four — separate jobs.

—John Darnton, "Madrid's new working class: the bureaucrats," The New York Times, February 7, 1983

surgiholic　n.

English definition：a person who seeks plastic surgery, from head to toe, and is never satisfied

Chinese equivalent：整形狂

type of word formation：affixation of -holic to Surgery

context：Choosing the appropriate patient is as important as selecting the correct procedure. Physical appearance is one clue to determine whether he or she is a good candidate. Is the patient disheveled? Does he or she have a defect which is only minimal? Has the patient already had a number of plastic surgery procedures performed? In other words, is he or she a plasti-surgiholic?

—Sheldon J. Sevinor, "The psychology of beauty: what are the right reasons for plastic surgery?," USA Today (Magazine), September, 1994

taikonaut　n.

Engllish definition：a Chinese astronaut

Chinese equivalent：太空飞行员

type of word formation：loan words from Chinese

context：Wu and Li already have a moniker — taikonauts — that appears on a Web site run by a Chinese software engineer in Singapore named Chen Lan.

257

The term, Chen explains, comes from the Chinese word "taikong," which means space or cosmos.

—Paul Hoversten, "China looks to blast off into the Space Age elite," USA Today, June 28, 1999

teacup n.

English definition: a college student with a fragile, easily shattered psyche

Chinese equivalent: 心理脆弱的大学毕业生

type of word formation: metaphor

context: Bright college freshmen arrive on campus as... "teacups" — sophisticated but overprotected... says Wendy Mogel, author of "The Blessing of a Skinned Knee," which is among the best-selling of a wave of new books about pressure.

"The teacups break because they literally don't know when to eat, and what to eat and when to sleep," says Mogel, a Los Angeles psychologist.

—Jennifer Sinco Kelleher et al., "Lessons in How to Chill Out," Los Angeles Times, April 17, 2002

technosexual n.

English definition: a male with a strong aesthetic sense and a love of technology

Chinese equivalent: 技术美男

type of word formation: blend from technology and sexual

context: A technosexual is not simply in touch with his feminine side but is connected to it on multiple platforms. He likes gadgets that have lots of gigabytes but are still small enough to fit in his pocket.

—Eric Edwards, "A new kind of lingo for those who tango," Orlando Sentinel (Florida), May 7, 2004

text v.

English definition: to create and send text messages

Chinese equivalent：发信息

type of word formation：conversion

context："Some Americans wonder how you can actually punch letters on a small keypad," said Ayson. "Some Filipino teenagers can do it blindfolded. I can't do that — but I can text while driving."

—Benjamin Pimentel, "Cell Phone Craze May Be Key to Philippines' Future; Nation a hotbed of 'texting'," The San Francisco Chronicle, February 11, 2001

The Gotcha Day　n.

English definition：the anniversary of the day on which a child was adopted

Chinese definition：领养日

type of word formation：compounding from got you and day

context：The Gotcha Day anniversary is also commonly called Adoption Day. Other choices are Family Day and Adoption Anniversary Day.

http：//wordspy. com

third place　n.

English definition：a place other than home or work where a person can go to relax and feel part of the community

Chinese equivalent：第三地

type of word formation：compounding from third and place

context：The term third place was invented by sociologist Ray Oldenburg and first appeared in his 1990 book The Great Good Place, a celebration of the places where people can regularly go to take it easy and commune with friends, neighbors, and just whoever shows up.

http：//wordspy. com

tiger mom　n.

English definition：a loving but strict mother who demands from her children obedience, respect, and academic excellence

Chinese equivalent：虎妈

type of word formation：compounding from tiger and mom

context：Amid all the psychosocial caterwauling these days over the relative merits of tiger mothers and helicopter dads, allow me to make a pitch for the quietly dogged parenting style of the New Caledonian crow.

—Natalie Angier, "Nurturing Nests Lift These Birds to a Higher Perch," The New York Times, February 1, 2011

tofurkey　n.

English definition：tofu molded into the shape of a turkey

Chinese equivalent：豆腐火鸡

type of word formation：blend from tofu and turkey

context：Vegetarians in Montreal can go to l'Herberie, a vegetarian restaurant serving tofurkey, made from tofu. It comes with gravy but isn't stuffed, says owner Mark Fagen.

—Barbara Wickens, "Turkey isn't the only game in town on Christmas Day," The Toronto Star, December 4, 1984

togethering　n.

English definition：vacationing with one's extended family or friends

Chinese equivalent：全家一起度假

type of word formation：affixation -ing to together

context：... in the last five years, eight out of 10 travelers took at least one vacation with extended family or friends.

More and more, Americans are vacationing in a loving gang, it seems.

This trend toward mob bonding is called "togethering," a novel word to my ear.

—Logan Jenkins, "NorthCounty the spot for 'togethering'," The San Diego Union-Tribune, April 29, 2004

trailing spouse　n.

English definition：in a relationship, the person who gives up their job in order to follow the other person to a new location where that person has found employment

Chinese equivalent：随迁配偶

type of word formation：compounding from trailing and spouse

context：In the past, companies primarily found jobs for wives of transferred employees. But now that too is changing. As women reach higher positions in corporations, more and more are being asked to transfer, and the husband ends up as the "trailing spouse."

— "Firms transferring employes often find jobs for spouses," The Wall Street Journal, January 21, 1982

trashout n.

English definition：the disposal of the entire contents of an abandoned house

Chinese equivalent：处理整个废弃房间的东西

type of word formation：conversion from verb to noun

context：Clearing out a house is called a trashout. But people leave behind much more than trash. They leave computers, printers, flat-screen TVs, new furniture, children's toys — all the stuff that used to be so easy to buy on credit. Charities don't want it, and so it all goes in the dumpster.

—Margaret Wente, "America's house of cards — make that, credit cards," The Globe and Mail, October 4, 2008

trophy children n.

English definition：a child used to impress other people and enhance the status of the parent or parents

Chinese equivalent：奖杯孩子

type of word formation：compounding from trophy and child

context：Hausner says some youngsters are often "trophy children" whose parents see them as nothing more than an extension of themselves.

"There is so much pressure to perform：They have to be in the best schools；they always have to look good." Hausner says.

—Frances Grandy Taylor, "Children of the rich suffer from wealth and neglect," The Record (Kitchener-Waterloo), November 23, 1990

turducken n.

English definition: a boneless turkey that is stuffed with a boneless duck that is stuffed with a boneless chicken

Chinese equivalent: 鸡鸭火鸡

type of word formation: blending from turkey duck and chichen

context: A turducken is a turkey, stuffed with a duck, stuffed with a chicken. Turducken is a dish popular in Louisiana.

—wikipedia. com

tweetup n.

English definition: a real world meeting between two or more people who know each other through the online Twitter service

Chinese equivalent: 推特网友见面

type of word formation: compounding from tweet and up

context: This is a blog entry that was inspired by a face-to-face meeting between two bloggers who connected via Twitter. What would you call that? A Twittermeet? A Tweetup?

—Scott Monty, "Be the Ball, Danny," The Social Media Marketing Blog, March 21, 2007

twilight mom n.

English definition: a mother who is a fan of the "Twilight" series of vampire novels

Chinese equivalent: 暮光之城妈妈迷

type of word formation: compounding from twilight and mom

context: Citing Shakespeare and Jane Austen as greater influences than Anne Rice or Stephen King ("I'm too much of a chicken" to read King, she says), Meyer noted that she already has some older readers, "'Twilight' Moms," she calls them.

—Hillel Italie, "Teen star Stephenie Meyer writes adult novel," Associated Press, April 30, 2008

two commas　n.

English definition: one million dollars

Chinese equivalent: 百万美元

type of word formation: compounding from two and comma

context: But who outside the US would recognise C. Everett Koop or Todd Krizelman? They both have their two commas — the latest American shorthand for millionaire status — after floating their infant Internet businesses on Wall Street.

—Adams Jones "Fortune favours the dreamers with the Big Internet Idea," The Times (London), July 22, 1999

ubersexual　n.

English definition: a heterosexual man who is masculine, confident, compassionate, and stylish

Chinese equivalent: 异性恋美男

type of word formation: affixation of uber- to sexual

context: Men are trying to be metrosexual, ubersexual, gay vague — where the lines are blurred and they are trying to adapt. At the office, men are adopting a lot of feminine traits. When I started working in the 70s, women couldn't talk about babies, shopping, and now men talk about babies and shopping at the office all the time.

—Maureen Dowd, quoted in Brooke Adams, "Whither the Y?," The Salt Lake Tribune, December 3, 2005

uninstalled　adj.

English definition: a euphemism for being fired

Chinese equivalent: 辞退（委婉语）；没有被安置

type of word formation: new meaning in old words

context: He offers ways to fight doublespeak, as simple as highlighting it in memos, rewriting the offending phrase in understandable language and placing it on the bulletin board. But be careful when you do this with management—you might find yourself "being walked" or "uninstalled" — that's "fired" to plain talkers.

—Judyth Rigler, "Books in Brief," San Antonio Express-News, July 30, 1996

universal release　n.

English definition: the simultaneous release of a new movie in theaters, on DVD, and on pay-per-view television

Chinese definition: 全球同步首映

type of word formation: compounding from universal and release

context: Mark Cuban says digital distribution and universal release will expand both the audience and the profits, while curbing piracy.

— "Hollywood Blues: Finding an Audience," ABC News Transcripts, July 17, 2005

unturkey　n.

English definition: a vegetarian substitute for turkey, particularly a turkey-shaped "bird" made with wheat gluten, soy, and other vegetarian ingredients

Chineseequivalent: 素食火鸡

type of word formation: affixation of un- to turkey

context: One of Open Harvest Natural Foods Cooperative Grocery's biggest sellers for Thanksgiving this year is a turkey substitute called unturkey. This bird-friendly holiday entree is a mixture of soy and wheat.

—Andrea Dukich, "Turkey Day creates other traditions for vegetarians," Daily Nebraskan, November 25, 2003

unwedding　n.

English definition: a formal ceremony held to celebrate a couple's divorce and to acknowledge their married life

Chinese equivalent：婚姻解除仪式

type of word formation：affixation of un- to wedding

context：Increasing numbers of incompatible Americans are choosing to solemnise the break-up of their marriages with an "unwedding ceremony" — often in church with a reception afterwards — which acknowledges their shared life and marks their amicable separation as a couple.

——Dermot Purgavie, "More and more divorcing couples are opting to end their union with a formal ceremony," Sunday Express, June 17, 2001

vegivore　n.

English definition：a person who craves or has a special fondness for vegetables

Chinese equivalent：食菜素食者

type of word formation：affixation of -vore to vegetable

context：For the vegivore, a vegetable can occupy the center of the plate, with meat adding flavor or functioning as a condiment.

——Robin Raisfeld and Rob Patronite, "Vegetables Are the New Meat," New York Magazine, November 15, 2010

vig　n.

English definition：a small fee charged to a buyer or seller by a third party whose software or technology was used to implement the transaction

Chinese equivalent：佣金

type of word formation：shortening of vigororish

context：To please the Street, and to make these evanescent windfalls appear recurring, Enron had to keep expanding into new (and ever more implausible) markets — a costly proposition that required the company to assume ever more debt. And here's the rub: Enron was not merely a toll-collector, a middleman skimming the vig off every transaction. It was a "counterparty" — that is, technically, it bought and then sold all the underlying goods that were traded under its aegis.

——Stephen Metcalf, "The How and Why of Enron," New York Observer, July 1, 2002

vishing n.

English definition: attempting to fool a person into submitting personal, financial, or password data either by sending an email message that includes a scammer-controlled phone number, or by spoofing an automated phone call from a financial institution using the voice-over-IP system

Chinese equivalent: 语音钓鱼

type of word formation: blend of voice and phishing

context: According to the FBI, there is a sudden rash of vishing across the country, the BBB reported in a release. "Vishing" is the term for automated calls or text messages to phones and cell phones with the specific goal of gaining personal information for the purposes of identity theft. "Phishing" is when the scam is perpetrated by e-mail.

http://wordspy. com

visitability n.

English definition: the extent to which a building is accessible to the disabled

Chinese equivalent: 残疾人友好

type of word formation: compounding of visit and ability

context: The three basic components of visitability are an entrance with no steps, ground-floor hallways and doorways wide enough for wheelchairs, and a ground-floor bathroom big enough for a wheelchair to enter and turn around.

—Jodi Wilgoren, "Wheelchair Users Achieve Milestone in 2 Ordinances," The New York Times, February 7, 2002

Volvoid n.

English definition: a white, moderately affluent, suburban professional who is politically liberal

Chineseequivalent: 富裕支持自由党的白人专业人士

type of word formation：affixation of -oid to Volvo

context：Weybridge writer Bo Knepp deserves more recognition than he ever got for his invention of the word Volvoid, a neologism which requires no translation or interpretation.

— "The Bike-Path Left," http：//www. addisoncountygop. org/

volun-tourism　n.

English definition：travel that also includes volunteer work

Chinese equivalent：含有志愿工作的旅游

type of word formation：blend of volunteer and tourism, or a play on volunteerism

context：Two other individuals honored in special awards categories were... Ray Fox of Las Vegas, owner of Certified Folder Display Service, Inc., who received the VolunTourism Veteran Award for donating his time, labor and service to the benefit of communities, territories and the state.

— "Rural conference honors tourism builders," Reno Gazette-Journal, April 12, 2002

xerocracy　n.

English definition：1. a society in which censorship is so pervasive that the only way to disseminate information is via photocopied documents and newsletters that have be written clandestinely; 2. rule by whoever feels like doing the photocopying

Chinese equivalent：复印社会；用复印机复制大量宣传品，动员群众争取民主

type of word formation：affixation of -cracy to xerox

context：Critical Mass was started by Chris Carsson in San Francisco in 1992 and he also had the concept of "xerocracy" — which means that anybody who can be bothered to pick a time and have the fliers Xeroxed is in charge.

—George Barber, "A charm offensive on city streets," The Independent, November 1, 1994

waitress moms　n.

English definition：a woman who is married, has children, works in a low-income job, and has little formal education

　　Chinese equivalent：低薪服务行业的妈妈

　　type of word formation：compounding from waitress and mom

　　context："There are more than twice as many Waitress Moms as Soccer Moms," said Ms. Lake, referring to blue-collar working women without college educations supporting children. "Right now they are voting Democratic, but many of them are undecided. . . . If you want to know the truth, it is now the Waitress Moms who are critical."

　　—Neil MacFarquhar, "What's a Soccer Mom Anyway?," The New York Times, October 20, 1996

Wal-Martian　n.

English definition：a person who does most of their shopping at Wal-Mart

Chinese equivalent：专门在沃尔玛购物者

　　type of word formation：affixation from Walmart and -ian

　　context：Just as the Romans imposed their culture on the nations they conquered, Wal-Mart wants to make Wal-Martians of us all. . . .

　　—Dominic Rush, "Wal-Martians," Sunday Times, June 10, 2001

wardrobing　n.

English definition：the practice of purchasing an item such as a piece of clothing or a device, using it briefly, and then returning it to the store for a refund

　　Chinese equivalent：穿后退货

　　type of word formation：new meaning in old word

　　context：A common problem for stores is consumers attempting to return merchandise that has been used but not defective. This practice, called "wardrobing," has affected more than half of companies during the past year and can include returns of everything from once-worn dresses to used laptop computers.

—Michele Chandler, "Tis the season for return fraud," San Jose Mercury News, October 31, 2006

warmedy n.

English definition: a comedy that features warm-hearted, family-oriented content

Chinese equivalent: 温馨家庭喜剧

type of word formation: blend from warm and comedy

context: "The 'creative team' that set out in the fall of 1978 to put Shirley together began with commensurate ambitions. The show was to be at once witty, happily emotional, and dramatic — a sort of classy example of the genre that one TV Critic has dubbed 'warmedy.'"

—Walter Kiechel III, "P. & G. Stars in a Prime-Time Cliff-Hanger," Fortune, December 31, 1979

warmist n.

English definition: a person who believes that the current global warming trend is the result of man-made factors

Chinese equivalent: 相信地球变暖是人为造成的人

type of word formation: affixation of -ist to warm

context: Some kind of deal is expected because while most countries accept that the earth is getting warmer, the debate as to what extent it will change our climate and impact on our lives has not been settled. "Warmists" (those who believe) and "deniers" largely agree on the basic science.

—Paul Melia, "The climate sceptics may be right — but are we willing to gamble?," Irish Independent, December 5, 2009

wasband n.

English definition: woman's ex-husband

Chinese equivalent: 女性的前夫

type of word formation: blend from was and husband

context: After reading here about the guy who calls his wife's ex her "wasband," Rosemary Wolohan confides that she refers to her two exes as "hasbeends."

—Herb Caen, "Plenty of Monday," The San Francisco Chronicle, March 12, 1990

webrarian   n.

English definition: a person who is an expert at not only finding information on the World Wide Web, but also at prioritizing, organizing, and cataloguing that information

Chinese equivalent: 网络技术应用专家

type of word formation: blend from web and librarian

context: Most Web pages are not indexed or retrieved by major search engines. This places a premium on the ability to ferret out resources buried in remote areas of the Web. An in-house "Webrarian" may be quite adept at such techniques.

—Brett Lockwood, Web-savvy lawyers

weddingmoon   n.

English definition: a vacation that includes both a wedding ceremony and a honeymoon

Chinese equivalent: 婚礼加蜜月度假

type of word formation: blend from wedding and honeymoon

context: Many Caribbean islands have reacted to the growing popularity of "weddingmoons" by agreeing to waive waiting period requirements so that, in some instances, tourists can marry the day they arrive.

—Harry Shattuck, "Not all couples wed to tradition," The Houston Chronicle, March 12, 1995

white food   n.

English definition: processed foods such as white sugar and all-purpose flour, or starchy foods such as potatoes, rice, and pasta

Chinese equivalent：白色食品

type of word formation：compounding from white and food

context：He also preaches a "no white food" diet to his patients, urging them to choose whole grains, fruits and such rather than starchy white potatoes, pasta and rice.

——Karen Feldman, "the newest four-letter word: CARB," The News-Press (Fort Myers, FL), January 14, 2004

white pollution　n.

English definition：litter, particularly plastic bags, but also papers, cups, and food containers

Chinese definition：白色污染

type of word formation：compounding from white pollution

context："White pollution," or improper disposal of rubbish such as food containers and wrapping paper in railway stations and along the rail lines, has aroused much concern, he added.

——Yang Yingshi, "Railways sprucing up sanitation," China Daily, April 10, 1995

whitelisting　v.

English definition：to place a name, e-mail address, Web site address, or program on a list of items that are deemed spamor virus-free

Chinese equivalent：加入白名单；加入名单

type of word formation：analogy from balcklist

context：Apple and Microsoft have pretty good but far from flawless filters in their mail clients. Measures taken before the junk gets to the in box include "blacklisting," which blocks stuff from known spammers, and "whitelisting," which permits only e-mail from preapproved senders.

——Stephen Levy, "How to Can the Spam," Newsweek, February 24, 2003

wife　v.

271

English definition: to downplay a women's career accomplishments in favour of her abilities as wife and mother

Chinese equivalent: 退居在家做全职太太

type of word formation: conversion

context: While we are on the subject of success, a Media Culpa is due Liddy Dole. I was among those who publicly feared that she would be "wifed" into oblivion after she quit her job to follow her man down the ole campaign trail. But Ramrod and Rainbow, as the Secret Service calls them, are now in reruns as the Senator and the Secretary.

—Ellen Goodman, "It's media-culpa time again," The Boston Globe, December 29, 1988

Wi-Fi n.

English definition: a networking scheme that creates a wireless connection between a device and a network or the Internet

Chinese definition: 无线上网

type of word formation: analogy from hi – fi

context: Working with companies like Wayport, MobileStar, and Airwave, hundreds and hundreds of airports, hotels, and even restaurants are rolling out Wi-Fi access. On Jan. 3, Starbucks and Microsoft announced that in early spring each coffeehouse would begin offering Wi-Fi access for its patrons.

—J. William Gurley, "Why Wi-Fi Is The Next Big Thing," Fortune, March 5, 2001

wiki n.

English definition: a collaborative web site that allows users to add, edit, and delete the site's content; the software that enables such collaboration

Chinese definition: 维基网

type of word formation: Hawaiian

context: Yahoo relies more on a Wiki-type model in which the community polices itself by correcting errors it finds in others' answers.

—Susan B. Shor, "Yahoo Brings Questioners Together With Answers," Technology News, December 9, 2005

word of mouse　n.

English definition：communication via computer-based means, such as e-mail, chat rooms, or newsgroups

　　Chinese equivalent：电脑鼠标交流

　　type of word formation：analogy from word of mouth

　　context：Given the clutter on the Internet, "how will people find it?" said Tom Beeby, creative director at Modem Media in Connecticut, an agency that specializes in Internet advertising. "They are trying to generate word-of-mouse, but I am skeptical."

　　—Denise Gellene, "Diversionary tactic," Los Angeles Times, September 18, 1997

wordrobe　n.

English definition：the words and phrases that comprise a person's vocabulary

　　Chinese equivalent：词汇橱

　　type of word formation：analogy from wardrobe

　　context："He spent his idle hours tailoring new words and stitching together new phrases in an effort to build up hiswordrobe."

　　http：//wordspy.com

worklesness　n.

English definition：the condition of being unemployed and having little or no prospect for employment

　　Chinese equivalent：无业

　　type of word formation：affixation of -lessness to work

　　context：Forget unemployment, the big challenge in deprived neighbourhoods is worklessness. There's a big difference. Unemployment is a temporary phenomenon：you may lose your job or fail to get one, but you're still actively

273

part of the labour market. ... Workless people, however, are out of the labour market completely.

—Rachel Spence, "Neighbourhood renewal," The Independent, January 23, 2002

yettie n.

English definition: a young person who owns or runs a technology company

Chinese equivalent: 雅帝；年轻有为的技术公司经营者

type of word formation: acronym from the phrase young, entrepreneurial, tech-based twenty-something

context: He carries a black computer bag stitched with a company name, has tightly cropped hair, wears tiny black glasses and frequently talks into a mobile phone about a double-chip switching router. Everyone has met him: he is a yettie, a Young, Entrepreneurial, Tech-based Twenty-something, and can be found tapping into his Psion while sipping a vodka and cranberry in a bar near you.

—Rupert Steiner, "Enter the abominable yettie," Sunday Times (London), February 13, 2000

YIMBY n.

English definition: a person who favors a project that would add a dangerous or unpleasant feature to his or her neighborhood

Chinese equivalent: 支持在自家后院建项目的人

type of word formation: acronym from the phrase yes in my back yard

context: You know about NIMBY's, Not in My Back Yard. These are the opposite, YIMBY's, by all means Yes in that same plot of grass.

— "... And the Year of the YIMBY," The Washington Post, February 19, 1988

zitcom n.

English definition: a television sitcom aimed at or featuring teenagers

Chinese equivalent：青少年情景喜剧

type of word formation：blend from zit and comedy

context：I find that despite the prevalence of antiseniorism in our society—evidenced by the preponderance of preadolescent zitcoms and other youth-oriented fare wherever I turn my bifocaled gaze.

In the2000 — Larry Gelbert, "The Seventh-Decade Stretch" The New York Times, 24 September 2000

zombie bank　n.

English definition：a bank that cannot lend money because its liabilities are greater than its assets, but remains in business thanks to government support

Chinese equivalent：僵尸银行

type of word formation：compounding from zombie and bank

context：Arguably, the only reason they haven't already failed is that the government is acting as a backstop, implicitly guaranteeing their obligations. But they're zombie banks, unable to supply the credit the economy needs.

—Paul Krugman, "Banking on the Brink," The New York Times, February 23, 2009

zombie computer　n.

English definition：a computer containing a hidden software program that enables the machine to be controlled remotely, usually to perform an attack on another computer

Chinese equivalent：僵尸电脑

type of word formation：compounding from zombie and computer

context：The danger is manifested in this version because the hackers are gaining control of as many as thousands of vulnerable zombie computers in order to magnify and direct their full-scale assault against a single victim from all directions.

—Brian Fonseca, "Denial-of-service attacks employ zombie PCs to hit networks," InfoWorld Daily News, December 9, 1999

zorb　n.

English definition：a sport in which a person is strapped inside a large sphere which is itself held inside a larger sphere by a cushion of air, and then rolled down a hill or along the ground

Chinese equivalent：左宾球

type of word formation：coinage

context：The latest zorb — made to look like a pumpkin — was completed this week and is on its way to wow the crowds at Euro Disney's Halloween celebration. Invented almost 10 years ago by Andrew Akers and Dwane van der Sluis, zorbing is now a global business with agents and franchisees in many countries. . . .

—Ellen Read, "Zorb inventors rolling in it," The New Zealand Herald, August 15, 2003

第十章　美语新词语翻译方法及原则

一　美语新词语翻译的方法

新词的翻译有两种方法。第一种是出版的英汉词典和新词词典提供新词的翻译方法和释义。第二种是国家行业或权威部门对一些新词或术语进行审定并发布标准译法。新华社、外交部和中国翻译杂志等也会对新词进行系统整理给出译名。但是这些翻译并不能涵盖飞速增长的新词，而且还有一定的滞后性。所以许多新词的翻译需要译者进行研究推敲，最终给出对等准确的译名。

英语中大量新词的出现给中国的英语学习者带来了新的困难。要使他们能够真正理解这些新词的内涵，归纳出行之有效的翻译方法是很有必要的。

（一）直译法

所谓直译，是指在符合译文语言习惯和规范条件下，在不引起错误的联想或误解的前提下，保留英语新词原文内容、它的文化内涵、修辞效果和语义表现。通过直译法，可以更好地保留英语中"原汁原味"的成分。例如把 money laundering 直译为"洗钱"，把 workaholic 译为"工作狂"，soft power 翻译为"软实力"，slow food 翻译为"慢餐"，couch potato 翻译为"沙发土豆"。更多的例子还有：

tiger mom 虎妈
road rage 路怒族
firewall 防火墙
bandwidth 宽带
passive overeating 被动多吃

mouse potato 鼠标土豆

lipstick effect 口红效应

dollarization 美元化

blue tooth 蓝牙

soft landing 软着陆

brain gain 人才获得

neighbourhood watch 邻里监视

chemotherapy 化学治疗

Clintonomics 克林顿经济政策

computer crime 计算机犯罪

frostbelt 霜冻地带

jobnik 工作狂

infowar 信息战

mouth feel 口感

green food 绿色食品

test-tube-baby 试管婴儿

visual pollution 视觉污染

teleholic 电视迷

netspeak 网语

web police 网络警察

zero tolerance 零容忍

white pollution 白色污染

green wash 洗绿

warming competition 热身赛

job hop 跳槽

ecocide 生态灭绝

（二）意译法

意译就是译文只保持原文内容而不保持原文形式的译法。由于文化差异，翻译在许多情况下难以找到对等的表达形式，新词的译语无法找到合适而简短的对应词时，就必须采取意译法了，有时还得采用一些很长或很复杂的解释性语言。例如把 happy house 意译为"公共厕所"，

wife 被翻译为"在家做专职太太"，warmist 翻译为"相信地球变暖是人为的人"，birther 被翻译为"奥巴马不是出生在美国的坚信者"，twilight mom 被翻译为"暮光之城影迷妈妈"，slugging 被翻译成"即时拼车"，sexting 被翻译成"发送性信息"，mouse race 被译为"轻松工作"，rat race 则被译为"激烈竞争的工作"。类似的例子还有：

all-nighter 开夜车

metrosexual 都市玉面男

meatloaf 群发信息

low hanging fruit 容易的工作

nest egg 小金库

Mcjob 低薪临时工

McMansion 超大房子

distance work 在家工作

brick and mortar 实体店

cruise 猎艳

kickbacks 回扣

left coast 西海岸

quiz kid 神童

apple picking 偷抢苹果系列通信设备行为

ape diet 素食

graze 少吃多餐

quit cold turkey 突然戒掉（烟、酒、毒品）

universal release 全球同步首映

dancing outreach 摇头丸

fat farm 减肥中心

furlough 裁员

brain trust 智囊团

make under 素颜

（三）阐述法

阐述法在翻译新词语时被广泛使用，主要用于翻译政治政策、科学术语、宣传口号等等。许多新词语在英语的口语和书面语中变得很流行，这是由于它们具有典型的现代精神和旺盛的生命色彩。一些新词新语因为有强烈的生命色彩，所以它们具有意味深长的文化内涵，这使得普通人很难理解，因此应该加上全面的解释来详细翻译原文的信息。20世纪60年代美国民权运动高涨，出现了来自英语副词 in 的后缀-in，表示"有组织的抗议或示威"、"公开的集体活动"，sit-in 的意思是"坐在地上表示抗议"。在此之后，出现了新的派生词语 lie-in, lock-in, swim-in, love-in, teach-in, shave-in，分别翻译为"（在大街等处）卧地抗议示威"、"把自己锁在房里以示抗议"、"游泳抗议或游泳示威"、"颓废派青年爱情聚会活动"、"教授或学者长时间不间断演讲以示抗议"、"剃头以示抗议"。

新出现的词语代表着一种全新的社会现象，新词语的使用还处于不被大众接纳和不稳定的状态，最合适的翻译方法就是进行阐释。这类词语的翻译也需要经过充分的摸索才能找到合适的词。比如 grup 是 grown-up 的缩写，来源于美国电视系列 Star Trek，被翻译为"装嫩族，特指那些实际年龄超过30岁，穿着打扮和行为举止却始终像少男少女的人"。

white collar 最早出现时，人们不知其为何意。通过在译名后注释的方法才能知道它的含义。现在经过时间的推移，它再也不是什么陌生的词汇。人们还以此类推创出 new collar（新领），golden collar（金领），grey collar（灰领），pink collar（粉领），open collar（敞领），green collar（绿领）等新词。

lame duck 最早翻译成"坡脚鸭"，给读者带来困惑，坡脚鸭到底是什么？这就很有必要作进一步阐述并把阐述的内容置于括号中。即在美国政界，常用 lame duck 来形容任期将届满的政治人物的窘境，尤其是第二任期快结束的总统。

一些词在最初翻译过程中为了易于理解，会在译名后加上括号注释。如 sandwich generation 如果译成"三明治一代"可能会让人迷惑不解，如果进行意译，在译名"夹心层"后面加上注释"同时扶养与照顾父母和子女的人"，新词则更为容易理解。

doughnut pattern 作为一个新词如果译为"多纳圈模式"让人不知所云，但是如果在后面加上注释"一种城市发展模式，即商业和富裕的居民居住在郊区，而穷人则居住在空空的市中心"，就会很容易理解，而且更加形象地描绘出这种城市发展模式。

（四）音译法

音译的方法是借用原文新词语的读音巧妙地译为合适的汉语对应词，同时保持原文的意思。许多新词汇被引进时没有对应物和对应词，译者常常采用音译的方法。这种音译方法直接且简易，同时具有异国风情。汉语中许多英语外来语都是采取音译的方法。例如：mosaic（马赛克），punk（朋克），latte（拿铁），twitter（推特），talk show（脱口秀），humor（幽默），copy（拷贝），fans（粉丝），parkour（跑酷），geek（奇客），inker（印客），bike（拜客），hacker（黑客），AIDS（艾滋病），clone（克隆），radar（雷达），vitamin（维他命），TOEFL（托福），gene（基因），bungee（蹦极）等。一些外来词刚被介绍到中国的时候，对中国人来说它们是新的事物和概念。当人们不想或找不到合适的翻译名称时，就会使用音译。因而在介绍新的思想和新事物时人们会使用音译法。商品名称的翻译尤为明显，例如：Bally（百利），Levis（李维斯），Dunhill（登喜路），Johnson（强生），Fendi（芬迪），GUCCI（古驰），Coach（寇姿），Canon（佳能），Adidas（阿迪达斯），Golgate（高露洁），Prada（普拉达），Paul Smith（保罗·史密斯），Ralph Lauren（拉夫·劳伦），Louis Vuitton（路易·威登）等。

（五）半音半意法

通过将原词一分为二，其中的一半采用音译的方法，而另外一半则采用意译的方法，这就是半音半意法。这种方法汲取音译法和意译法的优点，增加语言的魅力，避免它们各自的不足。例如 Blackberry（黑莓手机）曾经是一个全新的单词，如果使用音译，人们不会懂得它的确切意思，如果意译，也不能用几个单词就能进行全面的解释。为了避免两种方法的缺陷，给出一个较为明确易懂的翻译，人们把它翻译为黑莓手机。其他使用这种方法翻译的新词新语有：miniskirt（迷你裙），bungie jumping（蹦极跳），black humor（黑色幽默），reality show（真人秀），nano technology（纳米技术），salad oil（色拉油），internet（因特网），hula loop（呼啦圈），gene bank（基因库），X-ray（X 光），等等。

（六）音译加上汉语单词

为了给新词和表达附加上解释性的阐述，这种翻译方法把音译词和汉语中的单词连在一起，形成一种新颖且有异域风情的翻译方法。与此同时，它对信息的接收者来说也并不是完全的陌生，因为它保留了目标语言中的单词。下面的例子可以表明这种格式的运用：bowling（保龄球），sauna（桑拿浴），cartoon（卡通片），TOEFL（托福考试），pizza（比萨饼），golf（高尔夫球），zorbing（左宾球），yuppie（雅皮士），shaping（舍宾运动），等等。

（七）英语单词加上汉语解释单词

在现代生活中，人们经常使用下面的原语单词和汉语：POS 机，IC卡，IP 卡，B 超，X 光，NBA 比赛，MTV 决赛，CCTV 杯，Office 软件，MBA 考试，hi-fi 音响，GRE 考试，BEC 成绩，等等。这些都是英语单词和解释性的汉语单词的结合。

（八）省译

随着国际交流的频繁，许多英语新词尤其是缩略语已经家喻户晓，人们在日常生活中不再把它们翻译成汉语，而是直接使用这些词汇。体现了语言的经济性原则。汉语中越来越多地直接使用英语的词汇和缩略语，表明我国和外部世界经济、文化交流日渐密切，英语新词的引入和翻译也必将进一步促进这种交流。这类例子有：ATM，BBS，SOHO，GDP，GPS，WTO，CEO，NBA，MTV，VCD，E-mail，IT，等等。

二　美语新词语翻译的原则

（一）准确反映原词语

精确、准确是英语新词语翻译中应该遵循的原则，在可理解的基础上，译文应该尽可能准确地表达原文的意思。翻译者肩负着将正确信息传递给受众的重任，因此翻译工作必须要做到求实求真。只有这样才能实现国际间文化、经济、政治等的交流与学习。例如，如果把 cold turkey 翻译为冷火鸡，乍一看，似乎觉得是对等的译文，较为准确。但是，随后查证就会发现，这种翻译并不准确，让人不知所云。更为准确的翻译方法是"突然戒掉"（毒品、酒）。只有这样才能准确地表达原文的意思。

（二）遵从译语的语言习惯

遵从译语的语言习惯是翻译重要的原则。新词语进行翻译时必须考虑是否符合汉语语言习惯，能否被人接受。如果直接翻译，有的外来词语不能融入我国文化，例如 spend money like water，如果翻译成花钱如水，并不符合汉语语言习惯。更为恰当的翻译是"挥金如土"。meatloaf 是美国大众喜欢的具有美国特色的主食，作为动词如果被译为"做烤肉面包"，这种浓重的含有异国风情的译法不能融入我国的本土文化，让人不知所云。作为动词表示"群发"，只有这种翻法才是正确的。因此在引入新词语的时候不能背离汉语语言文化。

（三）尊重原文的语体语域

各种语言都有其不同的语体，而不同的语体之间存在着明显的差异。有些新词语只用于书面语，有些新词语只用于口语。交际身份、交际场合、交际内容以及交际心理差别会导致用词不同。在翻译过程中，必须把新词语中口语与书面语、正式语体与非正式语体之间的差异表达出来。

总之，随着国际交流的增加、科技文化的巨大发展，我国与世界将进行越来越密切的经济、文化交流，英语新词语将会大量出现并得到引进和翻译，更多的外来语会进入英语。英语新词的翻译反之必将进一步促进国际间的交流。翻译的时候，译者要使译文不仅在语义上准确，而且在语用上也要适宜。新词语的翻译要信守原文的内容意旨，遵从译语的语言习惯，还要遵循原文的语体语域。

第六篇
美语新词语及当代美国
文化发展趋势

第十一章　美语新词语发展趋势

根据美语新词网上字典 wordspy、美国方言协会、韦式英汉词典、牛津新词字典对于 21 世纪新词新语进行统计发现，它们大多数由复合法、派生法、缩略法、转化法等传统构词法构成。这些新词大量出现，越来越呈现简化、来源多样化、创新性强、系列化等特点。

一　美语新词语呈井喷趋势大量出现

人们对英语的总词汇量有各种不同的估计，1992 年版的《牛津英语词典》收词 50 万个，一般的估计是英语的词汇量已超过 100 万个。但是，如果把各种专有名称计算在内的话，数量就无穷无尽了。用"多若繁星"来比喻一点都不夸张。以地球上的物种（species）而言，已经命名的物种就达 150 万—180 万种，而且每年还以 13000 种的速度增加。根据不同的估计，地球上的物种在 300 万—1 亿种之间。估计的数字差距之大，难怪有人惊呼物种的数量是个 black hole（黑洞），物种数量估计是 armchair biology（坐在椅子里空想的生物学），纯属"pseudo-science"（伪科学）。更为严峻的是，我们无法确定地球上物种的数量，而且对已经确定的物种还了解甚微。1997 年 8 月 18 日的《美国新闻与世界报道》提供了若干已经确定的物种的数字：世界上有 4000 种哺乳类动物（mammals），4200 种两栖类动物（amphibians），6100 种棘皮类动物（echinoderms），6300 种爬行类动物（reptiles），9000 种鸟类（birds），12000 种蚯蚓（earthworms），18800 种鱼类（fish），26900 种海藻（algae），30800 种原生动物（protozoa），50000 种软体动物（mollusks），69000 种真菌（fungi），123400 种非昆虫类节肢动物（noninsect arthropods），248000 种植物（plants），751000 种昆虫（inoects）。要想记住那么多物种的名称绝非易事。21 世纪科学技术的发展速度将会更快，科技方面的新词必然会以更快的速度增加。

美国的科学技术突飞猛进，社会经济迅速发展，道德观念急剧转变。为了反映不断出现的新发明、新事物、新问题、新概念，以适应交际的需要，一大批独具特色的新词应运而生。例如：1990 年，美国耗资 21 亿美元发射的哈勃太空望远镜，首次为宇宙学中的黑洞理论和大爆炸理论提供了直接证据，并由此而产生了一批新词语。如：chaos（混沌状态），chaology（混沌理论），anti-matter（反物质），anti-proton（反质子），antiparticle（反粒子），supersymmetry（超对称性），squark（超夸克），slepton（超对称轻子），sparticle（超对称粒子），selectron（超对称电子），sneutrino（超对称中微子），kron（K 介子），muon（μ 介子），pion（π 介子），lepton（轻子），baryon（重子），quark（夸克），antimatter（反物质）等。人造卫星绕月出现新词 apolune（远月点）和 perilune（近月点）。太空船与太空站在空间会合对接，被称为 docking 或 linkup（靠泊）。其他太空术语有 CM（command module：指令舱，指挥舱），splashdown（溅落），space sickness（宇航病），deep space（深空间，远空间），quasar（类星射电源），pulsar（脉冲星），neutron strar（中子星）及神秘的 black hole（太空黑洞），astrionics（太空电子学）等。

数学和其他科学出现大量新词，如 NOT（"非"逻辑算子），parametric equation（变数方程），newmath（新数），artificial intelligence（人工智能），magnetocardiogram（磁性心动扫描记图），IC（集成电路），cryosurgery（冷冻手术），macrometereology（大气象学），ocean engineering（海洋工程学），phytochemistry（植物化学），biotelemetry（生物遥测学）等。

美国几乎在信息和通信技术的所有分支领域都处于世界领先地位。internet，局域网（Local Area Network），广域网（Wide Area Network）等均诞生于美国并获得广泛认可和使用，美国开发的个人计算机操作系统已成为事实上的全球标准。这些领域的新词语日新月异，层出不穷。如：intranet（内联网），extranet（外联网），cybercafe（网吧），website（网站），newbie（网上新手），guru（电脑高手），hardware（硬件），software（软件），mouse（鼠标），modem（猫），wired（上网），boot（启动电脑），click（点击），hacker（电脑黑客），virus（病毒），millenium bug

（千年虫），surfing the net（网上冲浪），fanzine（名人杂志），unicast（单播），multicast（多播），cellular phone（手机），beeper（寻呼机），swipe（刷卡）等。

人们对环境污染的重视在近年特别显著，环境学家倡议设立 Earth-Day（地球清洁日）和 Eargh Week（地球清洁周）。pollution 出现于各大报纸杂志上：heat/thermal pollution（热污染），internal pollution（体内污染），visual pollution（视觉污染），antipollutionist（反污染者），environmentalist（环境问题专家），dystrophication（河湖污染）等。由此，美国的环境监测评估技术、污染控制与避害技术在世界上均具有较高水平，有关的新词有：fallout（放射性尘埃），eco sphere（生态圈），reductionism（还原论），spriggina（原始细菌化石），eco-tourism（生态旅游），environmentalist（环境保护学家）等。

美国在医学技术和生物技术方面也创造了许多使人耳目一新的词汇。如：DNA（脱氧核糖核酸），anorexia（厌食症），lippo suction（手术减肥），trans-sexual operation（变性手术），plastic surgery（整容外科手术），genetic code（遗传密码），hospice（临终关怀医院），angiography（血管学），bionic organs（仿生器官），sperm bank（精子库），GM Human（基因人），diet pill（减肥丸），the pill（口服避孕丸），HIV（艾滋病毒），aids neurosis（艾滋恐惧症），euthanasia（安乐死），clone（克隆），hotoscanning（光扫描），open heart surgery（开心手术），picornabirus（换心人），microcirculation（微血管循环）等。

世界性的经济危机、通货膨胀和工商业的发展也是新词的重要来源之一。ASP（American Selling Price 美国售价），slumpflation（萧条膨胀），added-value tax（增值税），Eurodollar（欧洲美元），petrodollar（石油美元），revenue sharing（国库分享），Eurogeddon（欧洲末日），Federal deficit（联邦赤字），Federal shutdown（联邦政府关闭）等都是近期产物。

美国的社会生活五光十色，反映到新词新义上也是丰富多彩。美国政府在处理国际事务时热衷于 shuttle diplomacy（穿梭外交）和 mini summit（小型最高级会议），对不同的问题分别采用 high profile（高姿态）和 low profile（低姿态）。有时通过 psywar（心理战）或 trade war（贸易战），坚持 back yardism（排外主义）或 globalism（全球性干涉主义）。教育、体育、娱乐方面的新词琳琅满目，而且备受青年人的青睐。如：polyversity（多元大学），geeks（网络电脑精英），preppie（预科生），dropouts（退学生），flunkstein（屡次留级生），louse up（考试不及格），flunk out（因考试不及格被退学），salchow（滑冰单、双或三周跳），tankini（三点式泳装外套紧身透明背心的名牌泳装），slimnastics（减肥操），soap opera（言情连续剧），throat（歌唱家），infomercial（商业电视节目），songsmith（作曲家），noisesmith（音乐家），weeper（悲歌），top of the pops（最受青年人喜爱的歌曲），soft number（柔和或伤感的叙事曲），vidiot（什么电视节目都看的人），couch potato（终日看电视的人），square eye（电视迷）。家庭生活方面的新词也比比皆是：broken home（单亲家庭），nuclear family（核心家庭），split（离婚），leisure wear（休闲装），maxicoat（长女服），pullover（套头毛衫），rager（晚会），mosh（舞会），zit（青春痘），xerox（复印或复印机），nerd（书呆子），downsize（炒鱿鱼），snarfe（开怀大吃），viagrace divorce（男方服用伟哥导致妻子要求离婚）等。

可以预见，再过几十年，当 22 世纪来临的时候，地球上 100 多亿人口使用的英语将跟现在大不相同，不同的原因在于大量涌现的新词新语改变了英语词汇的结构，人们谈论的话题、常用的词语超出现在人们的想象。

二　美语新词语呈系列化趋势

众所周知，21 世纪的社会是信息社会，信息的产生、信息的存储、信息的分配和信息的应用已成为这个社会的基本特征，而网络技术是实现上述目标的基本手段之一。以 Internet 为代表的网络将更为广泛应用，并且极大地影响和改变着人们的生活方式和工作方向。现在学习、应用、参与网络的人越来越多，网络技术日新月异，伴随产生了许多新术语、新词语。它包括网络文化、网络技术、网络经济、网络生活、网络机构及组织等方面的新词新语。例如：

cyberspace 网络空间

cyberfood 电脑食品

cyberfraud 网络诈骗

cybernaut 网络用户

cybercafé 网际咖啡屋

cybermouse 三维鼠、遥控鼠

cyberphobia 电脑恐惧症

cyberpunk / cypherpunk 网际访客、网际浪人

cyber sales 网际行销

cybersex / cyberporn / cybersmut / cyberslut 网际色情

以 e/E-（electronic 电子的，网上的）为前缀构成的新词有：

e-shopping 网上购物

e-consumer 电子消费者

e-commerce 电子商务

e-market 电子市场

e-book 电子书籍

e-marketing 电子营销

e-business 电子商务

e-life 电子生活

e-cash 电子货币

e-currency 电子货币

e-fit （嫌疑犯人的）计算机模拟画像

e-mail 电子邮件

e-motion （电子邮件或互联网上用符号表示的）情感符

e-text 电子文本

e-services 电子服务

e-banking 电子银行

e-trade 电子贸易

e-wallet 电子钱包

再比如-ization/-fication 在现代英语中经常被添加到国名后，它可将一个国家的某方面重要特征或形势勾画出来，这是英美报刊常用的一种构词方法，具有高度概括的特点。例如：Iraqification（伊拉克化）指美国向伊拉克交权，以便脱身。美国 2003 年发动伊拉克战争并占领伊拉克后，发现想使之变成一个西方式国家并非易事。占领军到处受到打击

而疲于应付，实际上已受孤立，在国内也遭到批评与抨击。因此，美国想早日撤军，让伊拉克人自己去收拾这个烂摊子。《卫报》是这样使用这一词语的：Iraq will be central to Thuraday's meeting between our Bush and our Blair. The announcement this weekend that the Iraqification process is to be accelerated should be given a cautious welcome. （伊拉克问题将是布什总统与布莱尔首相周日会谈的中心议题。本周末将发表声明要加快伊拉克化计划，而这个计划将受到谨慎的欢迎）。类似的新词新语还有 Finlandization（芬兰化）、Vietnamization（战争越南化）、Colombianization（哥伦比亚化）、Lebanization（黎巴嫩化）、Copenhagenization（哥本哈根化）、blurbification（模糊化）、Coca-Colanization（美国文化殖民化）、casualization（休闲化）、cyberdisinhibition（网上放任化）、pseudoextinction（物种进化），等等。

三　美语新词语拼写简化

现代社会的生活和工作节奏加快，人们寻求在最短的时间内获取最大的信息量。美国人崇尚简单快捷的生活方式，媒体用语着重简洁明快。反映到新词上是，缩略语、截短词和拼缀词的大量使用。

（一）缩略语（Initialism）

缩略语有 DINs = double income no kids（双收入无孩子家庭），Kipper = Kids In Parents' Pockets Eroding Retirement Savings（啃老族），DWY = driving while yakking（开车打电话），SMUM = Smart, Middle-Class, Uninvolved, Mother（潇洒不愿照看孩子的中产母亲），SCAM = Smart Child Centered Active Mom（潇洒、活跃以孩子为中心的母亲），JOOTT = just one of those problems（仅仅是常见的问题而已），B2 = business to business（公司对公司），TGIM = thank God it's Monday（感谢上帝到了周一），UMPC = ultramobile personal computer（超移动个人电脑），HDTV = high-definition television（高清晰电视），ISP = internet service providers（网络服务提供商），TGIF = Thank God it's Friday（感谢上帝到了周五），SINK = single income, no children（单份收入没有孩子家庭），CIO = chief information officer（首席信息官），CEO = chief executive officer

（首席执行官），CFO ＝ chief financial officer（首席财务总监），CTO ＝ chief technology officer（首席技术总监），CMO ＝ chief marketing officer（首席销售总监），CHO ＝ chief human resource officer（首席人类资源执行官），COO ＝ chief operating officer（首席运行执行官）。美国人似乎最喜欢首字母连写，致使这类词的数量急剧增长。E. T. Crowley 等人1961 年编著 *Acronyms and Initialisms Dictionary*（第一版）时，只收入 16000 个，到 1970 年第三版时，已增加到 80000 个，到 1990 年第七版时，猛增到 30 万个。首字母缩略词的快速增加充分反映了美国人求简追新的心理趋向。如 BF ＝ best friend（最好的朋友），AL ＝ artificial intelligence（人工智能），PC ＝ personal computer（个人电脑），COBOL ＝ common business oriented language（面向商业的通用语），MSDOS ＝ Microsoft Disk Operating System（微软磁盘操作系统），CPU ＝ Central Processing Unit（中央处理器），ER ＝ emergency room（急救室），CD ＝ compact discs（激光唱片），VCD ＝ video compact disc（激光视盘），WWW ＝ world wide web（万维网），ESL ＝ English as a second language（作为第二语言的英语），SALT ＝ strategic arms limitation talks（限制战略武器谈判），GB ＝ Green Beret（美军在坎大哈附近的绿色贝雷帽行动），AASAH ＝ American Army Special Action Headquarters（美国陆军特别行动指挥部）。

（二）截短词（clipping）

20 世纪 90 年代，新潮美语中出现了一批为数众多的截成词，有的截头，有的裁尾，有的截头裁尾留中间。截成词因造词简练、使用方便而越来越受到人们的欢迎。截头去尾和截尾去头的有：bro ＝ brother（哥哥或弟弟），gram ＝ grandma（奶奶，姥姥），diff ＝ difference（不同），infor ＝ information（信息），prob ＝ problem（问题），expo ＝ exposition（展览会），mod ＝ modern（时髦的人或物），pol ＝ politician（政治家），cig ＝ cigarette（纸烟），doc ＝ doctor（医生），tab ＝ tablet（药片），pro ＝ professional（专业人员），memo ＝ memorandum（备忘录），deli ＝ delicatessen（熟食店），divi ＝ dividend（红利），limo ＝ limousine（大型轿车），fess ＝ confess（供认），phone ＝ telephone（电话），copter ＝ helicopter（直升机），con ＝ convention，decaf ＝ decaffeinated（去咖啡因的），vert ＝ vertical，amnio ＝ amniocentesis（羊膜穿刺术），techie ＝ technician，skell ＝

skeleton，sig = signature，scally = scallywag（饭桶），rad = radical，opto = optoelectronic（光电的）等。截去头尾留中间的如：flu = influenza（流行性感冒），tec = detective（侦探），frig 或 frige = refrigerator（电冰箱）。

（三）拼缀词（blending）

对两个词进行剪裁，取其中的一部分，或保持一个词的原形，与另一词的一部分组成一个新词。美国人现在越来越频繁地用这种方法创造出大量的新词。这类词主要出现在科技、政治、金融等发展迅速而又为人们敏感的领域。拼缀词的例子有：Chindia 来自 China 和 India，turducken 来自 turkey，duck 和 chicken，tofurkey 来自 tofu 和 turkey，Obamacon 来自 Obama 和 conservative，oppoguy 来自 opponent 和 guy，Barackphobia 来自 Barak 和 phobia，deleb 来自 dead 和 celebrity，celeblog 来自 celebrity 和 blog，groceraunt 来自 grocery 和 restaurant，Chimerica 来自 China 和 America，freeconomics 来自 free 和 economics，slowflation 来自 slow 和 inflation，recve 来自 Recreational vehicle，jumbrella 来自 jumbo 和 umbrella，tradigital 来自 traditional 和 digital，infomercial 来自 information 和 commercial，freemium 来自 free 和 premium，coopetition 来自 cooperation 和 competition，blogbrity 来自 blog 和 celebrity，abortuary 来自 abort 和 mortuary，vegelate 来自 vegetable 和 chocolate，emergicenter 来自 emergent 和 center，nutraceutical 来自 nutition 和 pharmaceutical，Whitewatergate 来自 White 和 Watergate，boatel 来自 boat 和 hotel，unabomber 来自 university 和 bomber，e-lancer economy 来自 electronic，freelancer 和 economy，infomediation 来自 information 和 intermediation，simputer 来自 simple 和 computer，eddress 来自 email 和 address，ringxiety 来自 ring 和 anxiety。拼缀词分为以下几类：

1. 一整词 + 另一词尾部分。如：boatel（码头旅馆）= boat + hotel，airmada（机群）= air + armada，radiogram（无线电报）= radio + telegram，mooncraft（旅月飞船）= moon + aircraft，sportscast（体育节目播报）= sport + broadcast，peek scope（袖珍望远镜）= peek + telescope，plugola（广告贿赂）= plug + payola，glideriter（滑写笔）= glider + writer，travelogue（旅行见闻）= travel + monologue，Reaganomics（里根经济政策）= Reagan + economics 等。

2. 一词首部分 + 另一整词。如：autoindustry（汽车工业） = automobile + industry, gravisphere（重力场） = gravity + sphere, paraglider（降落滑翔机） = parachute + glider, commart（欧共体） = common + market, dishmobile（活动洗碟机） = dishwasher + mobile, bureaucrock（好摆架子而无能的官吏） = bureaucrat + crock, educare（为老年人办的教育） = education + care, garbags（可随便丢掉的垃圾袋） = garbage + bags, petrodollars（石油美元） = petroleum + dollars, cinemactor（男电影演员） = cinema + actor。

3. 一个词的词首部分 + 另一词的词首或词尾部分。如：recve（娱乐车） = recreational + vehicle, scifi（科幻小说） = science + fiction, telesat（通信卫星） = telecommunications + satellite, telecon（电话会议） = telephone + conference, interpol（国际警察） = international + police, teched（技术编辑）= technical + editor, wespac（西太平洋）= western + pacific, gox（气态氧） = gaseous + oxygen, lox（液态氧） = liquid + oxygen, telex（用户直通电报） = teleprinter + exchange 等。拼缀词在开始出现时往往大写，具有专用名词或术语的性质，在普遍使用之后，也就变成普通名词了。这种词形结构简单，符合美国英语日趋简化的要求。

4. 网络词汇别具一格，新奇有趣。在美国，计算机已成为普通家庭的消费品，成为家庭办公、交际和娱乐的重要工具。为了充分发挥计算机的效能，美国人创造了一套别具一格的计算机网络词汇。例如：AFAIK = As far as I know（据我所知），IHNI = I have no idea（我不知道），IMO = in my opinion（依我的看法），JAM = just a minute（请稍候），KISS = keep it simple stupid（长话短说），OIC = Oh, I see（噢，我明白了），TIA = Thanks in advance（先说谢谢了），TTYL = talk to you later（下回再谈），FAQ = frequently asked questions（常问的问题），FYI = For your information（谨此通知），SYL = See you later（再见），BTW = By the way（顺便问一下），THERE = Are you there?（你在那里吗?）。就连美国人创造的表情符号也因其简便实用、幽默风趣而风靡世界。如：":—)"代表 smiling, ":—("表示 very sad, "(8—)"表示 wears glasses, ":—O"表示 big surprise, ":—i"表示 smoker, ";—)"表示 winking, "%—I"表示 confused, ":—P"表示 tongue

sticking out。网络语言是美国进入网络时代新词语激增的集中体现。随着计算机网络的飞速发展，美国新网语的产生频率将会更高，传播手段和速度也将更加方便和快捷。

四 美语新词语来源多样化

（一）吸收大量外来语

美国被公认为世界大熔炉，来自世界各地的移民对于美国文化和语言的影响日益增大，国际间交往越来越频繁，英语成为世界上词汇最丰富的语种，它不但善于接受和吸收外来语词，而且还接受和吸收各个民族的风俗习惯和文化概念。英语吸收了大量的世界各地语言，包括希腊语、拉丁语、俄语、阿拉伯语、法语、德语、日语、汉语等词汇和语缀，给美语增添了丰富的色彩。这类词有来自日语的 Teppan yaki（铁板烧），manga（日本连环漫画册），aragotokaizen，ciabatta，aitech。源自意大利语的 trattoria（意大利小饭馆），bimbo，fatwa，hamas，Islamic，jihad 等进入英语，成为美语新词。更有许多法语外来语如 déjà vu，jamai vu，déjà dit 成为美语新词。近年来，印度语中的 bangle 取代 bracelet，cheetah 表示"印度豹"，guru 用来表示"宗教老师"，guru site 表示"专题网站"。此外还有德语的 Ossi，俄语的 pamyat，lasik（激光原位角膜磨镶术），阿拉伯语的 shawarma（沙瓦玛烤肉卷），intifada，菲律宾语的 Imeldific（依美尔达式的），刚果语的 funky（质朴无华的），荷兰语的 skeg（冲浪运动员，冲浪爱好者），西班牙语的 El Nino。

值得一提的是汉语外来语。据总部位于德克萨斯州的美国"全球语言监督"发布报告称，自 1994 年以来进入英语的新词汇中，"中文外来词"数量独占鳌头，正在以 5%—20% 的比例超过任何其他外来语言。该机构主席帕亚克表示："令人惊讶的是，由于中国经济增长的影响，中文对国际英语的冲击比英语国家还大。"

这些例子有汉语中的 taikonaut（宇航员），self-employed businessman（个体户），hukou（户口），Goji（枸杞），Maotai（茅台），Pao-tzu（包子），Chinglish（中式英语），Dama（大妈），Tuhao（土豪），guanxi（关系），long time no see，good good study day day up 等。

（二）旧词赋予新意

旧词赋予新意就是词义的引申。旧词的隐喻义往往生动形象、内涵深刻。mouse 本义是指老鼠，21世纪人们赋予它以新义，表示计算机手控光标的"鼠标"。plastics 本义是"塑料"、新义是"信用卡"。这些词语的本义都是大家所熟知的，增加新义后其音形不变，但让人认识了新事物新概念。动词 graze 的本义是"（牛、羊等）吃草"，受动物吃草方式的启发，新义是指"整天少量吃东西而不正常吃饭，或少吃多餐"。动词 flame 本义是"用火燃烧、传送，火焰发送器"（to burn with, send out, become like fire），新义是"在网上发送辱骂的信息"。splitters 旧义为"分开、分裂"，现在表示"离婚者"，see-through 本义是看透，现在表示"透视装"，hotel 旧义为"旅馆"，现在用来表示"临时办公地"。

（三）词类转换法

名词转动词：《新牛津美语词典》（*New Oxford American Dictionary*）选出2009年年度词语，互联网上社交网站中常用的一个动词 unfriend（删除好友）当选。其他名词转动词的例子还有 sexting（性短信），pie（打），dejunk（收拾打扫办公室），celeb（名人聚会），regift（转赠礼物），Dell（直销），blackhole（消失，失去联系），buddy（成为好友），friend（交友），text（发短信），badmouth（说坏话），demall（从购物单中去掉）。

形容词转名词：a moderate（一个温和派），a depressive（沮丧的人），friendlies（友好的人），hostiles（敌人），a physical（一次体格检查），a new high（一个新的高度），an innocent（一个无辜的人），the creative（创作人员），the injectable（血管注射剂）。

近几年还出现将某些副词转化为动词的用法，如 to down（击落，打倒，放下），to up（提高，增加，举起，拿起），to off（中止，取消，离开），to out（退出，外出）等。

（四）类推法构词

一些组合形式和新的组合形式颇为活跃。例如，以 super-用作前缀的有：super spike, super Tuscan, super centenarian, super distribution, super infector, super size, super soap, super taste, super weed。mega-类推的词有：megameal, megavitamin, megabucks, megabook, megahit, megarich, megasmash, megamarket, megamall, megafirm, megamerger, megatrends, megacarrier, megastore, megabudget, megaplex, megalithic, megachurch, megalomaniac, mega-death。作为后缀的以 holic 结尾的类推词有：beerholic, colaholic, movie-holic, teleholic, carboholic, loveholic, milkhaulic, surgiholic。复合词类推法例子有：scarlet collar worker, green collar worker, grey collar worker, pink collar worker, silver collar, black collar, open colar, dog collar 等。

五 美语新词语具创新性

在美国，新文化、新思想、新概念以井喷形势出现，在此影响下，新词出现创新性。这可以从牛津美语新词词典和美国语言监控组织发布的新词看出：podcast（播客），carbon neutral（碳中和），locavore（土食族），hypermiler（超级省油者），unfriend（删除好友），rufudiate（拒绝），selfie（自拍），GIF（图像文件），Eurogeddon（欧洲末日），Higgs-boson（希格斯波色子），MOOC（慕课），nomophobia（无手机恐惧症），superstorm（超级暴风雪），showroom（展厅现象），word of mouse（网络口碑），shopping boyfriend（购物男友）等。

以复合词形式出现的新词汇有：acid jazz（酸性爵士），bubble tea（泡沫奶茶），latte factor（拿铁效应），universal release（全球同步上映），economic downturn（经济危机），white coat effect（白大褂效应），pink slip party（失业派对），single brand store（专卖店），hot spot（热点地区），functional food（功能性食品），labelmate（同一签约公司的艺人），wave pool（冲浪池），big-box（大盒子式的商店），cut and paste（剪贴），lemon law（不良产品赔偿法），managed care（特殊照护），snail mail（传统邮递的邮件），warehouse club（批发店），window of opportunity（宽限期），tramp stamp（女性后背下方纹身），funemployed（快乐失业），bad tongue day（嘴不好使的一天），office spouse（办公搭档），quiet date（寂静约会），power nap（动力午睡），trophy wife（花

瓶），May December romance（忘年恋），hockey mom（冰球妈妈），Alpha mom（阿尔法妈妈），Alpha dog（领头羊），anchor store（锚店），unwedding ceremony（解除婚姻仪式），mancation（男士聚会度假），eye candy（养眼蜜糖），speed date（速配），Monday morning idea（周一早晨不成熟的想法），car pool（拼车），capsizing（裁员过度），rightsize（合理裁减），brightsize（优化裁减），cyberslacker（工作时间上网做私事的人），alpha earner（养家太太），shutter man（百叶窗男人），saty-at-home dad（家庭妇男、住家男人）。

派生法例子有：canyoning（悬崖跳水），unturkey（不吃火鸡行为），bootable（可启动的磁盘），Floridization（地区性老年化），worklessness（无业），Incubator（孵化器），demall（从购物单中去掉），supersize（超级大餐），trashy（蹩脚的），dejunk（收拾打扫办公室），regift（转赠礼物），T-shirtable（可在上面印字的T恤），deshopping（购物诈骗），houseblinging（庆贺圣诞打扮房子）。

美语新词语层出不穷，一些新词出现，另一些新词消失，还有些词汇改头换面，但它们均折射出美国社会的发展、文化思潮，是大千世界的客观反映，蕴藏了具有民族特色的思想价值观、文化和语言特征。新词新语的不断涌现要求我们每个外语学习者都应该密切注意到语言各方面的发展动态，及时学习、准确理解和恰当运用好新词新语，从而使我们的言语表述更加准确、生动、形象、新颖，更具有适时性和现代感，最终成功地进行跨文化交际。

第十二章 当代美国文化发展趋势

一 逃离压力,追求慢生活

进入 21 世纪,美国人迫切感觉到应该将生活节奏放慢,尽量过得更有价值。高级职员可能会突然中止手头的工作,从大城市的生活挣扎中解脱出来,而到小城镇去办一份小报纸、开个小旅馆、办个小学校或组织一个小乐队。人们摆脱压力是因为他们认为不值得生活在巨大的压力之下,他们充满怀旧之情,渴望回到小城镇的价值观中,寻求新鲜的空气、安全的学校和坦率的邻居。他们推崇 All the work and no play makes Jack a dull boy(只工作不玩耍聪明的孩子也变傻)。每年半个月左右时间的休假和其他节日中,许多人会到山里或海边小木屋过一个周末,还有些人会去欧洲度两周假期。

越来越多的美国人认识到快餐的危害。他们推崇慢餐的理念。除非万不得已,否则不会选择吃快餐。slow food 注重传统和有机种植方式,倡导美食和美酒、放慢进餐节奏、享受生活,主流食品减少了肉和土豆。越来越多的饭店增设了 salad bar(沙拉吧),供人们选择新鲜的蔬菜。

二 绿色生活,回归自然

人们总是想活得更长,活得更好。人们现在明白了也许自己的生活方式正是导致自己早死的原因——吃不合适的食品、抽烟、呼吸污染的空气、使用毒品等。他们现在对自己的健康更加负责,会选择健康的食品,光顾 whole food store,购买 organic food 和 green food,许多人选择吃 heirloom pork(有机猪肉),pharma food(含有保健药物的食品),deprivation cuisine（健康但无味的食品）。推崇 ape diet（素食）和 grazing（少吃多餐）。美国人发明了 tofurkey（豆腐火鸡），unturkey（素食火鸡）。做 ethical eater（有机食品和人道喂养鱼肉的鱼素食者），freegan（免费素食者），locavore（只吃当地食品的人），locapour（只喝本地酒的人）和 vegivore（蔬菜迷）。素食越来越受欢迎，素食者更是大行其道，flextarian 只是偶尔吃肉的素食者。lacto-vegetarian 食用奶制品素食者，但是拒绝蛋类食品。ovo vegetarian 不食肉类也不食用奶制品，但是食用蛋类和蜂类产品。vegan 不食用任何奶类、蛋类或任何动物食品，是严格的素食主义者。

近年来，美国掀起了在家中阳台或花园种植食物运动，如 100-foot diet（100 英尺以内的食物）和 garden to fork（花园产食物）。有些人在自家后院进行小块地密集种植，称为 SPIN，有些人租地种菜。城市里开始有了 window farm（窗口种农作物）和 farm scraper（楼顶种庄稼的高楼）。

100 miles menu 掀起了一种生活方式浪潮，这种生活方式的倡导者倡导人们计算运输食物的 food mile，重视本地生长的有机食物，成为 locavore（土食族）。而这些食材，则全部来自餐厅 100 英里范围内的农场，它们都是在原始自然状态下，适应动植物本性自然生长。烹饪用料就地取材，减少 cookprint，食物更加新鲜时令，同时也减少 carbon offset（抵消因长途运输带来的碳排放污染）。

近年来，green wedding 受到美国年轻人欢迎。环保婚礼中的新人非常关心生态环境，持有环保社交的概念，因而他们选择的婚礼是绿色婚礼。一般情况下，婚礼前，亲朋好友聚集在一座有机农庄，参加远足和环保旅游的活动。宾客行走路程时，所呼出的二氧化碳通过植树或向雨林保护项目捐款得以抵消。新娘花束和婚礼装饰要使用绣球花和其他应季花卉，而不是耗费燃料从其他远方城市运来的奇花异草。新娘不会浪费金钱买一件只穿一次的婚礼服，而是租一件婚礼服或向朋友借一件老式衣裙。举行婚礼的餐厅或农场主办人向客人提供有机蔬菜食品、当地酿造的啤酒和有机葡萄酒、再循环能源的礼堂，使用 degradable plates（可降解碗碟）。至于婚戒则用"百分之百可回收利用的黄金"制成或从古董店里购得。平均下来，一场婚礼的花费是 2.5 万—3 万美元，虽然比较昂贵，但它充分表明新娘新郎对地球的关爱。这种婚姻形式正在

301

以其独有的魅力吸引越来越多的新人。

LOHAS 一族。中文翻译是"乐活"。LOHAS 是由 Lifestyles Of Health And Sustainability 的每个单词第一个字母组成，中文意思就是健康和可持续性的生活方式。乐活努力支持环保、保持良好的心态、坚持做好事，这样的生活理念使他们身心健康，充满活力。他们爱地球、爱家人，也爱他人。乐活的生存宣言是：有事业，但不放弃生活；有一些金钱，但不被金钱支配；追求有品位之生活，但不矫揉造作和附庸风雅；接近自然但不离群索居；享乐人生，但对不幸之人心存同情和救助之情；不忘走向大自然赏略广阔世界。基于此，乐活族选择了练习瑜伽、绿色环保家居、纯棉生活方式。

LOHAS 作为一种生活理念，在美国已经十分普及。在这种理念的影响下，环境友好的混合动力汽车和氢燃料汽车竞相出现，有机食品、健康食品更是争先恐后地往 LOHAS 概念上靠拢。另类疗法，如温泉浴、氧吧理疗、瑜伽大行其道，甚至旅行社也频繁打出绿色的自然生态游，迎合乐活族需求。随着社会发展与人们道德环保意识水平加强，越来越多的人会加入这一队伍。

三　全民健身，注重生活质量

鉴于美国小胖子越来越多，美国卫生组织致力于在学校推广健康午餐。美国国会通过了一些解决肥胖问题的议案，许多州也设定了 school food standard（校餐标准），规定学校向学生提供水果和蔬菜等健康食品。美国卫生组织还在社区范围内推动健康计划，如在社区中修建更多人行道，鼓励人们步行，在公园中修建 jogging trail（跑步小道）。在政府的教育及推动下，全民健身运动意识得到提升。许多美国城市在城建规划中都对体育设施分布作了明确的规定，市政府必须在预算中投入资金兴建体育场馆和体育设施。美国城市的每一个街区几乎都有一座小型的体育场所，免费向公众开放。

走在美国的各个公园，人们都会看到市民着运动装进行体育锻炼，各种形式的体育活动不断推陈出新。如 aerobics（有氧运动），sightjogging（观景慢跑），strollerobics（推婴儿车有氧运动），chariobics（椅子运动），core training（肚皮后背运动），retro running（倒走），off road skating（越野滑冰），parkour（跑酷），slacklining（走尼龙绳），fastpack-ing（背包跑步），dancesport（室内舞竞赛），glaming（豪华露营），zorb-ing（左宾球锻炼）等。

更多的城市开设自行车道，为骑车人乘 ten speeds（十变速自行车）锻炼提供方便。

四 追求个性化和个人自由

人们希望能发展自己的个性，从而使自己看起来与众不同。他们希望通过自己的经历和所拥有的东西来使自己具有个性。人们越来越喜欢订阅比较专业的杂志，参加特定活动的小团体，购买有特色的衣服、汽车和化妆品。老年人会花更多的钱来购买显得年轻的衣服，成为 grups（装嫩族）。有些人会去染头发或做整容。他们热衷于有趣且有个性的活动，其行为可能在以前会被认为与其年龄不相称。如购买成人玩具，参加野营、健身俱乐部和假日探险。

越来越多的州立法承认同性恋婚姻。不少州还在每年的春夏之际举行规模宏大的 gay parade。越来越多的美国大众以平常心接受这种生活方式。据 1990 年社会性别组织估测，美国大约有 170 万—340 万女性的丈夫曾经或正在与男性同性有性关系。芝加哥大学社会学家 Edward O. Laumann 估测，大约 2%—4% 的美国已婚女性公开或秘密地经历过 bi-sexual（双性）婚姻。他们领养孩子，借腹生子，生活方式另类。

美国人在婚姻上也很有个性。有人推崇双收入无形家庭，有人愿意做丁克族，有人寻求公司举行赞助婚礼，有人举办婚礼加蜜月旅行，有人重组家庭，带着各自婚前所生孩子一起度蜜月。

divorce ceremony 流行于 20 世纪 80 年代，表示"解除婚姻仪式"。到了 21 世纪人们更倾向于使用 unwedding 而不是 divorce，它的使用更加显示出人们对离婚的豁达及释怀。在美国、德国等西方国家，离婚夫妇举办离婚仪式，以快乐友好的方式结束婚姻已经渐成时尚。

apha mom 是母亲团队中的带头人。出现于美国各大城市。她们有强大的经济购买力，受过高等教育，为了培育完美的孩子，放弃大公司的繁忙工作。她们利用制订的计划、适当的资源，还有严格的精神及道德观念追求完美。在美国还出现了标准行为的收费电视台 Alpha Mom

TV，颇受女性欢迎。

女人有性感的、强悍的、倾城的、温柔的。现在，时尚界的命名癖们，同样给男人创造了诸多类型的词汇。他们乐此不疲玩着这类造词游戏：metrosexual（都市玉面男），ubersexual（粗犷阳刚男），technosexual（科技美形男）。许多男人们刚刚了解 metrosexual 的定义，开始关心品牌、美容和品位，努力向 homosexual 看齐，时尚预言家们又纷纷宣布：精心甚至过度修饰自己外表的 metrosexual 风潮，典型如贝克汉姆，已经过时了。现在，男人们必须要 ubersexual——具有男人阳刚之气，但仍然得保持女性化的那一面。而不久以前，时尚预测专家又宣布，technosexual（科技男）已取代都市粗犷男，成为现代流行词。可以预见的是，新人类不断出现，描写这类人的词汇会层出不穷。

许多美国人认为外面的世界会变得十分艰难与恐怖，而宁愿待在家里。许多人把家弄得像个"巢"，他们会重新装修他们的房子，喜欢在家看录像而不是去电影院，在网上购物，而不是去购物中心；他们常常利用 answering machine 来获取外面的信息。另一类人是 carcoon（车茧），他们在汽车里吃买来的食物并通过车载电话与外界联系，这种社交型 cocooning（做茧者）一般有少数的朋友，并经常为了交流而聚会。有些人是 couch potato，在家边看电视边吃 junk food，成为肥胖消极的一群人。随着互联网的发展和普及，indoorsman（宅男），indoorswoman（宅女），distance worker（在家办公者）会越来越多。

五　女性在美国社会地位逐渐上升

越来越多的女性担任高级职务，有的比丈夫收入还要高。在美国双职工家庭中，妻子收入高于丈夫的家庭占 1/3。这些妇女拥有大学学位和工商硕士学位。她们就职于华尔街或芝加哥的大公司，位居要职。研究结果表明，如果妻子的收入占家庭收入的 60% 或以上，这个家庭的妻子就可称为 alpha earner。造成这种现象的原因有两个：一个是社会已经接受男人可以做家庭妇男这一事实；二是在过去的几年中，技术金融及媒体行业白领男性职员过剩。

高技术产业是新兴产业，风气相对自由开明，晋升与否更是取决于个人的成就。这个行业的女性高级管理人员尤为多见。梅格·怀特曼的公司 eBay，是网络上最受欢迎的网站之一，卡莉·菲奥瑞娜是惠普公司的首席执行官，施乐和朗讯也是两家由女性经营的大科技公司。

在美国参议院，妇女当选参议员的人数从 1991 年的 2 名增加到 2001 年的 13 名，在 10 年中增加了近 7 倍。到 2004 年，在参议院中的 100 个席位里拥有 14 席，占 14%，在众议院中的 435 个席位里拥有 60 席，占 13.8%。2008 年大选后，美国女性在国会中占有的席位创下了历史新高，其人数在参议院中达到 17 人，在众议院中则为 74 人。2010 年，经奥巴马总统提名，埃林娜·卡根在参议院的投票选举中，顺利成为美国最高法院第 4 位女大法官。1997 年，马德琳·奥尔布赖特就任国务卿，成为美国历史上第一位女国务卿，也是美国有史以来职位最高的妇女。之后，在 2005 年，赖斯成为美国历史上第二位女国务卿。希拉里·克林顿成为美国历史上第三位女国务卿，虽然在民主党总统提名初选棋逢对手的对决中，希拉里遗憾告负，然而她的才能、魅力、硬朗作风让奥巴马最终决定提名她为国务卿。希拉里不但有众多支持者的拥护，也是美国历史上迄今为止最成功的女性总统候选人。

随着美国妇女运动进一步发展、社会的进步，美国妇女政治地位会不断提高。美国在不久的将来一定会迎来第一位女总统。

社会的发展和科技突飞猛进，迫使人们必须竭力设法同时承担多种角色和责任。妇女更是如此。如 supcr mom（超级母亲），她们必须工作，还要同时照顾好家庭和孩子，常常感觉时间不够用。她们常常在影视城的 laundromat（自助洗衣店）洗衣，还同时会光顾日光浴室、健身中心，在洗衣同时还会使用复印机和传真设备进行工作。

六 创新能力持续增强

进入 21 世纪，美国的创新出现了许多新的特点，这些特点在未来尤为突出。一是创新加速度。如电话普及用了 35 年，手机用了 3 年，互联网仅用了 7 年。二是学科交叉日益明显，合作尤为显得重要。三是多学科及领域交叉现象日益增多。因为创新要求科学家、工程师、设计者之间加强合作与沟通。四是创新活动范围日趋全球化。未来的趋势更是如此。

未来科技和创新使美国实现宏伟远大的目标。未来人们的生活质量将会大大提高，并为未来的产业和就业奠定基础。如将药物准确送到指定组织的纳米技术；克隆技术可以结束人们对器官移植无休止的等待，战胜癌细胞；借助科技和创新人们能把阳光转化为碳，太阳能电池变得便宜并便利；人们可生产出其消耗的全部能源的绿色建筑；随着学生人数的增多，网上课程得到普及，并不断地改进；创新活动将会使得世界主要语种间进行准确、实时的自动翻译，大大减少国际间交流和商务活动的语言障碍。

这些创新不是虚无缥缈的，而是有着坚实的基础和保证。以教育为例，奥巴马总统承诺将建立一个教育体系，帮助每个孩子在新的全球经济中取得成功。奥巴马政府支持教学改革，确保学生掌握 21 世纪世界一流的知识和技能。强化教学，奖励教学先进工作者，推动美国课堂中的创新活动。通过推广成功先进的教学改革经验，普及先进教育育人经验，提高美国初高中学生的成绩。总统还在美国学校实施 Race to Top（力争上游）计划，对各州提供投资，并要求它们制定和实施更明确、更高的标准和目标，引入顶尖人才，留住优秀教师，采取有效的方法改变差校，恢复美国高校毕业生人数居世界之首地位。

具体到民众的生活，有许多人认为有必要找到能改变枯燥日常生活的情感逃避方式。人们也许会去度假，吃异国情调的食品，去迪士尼乐园或其他有趣的乐园，或重新装修房屋使其有远离喧嚣的感觉。创造异想天开的产品和服务的机会。如美国创新网站推出各种才华横溢的创意，有人设计出以运动产生能为手机充电的设置，还有人设计出以尼龙珠球洗衣而不是水的机洗方法。总之，美国创新精神和土壤会培育出更多的创新人才。

七　网络数码技术发展更为先进，功能强大

在线看电视和电影仍然是一个更重要的大众行为。汽车制造商、生活消费品公司、电器制造商等，会增加网络广告投入。小应用软件继续受欢迎，为互联网发行人提供了更多上网和搜索途径。随着智能手机和新产品的推陈出新，如 IPhone 和 Android devices，移动互联的市场占有率将会继续飙升，将使移动网站频道手机银行等业务大量增加。此外，美国在线零售额的增长率也会持续增加。由于在线销售商通常比零售商

成本更低，加上他们通过打折、促销等方式吸引到更多消费者，能获取更大利润。未来美国人与网络对话将成为现实。人们只需对电话网络发话，就可以轻松创建和浏览网页，甚至可以进行商务交易。语音网页将为那些没有可靠网络基础设施的人们和没有太高文化能力的人们提供益处和方便。此外，互联网将走向无线互联网时代，无线互联网将使用户从桌面电脑转向移动互联网。手机逐渐和笔记本进行融合，无线通信速率更为高强，人们可以通过无线电脑设备随时查询信息、购买商品和服务，支付银行资金。

来自美国联邦劳动部下属的劳工统计局的信息表明，电子计算机的迅猛发展，预示21世纪美国职业结构将发生较大的变化。一些迅速发展的高新技术行业向掌握高深技术的人才敞开大门。未来美国各行业需求大量的计算机维护保养、程序编排、设计创造人才。尖端电子技术方面的物理学家和工程师大受欢迎。有关环保工程，如太阳能、核能以及生产研制合成燃料的能源工程师会有更多的就业机会。同时，仍有许多行业需要大量的普通工人。如秘书、护理员、房屋管理员、出纳员、售货员等服务性行业的雇员。社会仍然需要大量的快餐业从业者、卡车司机、汽车修理工、打字员、木工、房地产经纪人。

总而言之，开放、包容、创新，追求健康、绿色、高质量生活，追求个性和自由，女性地位提升、网络数码技术的加速发展是美国文化的发展趋势。它们有利于美国现代化的推进，有利于美国多元文化的形成与发展，有利于文化的丰富多彩，有利于美国人战胜困难、不断追求美好的生活。可以说，美国文化的优势是美国发展的动力。

主要参考文献

Christine Ammer, *American Heritage Dictionary of Idioms*, Houghton Mifflin Harcourt, 2003.

A. P. Cowie, *Oxford Dictionary of Current Idiomatic English*, Oxford University Press, 1975.

Cumming, J. D. , *The Internet and the English Language*, English Today, No. 1: 3 - 7. 1995.

E B Tyler, *Primitive Culture*, Cambridge University Press, 2010.

Goodnough, W. H, *Cultural Anthropology and Linguistics*, Bobbs-Merrill Reprint Series in Language and Linguistics, 1957.

Gozzi, R. Jr, *New Words and The Changing American Culture*, Columbia University of South Carlina Press, 1990.

Halliday, M. A. K, *Lexical Relations*, *System and Function in Language*, Oxford, Oxford University Press, 1976.

John Ayto, *A Century of New Words*, Oxford University Press, 2007.

Jackson. H and Amvela E. Z, *Words Meaning and Vocabulary: An Introduction to Modern Lexicography*, London and New York: Cassel, 2000.

May, H. et, *The facts on file Dictionary of New Words*, New York: Facts on File, 1998.

Pearson Longman, *Longman Dictionary of Contemporary English*, Fourth edition, Longman, 2003.

Rosaemary Courtney, *Longman Dictionary of Phrasal Verbs*, Addison-Wesley, 1983.

S. Butler, *Macquarie Dictionary*, Macquarie Dictionary Publishers Pty Ltd, 2009.

M. J. , *Pragmatics*, *An Introduction*, Blackwell, 1993.

Noam Chomsky, *Syntactic Structure*, Mouton de Gruyter, 2002.

A S Hornby, *Oxford Advanced Learner's Dictionary*, Seventh Edition, Oxford University Press, 2005.

Judy Oearsall, *New Oxford Dictionary of English*, Oxford University Press, 1998.

Merriam-Webster, *Webster's New Collegiate Dictionary*, G. & C. Merriam Co. , 2003.

Michael E. Agnes, *Wester's New World Dictionary*, Rocket, 2003.

Philip Babcock Gove, *Webster's Third New World International Dictionary*, Merriam Webster, 1976.

爱德华·萨丕尔：《语言论》，陆卓元译，商务印书馆 1964 年版。

楚至大、王东风：《英汉美国俚语大辞典》，安徽科学技术出版社 1996 年版。

丛莱庭：《英语委婉语详解词典》，湖北教育出版社 2001 年版。

董小川：《美国文化概论》，人民出版社 2006 年版。

费尔迪南·索绪尔：《普通语言学教程》，高名凯译，商务印书馆 1981 年版。

洪堡特：《论人类语言结构的差异及其对人类精神发展的影响》，姚小平译，商务印书馆 1999 年版。

贾玉新：《跨文化交际学》，上海教育出版社 1997 年版。

金圣华：《英语新词词汇》，辰衡图书公司 1979 年版。

克鲁克洪：《文化与个人》，高佳等译，浙江人民出版社 1986 年版。

李平武：《英语词缀与英语派生词》，北京外语教学与研究出版社 2002 年版。

陆国强：《现代英语词汇学》，上海外语教育出版社 1983 年版。

刘纯豹：《英语委婉语词典》，江苏教育出版社 1993 年版。

刘杰：《当代美国政治》，社会科学文献出版社 2011 年版。

刘永涛：《当代美国文化》，武汉大学出版社 2003 年版。

毛荣贵：《英语词汇热点透视》，上海交通大学出版社 1999 年版。

马林诺夫斯基：《文化论》，费孝通等译，中国民间文艺出版社 1978 年版。

钱歌川：《英文疑难详解续篇》，中国对外翻译出版社 1981 年版。

萨丕尔：《语言》，陆卓元译，商务印书馆 1999 年版。

束定芳：《隐喻学研究》，上海外语教育出版社 2000 年版。

索绪尔：《普通语言学教程》，商务印书馆 1980 年版。

王恩铭：《当代美国社会与文化》，上海外语教育出版社 1997 年版。

王锦瑭：《美国社会文化》，武汉大学出版社 1996 年版。

王作民：《美国万花筒》，新世界出版社 1988 年版。

汪榕培、卢晓娟：《英语词汇学教程》，上海外语教育出版社 1999
年版。

汪榕培：《英语词汇学研究》，外语教育出版社 2000 年版。

吴菲：《美国社会与文化》，武汉大学出版社 2003 年版。

徐昌和：《英语新词新语导论》，上海交通大学出版社 2009 年版。

袁晓红、戴卫平：《美语词汇与美利坚文化研究》，吉林大学出版社
2010 年版。

郑立信、顾嘉祖：《美国英语与美国文化》，湖南教育出版社 1993
年版。

周学艺：《英美报刊文章阅读》，北京大学出版社 2004 年版。

朱世达：《当代美国文化》，社会科学文献出版社 2011 年版。

http：//www. alphadictionary. com/slang

http：//www. americandialect. org

http：//www. answers. com

http：//www. askoxford. newwords. com

http：//www. dictionary. cambridge. org

http：//www. emory. edu

http：//idiomsite. com

http：//www. ruf. rice. edu/kemmer/words04/neologisms

http：//www. merriam-webster. com/dictionary

http：//www. neologism. deri. ie

http：//www. neologisms. us

http：//www. netlingo. com

http：// urbandictionary. com

http：//www. unwords. com

http//www. vappingo. com/wprd

http：//www. wikipedia. org

http：//www. wordspy. com

http：//wordwatch. com

http：//wordexplore. com